NOONGAR PEOPLE, NOONGAR LAND

THE RESILIENCE OF ABORIGINAL CULTURE IN THE SOUTH WEST OF WESTERN AUSTRALIA

NOONGAR PEOPLE, NOONGAR LAND

THE RESILIENCE OF ABORIGINAL CULTURE IN THE SOUTH WEST OF WESTERN AUSTRALIA

Kingsley Palmer

First published in 2016 by AIATSIS Research Publications

Reprinted 2021

Australian Institute of Aboriginal and Torres Strait Islander Studies (AIATSIS)
GPO Box 553, Canberra ACT 2601

Phone: (61 2) 6246 1111
Fax: (61 2) 6261 4285
Email: research@aiatsis.gov.au
Web: www.aiatsis.gov.au

National Library of Australia Cataloguing-in-Publication
Creator: Palmer, Kingsley, 1946- author.
Title: Noongar land, Noongar people: the resilience of Aboriginal culture in the South West of Western Australia / Kingsley Palmer.

ISBN: 9781922102294 (paperback)
ISBN: 9781922102478 (ebook: pdf)
ISBN: 9781922102485 (ebook: epub)

Subjects: Noongar (Australian people)—History. Noongar (Australian people)—Land tenure. Noongar (Australian people)—Social conditions. Native title (Australia)—Western Australia—South-West. Aboriginal Australians—Land tenure—Western Australia Aboriginal Australians—Western Australia—History.

Dewey Number: 305.89915

Front cover images: Each of the six photographs on the front cover shows an important place within the six main regions of Noongar country. These places have been of significance to Noongar people since *kura* (a long time ago), continue to be so *yeye* (today) and will be important *boorda* (tomorrow) and into the *boordawan* (future). Top (from left): Whadjuk country — Floating sculptures on Dyarlgaroo Beelya (the Canning River) show the contemporary artistic cultural expression of Noongar artists; Yued country — Sunset at Mogumber, site of the Moore River Native Settlement; Gnaala Karla Booja country — Minningup (on the Collie River), a place of mythological and spiritual significance for Noongar people. Bottom (from left): South West Boojarah country — Nannup Cave, Caves Road, Boranup Karri Forest; Ballardong country — Wave Rock, an iconic feature for Noongar people, a part of their natural and cultural geography, serving as a ceremonial meeting place; Wagyl Kaip/Southern Noongar country — Sleeping Beauty (Stirling Ranges), the outline of the many peaks of the ranges illustrates and testifies to one of many Noongar Dreaming stories handed down through the generations. Photographs courtesy SWALSC. Captions by Sarah Bell and Sandra Harben, SWALC.

Typeset in Minion Pro by Midland Typesetters, Australia
Printed by SOS Print + Media Group

CONTENTS

TABLES AND FIGURES

ABOUT THIS BOOK

This book, *Noongar people, Noongar land*, arose out of the protracted struggle by the Indigenous Noongar people of the South West of Western Australia to gain recognition of their native title rights and interests under the Australian federal government's *Native Title Act 1993* (Cth) (NTA). The claim, known as 'the Single Noongar Claim', was heard in 2005. The case resulted in a historic judgment in favour of the Noongar people, in which Justice Wilcox of the Federal Court found that native title continued to exist (*Bennell v State of Western Australia* [2006] FCA 1243). The area ruled by Justice Wilcox to be subject to native title rights included parts of the city of Perth. This was the first judgment to recognise native title over parts of a capital city and its surroundings.

This success was to be short-lived, however, as the state government of Western Australia appealed the decision to the Full Bench of the Federal Court. This appeal was heard before three Federal Court judges who, in April 2007, set aside Justice Wilcox's judgment. The Full Court held that Justice Wilcox was wrong to focus on the continued existence of a Noongar community and should have instead concentrated on whether or not Noongar people continued to observe and acknowledge traditional law and custom. Demonstrating this ongoing exercise of traditional law and custom had become an essential component of the proof of native title since a case commonly referred to as the *Yorta Yorta* case (*Members of the Yorta Yorta Aboriginal Community v Victoria* [2002] HCA 58). The Full Court also said that Justice Wilcox was mistaken in assuming that simply because the claimants had demonstrated their connection to the broader claim area as a whole they had also proven their connection specifically to the Perth metropolitan region (*Bodney v Bennell* [2008] FCAFC 63). No finding was made that rejected or dismissed the claim, but it was reassigned to a fresh hearing before another Federal Court judge. Discussions with the state government of Western Australia then followed, with a view to settling the claim out of court. Negotiations between the parties were conducted between 2009 and 2014, ultimately affording Noongar people the opportunity to decide whether to proceed with their claims in court or exchange their native title rights and interests for rights contained in Indigenous Land Use Agreements (ILUAs). These ILUAs were approved by Noongar people at six authorisation meetings held across Noongar country between January and March 2015.

Part of the evidence required for proof of native title in a court is an expert anthropological report. The South West Aboriginal Land and Sea Council (SWALSC), the native title representative body for the South West of Western Australia, commissioned Dr Kingsley Palmer to research and prepare this report, which was filed in the Federal Court in 2004. SWALSC researchers Kate Morton, David Raftery and Ophelia Rubinich worked under Dr Palmer's direction to collect some of the data used in the report. It is this report, *Single Noongar Native Title Claim (W6006 of 2003 & W6012 of 2003): Anthropologist's Report*, that has been adapted and edited to become this book. SWALSC has also published a book based on the report of the expert historian, Dr John Host, whose account was submitted as part of the evidence for the Single Noongar Claim, in the form of the report *Single Noongar Native Title Claim (W6006 of 2003 & W6012 of 2003): Applicants' History Report.* This published historical account, *It's still in my heart, this is my country* (SWALSC 2009), has shed new light on the struggle that Noongar people have endured over the decades to gain recognition of their rights to country.

The preparation of anthropological materials for a native title claim to the whole of the South West of Western Australia posed particular challenges for SWALSC. How can one of the largest groups of Indigenous people, whose members have been subjected to nearly two centuries of colonial domination, be understood anthropologically? How can these understandings be translated into a form that can be presented as evidence in a legal proceeding?

The significance of the research achievement presented here should be understood in the context of the history of disinterest shown by some earlier anthropologists in the people of the South West and the pessimistic view expressed by some about the viability of their culture. Daisy Bates, for example, was a complex yet forceful exponent of the idea that Aboriginal culture was doomed to extinction (Bates 1966). This same pessimism and failure to appreciate the richness of the culture of Noongar people can be observed in the work of subsequent researchers. For example, Professor Ronald Berndt, writing in 1979, declared that the South West contained 'primarily a part-Aboriginal population — few of them directly descended from the original local people . . . and all possessing little or nothing of their traditional heritage' (Berndt 1979, p. 87). Later, a handful of anthropologists provided correctives to this deficit view of Noongar culture, but for the most part their work was not widely published (Baines 1987; Birdsall 1990).

Earlier predictions and claims that the Noongar people have 'lost their culture' do not accord with the present-day reality. There are some 30,000 Noongar people living in the South West, participating in hundreds of kin-based networks of Noongar family groups, raising Noongar families, looking after Noongar land and maintaining distinctive Noongar practices. Noongar people who informed the content of this book, some of whom have not survived to see its publication, bear witness to the continuing vibrancy of Noongar tradition. This collective account of Noongar people's relationships with each other, and with the country to which they remain connected, is testimony to an enduring Indigenous tradition that continues to survive despite the odds.

The book represents a scholarly alternative to the dominant themes of assimilation and demise that have influenced not only the formation of Indigenous policy in Western Australia, but also to the popular imaginings of the history and culture of people who are indigenous to Australia's South West. It demonstrates how the Noongar community has met and adapted to the challenges of modernity. It is also hoped that the publication of this book will provide a valuable record for the Noongar people and enable not only them but also Indigenous people elsewhere in Australia, and researchers commissioned to carry out research with them, to better understand how anthropological research can assist in the successful determination of native title claims.

South West Aboriginal Land and Sea Council

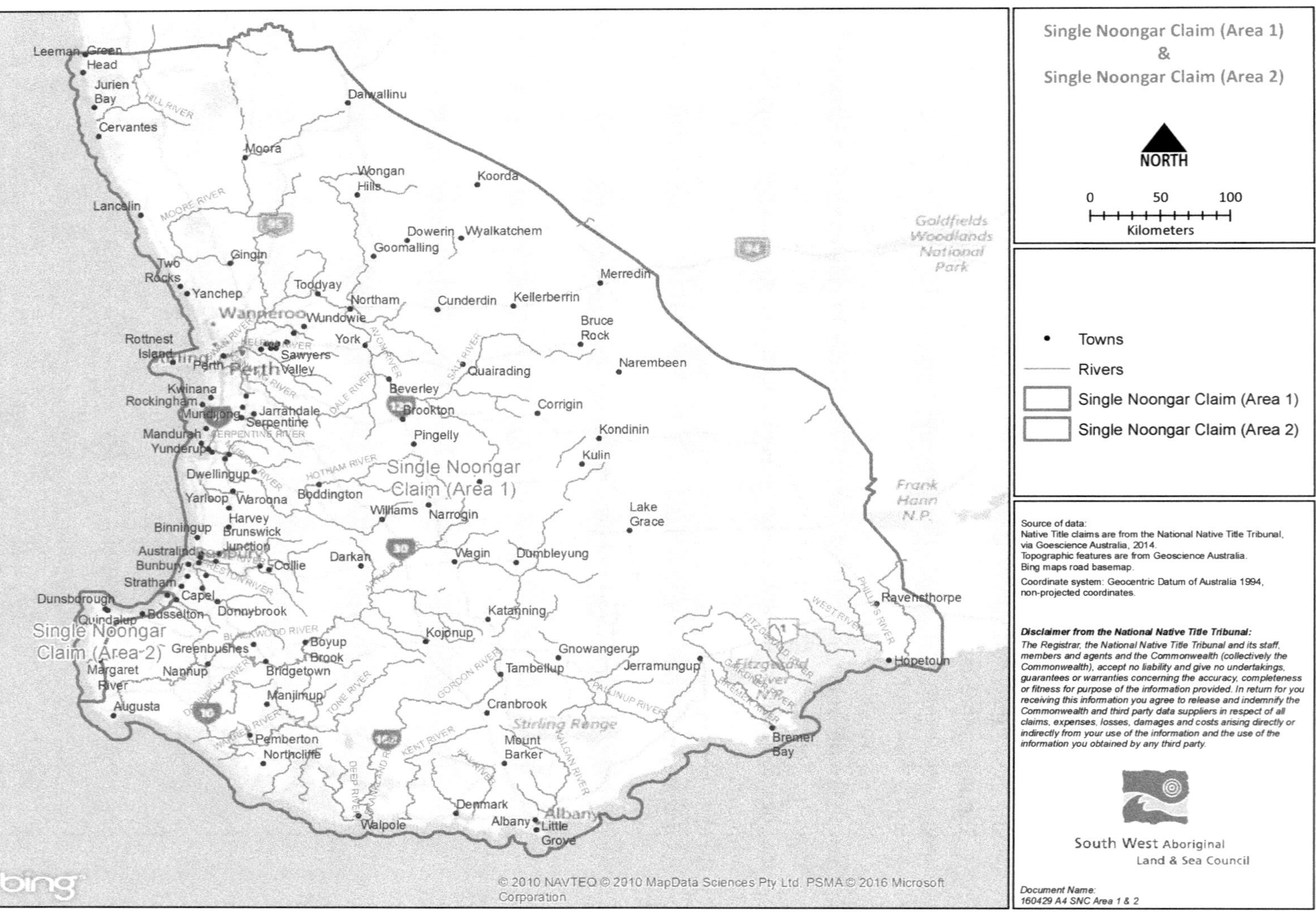

Map of the claim area

WRITING AND PUBLISHING EXPERT ANTHROPOLOGICAL REPORTS IN THE NATIVE TITLE CONTEXT

This book is an edited version of an anthropologist's expert report researched and written for the purposes of a native title claim. While it provides an account of many aspects of Noongar culture it is also an example of how an expert anthropological report can be prepared and presented to the Federal Court of Australia under the *Native Title Act 1993* (Cth) (NTA). For readers not familiar with the native title process in Australia, some introductory comments may be of assistance.

Native title in Australia

The NTA provides a statutory basis for the recognition of native title in Australia. Following the High Court's decision in *Mabo v Queensland (No. 2)* (1992) 175 CLR 1, the Act was designed to 'accommodate native title and the aspirations it has generated, into existing systems, especially those for land and resource management' (Williams 1998, p. iii). It was to reflect the common law recognition of native title 'in areas where Australia's Indigenous people have maintained a traditional connection with land' (p. iii).

Section 223 of the Act defines 'native title' or 'native title rights and interests' as,

> . . . the communal, group or individual rights and interests of Aboriginal peoples or Torres Strait Islanders in relation to land or waters, where:
>
> (a) the rights and interests are possessed under the traditional laws acknowledged, and the traditional customs observed, by the Aboriginal peoples or Torres Strait Islanders; and
>
> (b) the Aboriginal peoples or Torres Strait Islanders, by those laws and customs, have a connection with the land or waters; and
>
> (c) the rights and interests are recognised by the common law of Australia.
>
> (*Native Title Act 1993*, s. 223)

Applications for the recognition of native title which are not settled through mediation and negotiation, particularly with state and territory governments, eventually go to trial in the Federal Court. Over the years, the developing jurisprudence has established some of the key elements required for the successful recognition of native title. One of these emerged from a High Court judgment in the Victorian *Yorta Yorta* case (*Members of the Yorta Yorta Aboriginal Community v Victoria* [2002] HCA 58). This established that the traditional laws and customs, including those relating to rights in country, are those of a 'society' or group whose members share those laws and customs. The *Yorta Yorta* case also established that for native title to have survived there had to be a demonstrable continuity of the society and its laws and customs since the date of acquisition of sovereignty by the British Crown to the present day. The proof of that continuity and of the society and its members' laws and customs has to be provided to the court by the applicants. While Aboriginal or Torres Strait Islander claimants provide the principal source for this evidence, anthropologists have been quickly drawn into cases as it has become apparent that their services as experts are required to collect, analyse and present field data as well as provide opinions on key issues relating to continuity, society, normative values and change.

Typically, anthropologists are commissioned by applicants (or their legal representatives) to undertake field research with the claimants and write a report that addresses issues relevant to native title. They are also commissioned by respondent parties (particularly the state and territory governments) to review the work of the applicants' anthropologist.

Since proof of native title has been seen to lie in establishing the continuity of a customary normative system, much reliance has been placed on the examination of the writing of earlier scholars, diarists and settlers, as well as on other archival materials. In this way the anthropologist can build up a picture of the likely nature of the society and its laws and customs at the time of sovereignty, or as close to that date as possible, depending on the availability of early source materials.

The role of the expert anthropologist in native title inquiries represents a growing field of endeavour for practitioners in the field. As a practical application of the discipline of anthropology, it provides an opportunity to apply research and scholarship in ways that may assist the courts to reach positive outcomes in native title applications. As a result of the particular constraints of the legislation and the legal process, which require opinion relating to specific technical matters, it is also subject to limitations regarding the form and content of the research findings. Anthropologists seek to address issues identified through legal processes as being significant to native title inquiry. One consequence of this is that some technical terms of anthropology, such as 'society', have to be recruited to perform novel functions (Palmer 2010a). Other terms are borrowed direct from the legal parlance and include 'rights and interests' (i.e. 'rights'), 'laws and customs' (normative action) and 'traditional' (perhaps customary) (see Sutton 2003, p. xvii for a discussion).

The requirement for correspondence between what is meant in matters of law and in anthropological thinking necessitates that such terms be used definitively in expert reports, and this is the intention in what follows. Terms of art in anthropology, like 'filiation' and 'descent', are distinct anthropological concepts (Sutton 2003, pp. 188–9), although, as Sutton points out, they are often 'confounded' (p. 191). In relation to these and other similar terms, courts, and judges in particular, are less interested in theoretical debates about technical differentiation than in how a system works and whether it is founded or rooted in tradition. Thus a native title report is not the place to seek out arcane debate, and if a report contains such debate it is probably not doing the job it was commissioned to do.

This means that good anthropological reports for a native title matter have a number of required foci and cannot readily expand to consider all aspects of the culture under consideration. Despite the limitations, many of the reports prepared for native title cases for the claimants contain a wealth of ethnographic material, gathered from the past as well as from the present, which provides an invaluable resource for community members and, perhaps in time, for the broader scholarly community.

Expert reports and connection reports

Reports prepared by anthropologists for native title claims are generally called 'expert' or 'connection' reports, the two terms being used somewhat indiscriminately despite the fact that they are quite different in form. A 'connection report' usually refers to a report submitted to a state or territory government in negotiations towards a consent determination of native title. An 'expert report' refers to a report prepared for a litigated determination before the Federal Court.

In native title proceedings the state and territory governments are the principal respondents. Should the state and other respondent parties, sometimes represented by the state, come to accept that native title is evident from the materials provided to them by the applicants, it is possible for the matter to be settled by consent before the Federal Court as a 'consent determination'. Most states have issued guidelines which set down the sorts of materials they require for an assessment of 'connection'. In response to these guidelines anthropologists have been asked to write 'connection reports' which set down the bases upon which such continuity of connection is typically matched against the state's guidelines. As reports for assessment by the state, they are not usually filed in the court and are not subject to the strictures which apply to documents that are to be used as evidence.

Should the state or other respondent parties not accept the connection evidence for a consent determination, the report has to be remodelled into an expert report for hearing before the Federal Court for a litigated determination. An expert report must be prepared according to the court's stringent rules for expert evidence (discussed below). Transforming a 'connection report' into the form required by the Federal Court is not always easily achieved, and the rewriting and additional research required may cost considerable time and money. To avoid duplication, most claimant groups opt, at the outset of their claim process, for the preparation of evidence of their connection to country in the form of an 'expert report' in the event that, if they do not gain a consent determination, they will be ready to go to the court.

The writer of an expert report is an expert to the court and is governed by directions of the court.[1] The writer owes his or her first duty to the court and should not be an advocate for any party. Experts may not advance views or opinions on matters that lie outside of their expertise (Palmer 2011).[2] Expert opinion evidence is consequently a particular sort of evidence and subject to rules regarding its nature and derivation; for example, there is a distinction between a 'fact' and an expert opinion based on that fact, which is developed according to the particular training and experience of the expert. Expert views must be based upon identifiable data (facts), which are recoverable, and the reasons for all opinions proffered must be provided to the court. Generally, reports written prior to 2004 did not pay attention to issues of admissibility or the strict rules that now apply to expert evidence given in native title matters. In a native title case known as *Jango* (*Jango v Northern Territory (No. 2)* [2004] FCA 1004), the admissibility of the expert report written by Peter Sutton and Petronella Vaarzon-Morel was challenged successfully (Palmer 2007). This changed the way anthropologists now write expert reports, as the application of the *Evidence Act 1995* (Cth), the court's requirements and admissibility issues have come to the fore.

---

1 Federal Court of Australia. Practice Note CM7. 'Expert witnesses in proceedings of the Federal Court of Australia.' JLB Allsop, Chief Justice, 4 June 2013. These Practice Notes are updated from time to time.

2 See <http://www.aiatsis.gov.au/publications/products/anthropologist-expert-native-title-cases-australia> (viewed 18 September 2015).

Why publish an expert report?

The report prepared for the Single Noongar Claim was written as an expert report, and so for a particular purpose in a native title context. While it conforms to the requirements of an expert report it contains substantial information about the Noongar people of the South West of Western Australia. This includes accounts of their cultural practices taken from the early ethnographic literature, some dating back to the time of first settlement at King George Sound (now the site of Albany) and the Swan River colony. The report describes something of the complexity, diversity and richness of an enduring contemporary Noongar culture. These data provided the basis for the expert's opinions. SWALSC considered that this account of Noongar culture, so long ignored and neglected by other Australians, should be published as a book so that Noongar people would have a written record of their heritage. Others, too, might learn something of the richness of Noongar culture and life, both past and present.

There is a second reason to publish the original report. Expert reports are usually only made available to those directly involved in the case and may be subject to court orders or other restrictions. These restrictions have meant that there are few examples of expert reports that can be accessed and used as examples for developing the expertise required for this specialist task. In the case of the Noongar expert report, the Federal Court had issued orders that restricted its publication. SWALSC was obliged to make application to the Federal Court to have the orders lifted, which they were on 8 May 2012.

There are two examples of expert reports that have been published, but both predate 2004 when the Federal Court requirements for expert reports were clarified. The first was based on a report written by Scott Cane for a native title application by the Spinifex people to parts of the Great Victoria Desert. Subsequently, a revised version of the report was published along with splendid illustrations (paintings and photographs, see Cane 2002). The book contains some useful materials on desert systems of land ownership and is a helpful reference in this regard. However, the book is not presented as an expert report and pays no attention to the stringent requirements for an expert report. The claim was settled by consent, and the matter did not proceed to trial.

A second report, written for the Karajarri native title claim, was published by Geoffrey Bagshaw as an Oceania Monograph in 2003, following the successful determination of the claim (Bagshaw 2003, pp. 1–8). This report is contextualised by the author in terms of its origins, amendments and the purpose of its publication. The report provides a detailed and thorough account of Karajarri culture, and is the result of patient and exhaustive fieldwork and scholarship. However, like Cane's work, it does not address the evidentiary requirements of an expert report, as these had yet to be called into question. Nor does Bagshaw's report really tackle the difficult problem of the proof of continuity.

While the legal requirements for some aspects of the native title process will no doubt change as time passes, it is hoped that many of the principles addressed in this report on the Noongar people of the South West of Western Australia will remain relevant. The way in which the historical ethnographic material is presented and its relationship to the reporting of contemporary Noongar culture are fundamental to the demonstration of continuity. It is hoped that the topics covered, their manner of presentation and the framing of an expert view may provide a guide to others seeking to prepare connection materials for native title cases. Needless to say, the requirements for the production of an expert anthropological report do not encourage imaginative or fluid writing, and some might say that the result is sometimes far from readable.

Revisions and edits

The original expert report had to comply with the requirements of both the *Native Title Act 1993* and the *Evidence Act 1995*. In preparing it for a more general readership, aspects of the original report have been modified while some materials have been removed. Those who wish to consider this book a guide to writing an expert report should be mindful of these revisions and omissions.

The original report featured at times repetitive and technical qualifications relating to statements made in the report that clarified the evidentiary bases on which the author formed his expert opinions. These qualifications and associated terminology have been removed from the text of this book, although the sense remains, in some places, less fluid and more constrained than might otherwise have been the case. It was also necessary to explain the bases upon which expert opinion was developed, requiring discussion of methodology, responsibility and the theoretical bases of some anthropological thinking that might not normally be included in an ethnography. All statements had to be referenced to the field data or other sources upon which they were based, necessitating the inclusion of multiple footnote references. Indeed, the original report had some 624 footnotes. These have been substantially reduced by omitting references to the source of the field data.

Adding to these cumbersome requirements is the fact that the original expert report was presented in numbered paragraphs, as that is a requirement for such reports that are provided to the court. While this numbering has been removed for ease of reading, it has resulted in a rather syncopated style.

The original report contained some material that for reasons of confidentiality has been excluded from this account. In this regard there are two principal documents. The first is a summary list of Noongar sites and a map showing their approximate location, which was appended to the expert report on which this book is based and submitted to the Federal Court. This list and the map have been excluded from this book in order to safeguard the confidentiality of this information. In cases where information about sites is discussed publicly by Noongar people as a matter of course and is relevant to the issue under consideration, it is included in the text (see, for example, Chapter 13).

The second document to be excluded from this book for reasons of confidentiality is a collection of Noongar genealogies. The author and co-researchers dedicated much time to compiling genealogies of the Noongar families in order to provide a basis for expert opinion regarding the continuity of connection with ancestors who might reasonably be supposed to have been in possession of the claim area at or about the time of sovereignty. Such a mammoth undertaking was an important part of the preparation of the expert report. However, this account necessarily included much personal and confidential material, so it has been excluded from this published account.

A final editing matter has been the spelling of the word 'Noongar', which has been subject to much debate over many years. One view is that 'Nyungar' might be a more accurate reflection of the original pronunciation. However, the spelling 'Noongar' reflects the original name the claimants gave to their application for recognition of native title and the spelling reflects a compromise between claimant groups as to how best to represent, in an alien form, the name by which they identify. Thus in the report, and in this book, the spelling 'Noongar' is employed to describe the Indigenous people traditionally associated with the South West of Australia. However, the terms 'Nyungar', 'Nyoongar', 'Nyungah' and 'Yungar' are used according to how they are spelt in the original texts to which reference is made.

Noongar knowledge and permission

The ethnographic materials set down in this book belong to the Noongar people of the South West of Western Australia. Had they not shared their knowledge with the researchers, this contemporary account of Noongar culture would have remained unknown to the wider reading public and largely unacknowledged. The original report contained footnote references for every piece of information, sourced to the specific individuals who participated in the research. In order to protect the privacy of these individuals, these footnotes and other source references have been removed from this book.

Prior to the preparation of this book, SWALSC commissioned Dr David Raftery to contact those who participated in the research, who were relied upon and who were specifically acknowledged in the text of the report. Their permission to publish information they had provided or that related directly to them was obtained, subject in a few cases to minor alterations to the text. Appendix A contains a list of the names of the Noongar claimants who gave their permission to SWALSC for their material to be included in this book. In cases where informants were deceased, permission was sought and granted from appropriate close relatives. Where it was not possible to locate individuals who should be consulted, their names were removed from the text. Each informant or relative was provided with the relevant sections of the expert report and given time to digest its import. In some instances, face-to-face consultations concluded the permission process, while in others the process was finalised through written or phone correspondence.

Some of the Noongar people whose names are recorded in this book have passed away since the research was undertaken. The author and SWALSC regret any offence that may be caused by the viewing of these names in print. It is hoped that these acknowledgments will provide a lasting testament to these individuals and their store of cultural knowledge.

Kingsley Palmer

A NOTE ON THE ORTHOGRAPHY USED IN THIS BOOK

A wide variety of spellings occurs in written representations of the Noongar language. In part this may represent regional variations in pronunciation. However, it also reflects the fact that there is no single orthography generally accepted for use by those who write the language. In this book, I adopt, for the most part, the orthography set out by Dench (1994, pp. 175–6). This orthography distinguishes five vowels and their long forms (where recorded), shown in this book by a doubling of the letter.3 It also distinguishes between voiced and voiceless stops (p, t, k and b, d, g). Interdental d and t, l and n are shown by the use of h, thus dh, th, lh and nh, there being no equivalent sounds in English. Alveolar palatal l (like the 'li' of million), n (like the 'ni' of onion) are both shown by the use of y following the consonant. English j (as in 'jam') is shown as j, while Dench differentiates dj and tj. Retroflex is shown by the use of r before the consonant; thus rl (as in American English 'Carl'), rd (as in English 'lard'), rn (as in English 'barn') and rt (as in American English 'garter') (see McGregor 1994, pp. xxvii–xxviii). However, rolled r (as in Scottish 'bright') is not distinguished in what follows from retroflex r.

Exceptions relate to the following circumstances. Terms that are well established within the literature will be spelt consistent with that convention. Personal names in general use are spelt consistent with current use. Other names, usually from the historical record, follow the preferred spelling adopted by Hallam and Tilbrook (1990), Green (1989) or Green and Tilbrook (1990). In the context of a discussion of the work of another writer, a Noongar term that is the subject of that discussion will be presented according to the author's spelling for the duration of that review.

3 Dench suggested that long e and long o be shown by 'e:' and 'o:' respectively.

A NOTE ON METHODS AND SCOPE

Methodology and fieldwork

The Single Noongar Claim sought recognition of native title over the South West of Western Australia. This represents an area of about 186,000 square kilometres; a substantial area involving many potential claimants. The research and expert report had to be finalised within a 12-month period, and as a result the research methodology had to accommodate a requirement to gather data efficiently over a wide area and from many Noongar people. The data also had to be consistently gathered, reliable and accessible. We decided to adopt a team approach. Three researchers assisted me: Kate Morton, David Raftery and Ophelia Rubinich. All were employees of SWALSC at the time of the research. The claim area was divided into six areas, with each researcher being assigned responsibility for two areas.

We then organised a workshop to decide upon our research methodology, attended by both the researchers and the legal staff involved in the claim. This collaborative approach resulted in a research pro forma to be used by each researcher. The pro forma identified 16 'key concepts' relevant to the inquiry. Each key concept had listed beneath it a series of related issues, which were characterised as prompts. The purpose of the pro forma was to ensure that each researcher collected data relating to the same issues and covered items for which data were required for the completion of the expert report. A second pro forma, termed an 'observation pro forma', provided an opportunity for the researchers to record details of any activity, relevant to the inquiry, observed during the fieldwork. Both pro formas provided for details of time, place and personnel to be recorded, along with a unique identification code. Copies of the pro formas are included in Appendix C to this book.

The pro formas were to be understood as guides to the type of information required. They were not questionnaires, nor was there an expectation that all key concepts would be covered in discussions with each claimant participating in the research. Methodologically, this is an important understanding. One of the characteristics of the anthropological approach (and one that distinguishes it from other forms of social science) is that it seeks to understand both structure and meaning in human cultures, as well as how these might relate, for example, to systems of rule-based action. It is axiomatic in this endeavour that both have to be discovered by close observation, participation and familiarity. Given the constraints of the research, long-term association with the claimants was not going to be possible. However, interactions were to be as open and unstructured as possible. Researchers were encouraged to take the claimants into the field whenever the opportunity arose, since it is a given of anthropological study that field visits provide a less formal and more relaxed atmosphere in which information that would not be forthcoming in a formal interview can be brought out. Researchers were also encouraged to make multiple visits to claimants, where this was possible and practical, so that some degree of rapport was established. In this way, the data sheet provided a template to assist the researchers to ensure coverage of the topics for which information was required. However, there was no intention that the data sheet be consistently and completely applied to all interactions.

This means that for some claimants data were not available for some areas represented in the data sheet. The absence of data in relation to a particular concept should not be taken to imply that no data were available. It may mean that the topic was not discussed. The semi-structured interviews, complemented by field visits, provided for a balance between an observational and participatory approach (favoured by anthropologists) and a need to ensure that the research remained focused. The anthropological opinions expressed in this book are based, in part, on the data contained in the data sheets.

In order to meet the stringent requirements for the admissibility of expert opinion in the court, it was important to be clear about who was responsible for the research and the views which would form a part of the evidence for the application. Consequently, I led this project and took responsibility for research design, research supervision, quality control, data assessment and processing. I was the sole author of the expert report. Questions asked by respondent parties to the application in court were then to be directed to me, as it was clear that the expert views expressed were mine, based upon both my own field data as well as other material collected under my supervision.

Anthropologists generalise from the particular. That is to say, they record or observe what some do, believe or think within the culture they study and, provided they are confident that the data are not anomalous, assume that they represent what might be the case more generally. If some social phenomenon is noted by a researcher on many occasions, it lends credence to the generality of its occurrence. This is desirable, but provided any conclusion developed from the subsequent generalising is falsifiable through subsequent inquiry, the proposition is legitimate as forming the basis for an understanding of an aspect of the society being studied.

Some social scientists, in seeking to understand the generality of, say, an opinion, have developed research methodologies which ask the same series of questions to a wide cross-section of the population being studied. These questionnaire surveys commonly are used for market research and by political parties. They depend for their accuracy on a number of factors, including a consistency in the manner in which the questions are both asked and understood by the respondent. They also depend upon the representativeness of the sample, as in these cases it is usually impractical to poll the whole population (except on election day). Needless to say, the reliability of market research is patchy. Moreover, while it may provide some insights in relation to questions which require a simple answer, it does not lend itself to complex issues like social structures, beliefs, customs and rights.

In the research reported here there has been a reliance on the anthropological practice of generalising from the particular to the general. That is to say, if some cultural trait is recorded that does not appear anomalous, it is generalised to the wider claimant community. Assessment of what might constitute an 'anomaly' is based upon the researcher's extensive experience in Australian Aboriginal cultures. Supporting data (historical or contemporary citations) are also of assistance here.

Given the nature of the research reported here and the limitations of social inquiry generally, it is neither possible nor practical to make definitive comment on the absolute extent of any particular belief or practice amongst the claimant community. Consistent with anthropological practice, I have based my conclusions on a reasonable assumption that the beliefs and practices on which I report here are likely to be found within the larger Noongar community, with variations and not without exception. In providing citations in support of the data set out, I in no way imply that the belief or practice is limited to those cited. Such a conclusion would be inconsistent with accepted anthropological thinking.

The scope and the extent of the research

The application area is extensive, comprising (as I have already noted) some 186,000 square kilometres. The direct distance from Jurien Bay to Perth is approximately 200 kilometres and from Perth to Albany, as the crow flies, is approximately 400 kilometres. Perth to Hyden is about 300 kilometres direct. Not only are the distances great, but the region is home to many Noongar families. The Form 1 of the Federal Court Application for determination of native title lists 99 different apical ancestors, from which hundreds of Noongar families are descended. Given the constraints imposed on the research by both time and resources, it was not possible to undertake exhaustive research that would include all claimants and provide for comprehensive coverage of all areas of the claim.

What was planned and executed was a detailed but partial coverage of both areas and persons. This provided for a representative sample of the total Noongar population and lands. This means that some Noongar families were not included in the interviews and site visits were not made to some areas of the application. While the research reported here is therefore not exhaustive, representative sampling is a common and acceptable anthropological method employed to gain data, reflective of a larger picture, where it is not practical to view all cases. Consistent with this methodology, the findings contained in this book are extrapolated to apply to all claimants and the application area as a whole.

The available literature relevant to the Aboriginal population of the South West is considerable. In Part I of this book I review some of this literature. Given the limitations of both time and resources, I exercised some discrimination over what was reviewed and what was not. For example, I decided not to use material collected by researchers investigating earlier native title applications over parts of what was later identified as the Single Noongar Claim area. This was because research conducted in relation to a claim different in geographic scope to the one considered here would have a focus which was significantly different from my own. Its potential usefulness might be called into question. In addition, if I were to base my views on such research, I would need to validate the work of the researchers. I judged this to be impractical, given difficulties occasioned by death and demography. It would also have been beyond the resources of the project. I have focused my attention on the better-known sources and those which seemed to me to provide the most copious commentary in relation to Aboriginal culture. The review is not exhaustive, and no doubt some texts which might have deserved a place were omitted. However, I am of the view that the range of materials which I have covered is adequate to provide a sound view of the early commentary on Aboriginal culture in the South West.

PART I

NINETEENTH- AND EARLY TWENTIETH-CENTURY ACCOUNTS OF NOONGAR CULTURE

Chapter 1

INTRODUCTION

In this section of the book I consider how the ethnographic accounts written within the first hundred years or so of settlement might assist in establishing the fundamental components constituting Noongar[4] laws and customs prior to 1829.[5] Reconstructive anthropology must be treated with caution, depending as it does on interpretations of interpretations. Moreover, the observations of the early writers present their own difficulties, which I will examine below. However, given the relative abundance of materials and their ethnographic content, it is relevant to consider what they might have to contribute to an understanding of the traditional laws and customs of the claimant community. These materials may also provide some indication of the continuity of those laws and customs since the acquisition of sovereignty by the British government. To this end, I will first outline the accounts which are my principal concern in this section and look at how they can broadly be categorised. Second, I address the limitations of these materials and the extent to which these limitations can be obviated. Finally, I set out methodological issues prior to commencing my analysis of the materials themselves.

The range of available materials

The South West of Western Australia was settled by Indigenous Australians tens of thousands of years ago, a fact attested by the archaeological record.[6] It was not

4 Consistent with the title of this application for a determination of native title, I will call the Aboriginal people of the South West of Western Australia 'Noongar people'. Further discussion of the use of this term, and others, is set out in Chapter 2.

5 The date of the acquisition of sovereignty by the British Crown over Western Australia. Prior to this date it could be assumed that native title existed unencumbered. It is therefore a significant date in the proof of the continuity of native title.

6 For a list of relevant citations, see Crawford and Crawford (2003, p. 10). See also Hallam (1975, pp. 5–8); Smith (1982, p. 117).

until 1826 that the British established a military outpost at King George Sound in the far south of the state and, three years later, a colony for free settlers on the Swan River. Since the early part of the seventeenth century, Europeans had touched on the coast of what is now Western Australia, from necessity or convenience. However, the two settlements at King George Sound (now Albany) and the Swan River (now Perth and Fremantle) marked the beginning of a permanent European presence in the South West, with significant consequences for the Indigenous inhabitants of the region.[7]

A number of the early settlers and staff of the garrison proved to be committed diarists and writers, leaving accounts of the inhabitants of the region they had colonised. These accounts provide a view of the European settlers' attitudes to and observations of the Indigenous culture within a few years of settlement. While, for obvious reasons, none of these accounts can be considered to pre-date European settlement, they represent contemporary accounts of a society within a few years of colonisation. Notable for the Perth region are the accounts of Moore (1978b, written in 1830), Lyon (written in 1833, see Lyon 1979), Armstrong (written in 1836, see Armstrong 1979) and Grey (1841). For the Albany region, early written accounts are provided by Barker (1992, written in 1828–31), Clark (1842), Collie (1834), Nind (written in 1831, see Nind 1979) and Wollaston (1975, written from 1848). These men were mostly from the professional classes: administrators, lawyers or clergymen with a good education but a limited understanding of trans-cultural issues. I will return to this point later.

Following the first decades of settlement, a number of writers recorded aspects of Noongar culture. Although coming from a variety of backgrounds and with varying degrees of expertise, these writers had in common a desire to provide an account of Aboriginal culture that reflected a growing awareness in Western thinking of the importance of understanding ethnographic materials and an increased interest in their public presentation. While at its worst this represented the Aborigines of the South West as colonial curios, material produced from the mid-nineteenth century to 1900 provides ethnographic data, collected from individuals who had either been born prior to 1829 or who could recall interactions with those who had. For the South West of Western Australia two writers are particularly significant from this era. One was Bishop Salvado and the other was EM Curr. Both attempted a degree of systematic recording of Aboriginal culture

7 A succinct account of European settlement of the South West is to be found in Green (1984, pp. 23–48).

(systematic at least by the standards of the day). Salvado lived in close proximity to Aboriginal people for a number of years. Curr assembled notes collected by others at his request from many areas of Australia, so attempting to provide a comparative analysis.

Salvado's memoirs relating to Australia cover the period 1846 to 1850 (Stormon 1977). The memoirs contain copious ethnographic observations resulting from Salvado's close association with the local people in the course of establishing the mission at New Norcia, developed as a result of his scholarly interest in their culture. Salvado also contributed to what was, arguably, the first attempt at a comprehensive Australian account of Aboriginal people, compiled by EM Curr in 1886–87. This work purported in the title to characterise the 'Australian race . . . its origin, languages, customs, places of landing in Australia, and the routes by which it spread itself over that continent'. Importantly, the work attempted to present ethnographic data, collected systematically to some degree, although Curr relied on correspondents across the continent so quality control was virtually impossible. Two other writers of this time were Browne (1856), who grew up in Albany and whose account had more in common with earlier writers from the region than with more scholarly accounts. Towards the end of the century, R Helms (1896) contributed to the report of the Elder Scientific Expedition in 1891–92, but his account is only marginally relevant to this application.

In 1878, Ethel Hassell, who was born in Albany, married a pastoralist from Jerramungup, where she lived until 1886. Hassell wrote an account of the lives of the Aboriginal people in whose traditional country her husband's property lay. This was finally published in 1975 (Hassell 1975). The American anthropologist Daniel Davidson edited parts of Hassell's manuscript, which he published in academic journals. They appear to contain the same material as the manuscript but lack Hassell's rather homely style (Hassell 1934–35, 1936). Hammond's observations date from the latter part of the nineteenth century, although his best-known work was not published until 1933 (Hammond 1933). The account contains numerous ethnographic observations, wrapped up in the author's own somewhat idiosyncratic notions (see also Hammond 1938). Frances Terry provided some material from the Margaret River area, dating from 1857 (Terry 1994; Terry n.d.). In the York area Mrs Edward Millett, writing in the 1870s, provided a quite extensive account of colonial life at Ballardong (York),[8] which included some details of the

8 The term Barladong is used by Millett for the York area. See, for example, Millett (1872, p. 72).

Aboriginal people she came to know (Millett 1872). Finally, the letters of Henry Lefroy provide some limited materials from the same area, but the account makes only passing reference to Aboriginal people in the region (Lefroy 1934).

The turn of the century saw extensive research on Noongar culture conducted by Daisy Bates in the South West of Western Australia. Although Bates was not an anthropologist, she considered herself an expert in Aboriginal culture and spent substantial periods of time living in close proximity to Aboriginal people. She attempted to present her account of their culture in a systematic manner, encouraged by correspondence with several eminent anthropologists of the day, including AR Radcliffe-Brown and Andrew Lang (see White 1985, pp. 5–6). Bates was probably one of the last researchers or writers to have worked with Noongar people born within a decade or two of European colonisation, and she certainly would have encountered men and women during her travels in more remote areas of the South West who would have lived beyond the borders of European settlement. Her writings are important in any attempt to understand how Noongar culture might have been before the changes wrought by colonisation. Unlike the writers considered above, Bates attempted a systematic and analytical study, influenced by the new methods and theoretical considerations of an emergent anthropology, promoted in particular in Australia by AR Radcliffe-Brown, the first Professor of Anthropology at the University of Sydney. She was also influenced by a number of other influential academics of the time (White 1985, pp. 14–18).

Two other writers warrant mention here. Radcliffe-Brown worked briefly and disastrously with Daisy Bates in the North West of the state in 1910 (White 1985, pp. 6–9). He wrote a brief piece on the Aboriginal people of the South West of Western Australia (Radcliffe-Brown 1930) and presented some limited material in a more extensive paper concerning the social organisation of Australian tribes (Radcliffe-Brown 1930–31). It is possible that Radcliffe-Brown drew upon Bates's material for his South West article, but if this is so it is not acknowledged. Also relevant to this period is a paper by WE Roth, published in the *Proceedings of the Royal Society of Queensland* in 1902. The paper was based on material provided to Roth from FR Austin, Assistant Surveyor in Western Australia, being 'reminiscences' that dated back to 'the years 1841–3' (Roth 1902, p. 45). Roth was an ethnographer, and he conducted an inquiry into the conditions of Aboriginal people in the North West of Western Australia (Horton 1994, pp. 955–96). The account provided by Roth is scholarly and covers a wide range of ethnographic materials.

The development of anthropology as a social science in Australia saw few field studies in the South West of Western Australia.[9] For the most part it was not until the latter part of the last century that any detailed field studies were undertaken in the region. These are not my concern at present but they will be discussed in due course. Many relied upon earlier writers, including Bates, to develop views as to the nature of Noongar culture prior to 1829. Some, however, have relied heavily on the early sources in presenting their own reconstruction of Noongar society. These accounts provide a means of access to earlier writers, while laying an additional layer of interpretation upon the original sets of observations. Ferguson (1987) interpreted data from Nind, Barker and Collie (see above), as well as from Dr Braidwood Wilson.[10] Ferguson does not reference his material specifically, and his account at times goes beyond a summary of his sources and is no substitute for reading the originals. Richards' book on the 'Bibbulmun' (1994) is based on the work of earlier writers, in particular Hammond (1933, p. 6). While the author provides no citations, he is candid in admitting that his is a work of 'dramatic narrative' — a style that will allow him to escape from the 'accusation of possible inaccuracies', considering as he does that the 'facts' are now impossible to recover (p. 5). Substantial reliance is also placed on early writers by both Le Souef (1993) and Crawford and Crawford (2003) when writing on aspects of Noongar culture. A scholarly work by Keen (2004) relies on the work of the early writers from the Albany area in its comparison of the reconstructed traditional economies of seven regions.

The categorisation I have adopted above is heuristic rather than definitive, and other ways of organising these data could be devised (e.g. see Brunton 2003, pp. 3–10). I have only included sources which I consider may assist in accomplishing the task at hand — that is, developing an appreciation of how early writers understood or perceived Noongar culture.

Limitations of the pre-1900 materials

Historians are aware of the limitations of the reliability of the accounts of the early settlers. Writing in 1984, Neville Green was well aware, as a historian, of

9 A deficiency that Professor Elkin (Professor of Anthropology at the University of Sydney) noted for the whole of Western Australia up until the 1920s, with the exception of Bates, whose work he regarded as 'tantalizingly incomplete' (Elkin 1979, p. 298).

10 Wilson was a colonial surgeon. According to Ferguson (1987, p. 130), he travelled 'extensively with Mokaré during 1829'. Ferguson does not reference his quotation, but his source is likely to be Wilson (1968).

the difficulty he faced when interpreting the accounts of the early settlers. He wrote with respect to both the 'tribal' groups of the Swan River and Noongar groups more generally that:

> few of the reports are reliable, most are lacking, some are contradictory and all are by non-Aborigines. The European writers are often observing customs they did not understand and which were explained to them in a foreign language. Consequently they tried to use their own cultural experiences and values to describe Aboriginal behaviour. (Green 1984, p. 9)

In the same book, Green expands on what he considers the early settlers' inclination to interpret the world according to their own standards. He writes that, 'The settlers' response to the Aborigines reflected a personal set of cultural values (p. 54).' He then gives an example of a female settler who was distressed at the idea of living among a 'low' and 'degraded race'. He continues:

> In common with many men and women of her times, she was inclined to measure a person's worth by his lands; his possessions; and by his degree of conformity to English middle-class concepts of acceptable social behaviour. (Green 1984, p. 54)

The point is well illustrated by Clark, who provides an account of Noongar culture by critical reference to the Ten Commandments, a process by which he judges its comparative worth (Clark 1842).[11] Other writers were concerned with what they considered to be elemental issues that related to humanity and civilisation. These included the belief in the existence of a deity, belief in an afterlife, a system of morality and a system of government (e.g. see Armstrong 1979, pp. 186–7; Barker 1992, p. 345, n. 30; Stormon 1977, pp. 126–30). In some respects, then, the accounts of the early settlers tells us more about these men and the moral, political and philosophical climate of their times than it does about the original inhabitants of Western Australia.

Keen, an anthropologist, is also cautious about the validity of these early sources. He notes that much information is not available. Of the Albany region in particular (the Minong people) he has this to say:

> There is no possibility of recovering the whole texture of Minong social life of the early nineteenth century — all we have are some oral traditions and the writings of

---

11 Lefroy (1934, p. 107) considered the Aboriginal people he encountered to be 'nearer to the gorilla than to Aristotle, St Paul or Newton'. For similarly prejudiced accounts, see Millett (1872, pp. 70–1).

> Scott Nind, Collet Barker, Daisy Bates and a few others. Their language provides a grid through which we can imagine Minong life, and the gaps remain unfillable, except by analogy and inference . . . The 'findings' then must be tentative, susceptible to revision in the light of new evidence or a re-reading of the old, and in the light of criticism of the categories, conceptual schemes, and theories that inform them. (Keen 2004, pp. 15–16)

I agree with Green that there was a huge disparity between European concepts of land ownership and that entertained by the Noongar people (Green 1984, p. 55). The worldview of the early colonial writers was bound by strongly Eurocentric views, at a time when patriarchy and patrilineal descent and inheritance were the norm. These writers generally were of the opinion that defined and bounded property was a feature of man's relationship to country and that estates were an exclusive property. Commonage was not a part of this ideology. While the writers recognised that there was a strong personal link between those they sought to dispossess and the country, they were only able to interpret it according to their own precepts. It is no coincidence that Barker concludes his journal with the first two lines from an early poem by Alexander Pope (see Barker 1992, p. 407):

> Happy the man, whose wish and care
> A few *paternal* acres bound,
> Content to breathe his native air
> In his own ground. (Pope 1956, p. 1, emphasis added)

Not only does the poem extol the virtues of a person's 'own' ground, but builds on the expectation that the ground will be patrilineally inherited.

There was also an assumption that a 'native' society would take the form of a named 'tribe', with little or no understanding of the variety of social formations and the plethora of names applied to social and regional groupings composed of 'tribes'. Howard remarked on this in his account of Noongar politics:

> Analyses and descriptions of traditional Aborigines have often utilized the term 'tribe' for a variety of socio-cultural, linguistic divisions. This seems to stem from a proclivity of Western man to see all 'primitives' as having tribes. That is, while all 'primitives' have tribes, so-called 'civilised' people are seen as having ethnic groups. As was the case . . . elsewhere, the early commentators on the south-west tended to identify the tribe with the local foraging unit, or band. For example, Nind (1979) and Bunbury (1930) mention numerous tribes with populations of between fifteen and forty individuals, which corresponded (it would appear) with

> local bands. Likewise, Browne (1856: 445-446) identifies four different tribes in the King George Sound area, each with its own territory and name. Later analyses sought to find the tribe at a higher level of articulation. (Howard 1976, pp. 17–19)

This is an understandable conclusion, particularly in light of contemporary accounts of social and local organisation, and it is one confirmed by Brunton (2003, p. 31).[12] However, the fundamental misunderstandings of the early writers must call into question other remarks that they made about Noongar culture, often with great certainty and apparent authority.

Without exception, the early writers were educated men who filled positions of authority in the new settler society. Barker was the commandant of the King George Sound garrison; Moore represented the legal authority of the colony, and admitted that he was recognised as 'one having authority' (Moore 1978b, p. 379); Collie was a surgeon; Hassell was the station owner's wife. To a greater or lesser extent, there was always an asymmetrical relationship between the original inhabitants and the new settlers where power over goods, services, resources and firearms was almost always in the settlers' favour. Even when the explorer Grey was *in extremis* and dependent on his Noongar guide, Kaiber, for his life, he was able to exert his authority over him by threatening him with his gun (Grey 1841, vol. 2, pp. 73–7). It may well have been an appreciation of the one-sidedness of the relations between the settlers and the Aboriginal people that led the latter to exercise caution over the release of information which some of the new settlers sought. There is some evidence that not all the data collected was sound. Armstrong is particularly damning of those with whom he worked, accusing them of making up information for the price of a meal or a 'few pence', then laughing at the settlers for their gullibility (Armstrong 1979, pp. 205–6). Hassell was similarly critical of the quality of the information provided to her (and presumably to others). She stated that those with whom she lived might tell only what they thought 'was good for you to know' or what they thought you wished to hear (Hassell 1975, p. 157), and that information about the ritual life, which was deliberately being kept from her, was hard to come by (p. 78). Salvado also provides examples of when he was deliberately misled (Stormon 1977, p. 125; see also Millett 1872, p. 289).

I agree with the observation of Hammond that 'without some knowledge of their language' it would be 'impossible to get a true account of the aborigines' (Hammond 1933, p. 9). He considered that the potential for misunderstanding

---

12 This conclusion was reached by Salvado in the mid-nineteenth century. See Stormon (1977, p. 130).

without some fluency in the language was high. Armstrong was appointed Government Interpreter some time prior to 1871 and was fluent in 'at least' five dialects of the Noongar language (Green 1979, pp. 181–2). However, early accounts attributable to Armstrong are limited. Hassell collected words from the local Wilmun language (as did many other early writers for other dialects), but there is no indication that she spoke the language herself. The degree of fluency in a Noongar dialect of other writers noted here is difficult to judge. From a reading of his journals, Grey would appear to have some facility in the language. Salvado indicates that he considered the 'study' of the language to be important to an understanding of the culture, but it is unclear whether study extended to any fluency in speaking the language. He certainly lived in close proximity to the people, particularly during the first years of the establishment of the mission at New Norcia, and this may have assisted him in gaining some knowledge of the language (Stormon 1977, p. 54). However, his view that the New Norcia language and that of Adelaide had a 'great number' of words in common indicates that his was more an academic study of a selected set of words, rather than one based on daily language use. On the whole, my reading of the texts is that in exchanges between the settlers and the Aboriginal inhabitants the use of English was the norm, supplemented by the interpolation of some Noongar words. Given the fact that Aboriginal people spoke little English, especially in the first decades of European settlement, this must have influenced both the quality and quantity of the information available to the early commentators.

Philosophical, social, political and practical issues qualify the validity of these early writings.[13] It would represent a misjudgment to accept the statements of the authors of these early materials without question. They should be critically examined in the light of other comparable writings and be subjected to close scrutiny. Yet these early accounts are the only record that we have of the culture of the Aboriginal people of the South West of Western Australia and, provided they are understood to be a product of their times, they can give some tentative indications of the way things may have been. Where there is agreement between several sources, the validity of the observations may be strengthened, unless of course one source relied upon another, which is a possibility. The early texts are best judged on the evidence provided within those texts, rather than resorting to an attempt to judge the worth of one particular writer by reference to what is known of his personality.

13 Berndt (1979, p. 81) called them 'anthropologically unsatisfactory'.

The Bates material

Daisy Bates can be seen to follow on from the early writers, but she also represents a departure from them. Bates lived many decades after the early settlers and collected her material in a manner and according to precepts that were different from those of the earlier diarists and writers. She attempted to provide a scientific account of the culture she studied. In this regard, she made notes while in the field and recorded genealogies. She lived with Aboriginal people and therefore had the opportunity to record their culture at firsthand. She published the results of some of her research and wrote unpublished manuscripts. However, measures of her success as an ethnographer have been subject to much debate.

Bates's materials are voluminous, diverse and often disorganised, spanning several decades. White (1985, p. 5), records that Bates arrived in Perth in 1899 and spent her first few years travelling in the north of the State (pp. 9–10). Bates became an employee of the state government in 1904. She was required to collect language and other materials from the Aboriginal people of the Perth area and elsewhere in the South West. She moved to the Maamba Reserve in Perth a year later (pp. 5–6) and, while it is possible that she collected field data before her move there, it is likely that her employment by the government gave impetus to her collection of data. Bates produced a manuscript of a book on the Aboriginal people of the South West in 1909, but this was not accepted for publication by the state government (pp. 9–16). The manuscript was retyped between 1936 and 1940; however, according to White, it 'remained essentially as Mrs Bates devised it in 1909' (p. 16). Bates published her best-known work, *The passing of the Aborigines*, in 1938, and numerous journalistic articles were published between 1907 and 1934 (see Bates 1992). Bates's collections of observations of Aboriginal customs and beliefs, as well as of their languages, cover many areas of Western Australia, as well as South Australia, and were not confined to the South West of Western Australia, although that is the focus of this discussion.

Bates had no anthropological training, although she was influenced by eminent scholars of the time (see White 1985, pp. 14–16). She was very much a product of her time, considering that the Aborigines with whom she worked were a doomed race, close to extinction (p. 22).[14] She also saw Aborigines as filling a particular niche in evolutionary terms, which, as a result, sometimes

14 See also 'Introduction' to *The passing of the Aborigines* (Bates 1966, p. xi) by Arthur Mee: 'She has given her life and her heart to this dying race . . . She has done it for the love of humanity and for England.'

caused her to denigrate them. She generally disregarded Aboriginal people of mixed descent (pp. 16–17).[15]

In 1910, Bates accepted an offer to join an anthropological expedition from Cambridge University, led by anthropologist Professor AR Brown,[16] accompanied by his colleague EL Grant Watson (White 1985, p. 7). The arrangement proved to be an unhappy one, as Radcliffe-Brown and Bates were unable to work together. Grant Watson reported that Radcliffe-Brown held the view that the contents of Bates's mind were, 'in his estimation . . . somewhat similar to the contents of a well-stored sewing basket, after half a dozen kittens had been playing there undisturbed for a few days' (Grant Watson 1946, pp. 105–6, cited in White 1985, pp. 7–8). Whether Grant Watson agreed with Radcliffe-Brown's account is unclear, although the fact that he set it down in this manner may indicate that he concurred.

White (1985, pp. 14–22) reviews Bates's contribution to our knowledge of the Aborigines of the South West of Western Australia and touches on some of the criticisms that have been levelled at her. White agrees that the organisation of Bates's materials was sometimes 'haphazard' (p. 21), but concludes that her materials collected from the South West 'remain her greatest contribution to our knowledge of Aboriginal life-styles before these were changed by contact with Europeans' (p. 19).

My own view is that White was correct, in that Bates did collect a substantial amount of material over a period of years from Aboriginal people in the South West of Western Australia and this material provides us with an indication of the society and culture that existed in the region prior to 1829. However, Bates's material lacks organisation, and the form in which the South West materials eventually saw the light of day when edited by White in 1985 is not always consistent with Bates's earlier notes and observations. I am of the view that Bates entertained a conceptual uncertainty with respect to some social structures, which made for an imperfect and sometimes contradictory analysis. Her work therefore must be treated with caution. I will set out my reasons for reaching this view below.

15 See White (1985, p. 19), for a list of some of her informants. In Bates's genealogies (Bates n.d.k), she generally does not record the names or details of 'half caste' children. Bates's view that the Aboriginal race was dying out discounted mixed-descent Aboriginal people as members of the Aboriginal race.

16 Later Radcliffe-Brown.

Chapter 2

THE ABORIGINAL SOCIETY OF THE SOUTH WEST

Early sources

The South West society and how it is named

Given the limitations of European settlement and exploration, early commentators in the South West of Western Australia were initially unable to gain a clear idea of the nature and extent of the Indigenous society that occupied the south-western triangle of the state. However, as the decades passed and the extent of colonisation progressed, views developed regarding both the homogeneity and heterogeneity of the Indigenous culture. Later writers like Bates were to state categorically that the South West of Western Australia was peopled by a single society, which she called Bibbulmun, and I will consider Bates's views in more detail subsequently. Later, Tindale (1940,[17] 1974, pp. 41, 254 and 297) was to identify the 'Njunga' as an alternative to Wudjari (occupying country to the east of Bremer Bay), recognising this group along with 12 others as comprising 'tribes' with geographic proximity whose members practised neither circumcision nor subincision. Tindale's so called 'circumcision line' extends northwards beyond the South West.[18]

---

17 Tindale based his findings on his own field studies as a member of the Harvard–Adelaide Universities Anthropological Expedition, 1939–40, as well as on early sources.

18 Two early writers make comment on the existence of what might be termed a northern boundary to the South West Noongar culture. Moore (1978b, p. 380) remarks that Aboriginal people told him that 'witchcraft' came from 'the north', indicating that things evil and undesirable came from some point north of Perth. Wollaston (1975, pp. 170–1) notes that the Aborigines in Geraldton were 'cannibals' and were 'different in some respects from our own natives' [from Albany]. While Wollaston's observations about cannibalism are unfounded, the comments reflect an appreciation of cultural difference between those living in the South West of the state and those living further north.

Berndt (1979) calls the Indigenous occupants of the South West of Western Australia 'South-West Aborigines' (p. 81), considering Tindale's 'tribal' distinctions were 'actually "dialectal units" of a common South-West language' (p. 82). He states that the linguistic (dialect) groups of the South West can, '*in toto* . . . be classified today as Nyungar (a word meaning "man" or "person")' and that 'it is also interesting that, according to Moore, in 1842 this was the name (he spelt it as *yung-ar*) the South-West people used for themselves' (p. 81).[19] Most subsequent writers have accepted that the Aboriginal occupants of the South West of Western Australia comprise a single cultural society (e.g. see Howard 1976, pp. 23–5; Toussaint 1987, p. 50; Birdsall 1990, pp. 1–2; Crawford and Crawford 2003, p. 11). Green provides a useful listing showing the ubiquity of the occurrence within the South West of Western Australia of the term 'Noongar' or its variants derived from EM Curr's vocabularies (Green 1984, p. 7). The component 'dialect units' (Tindale's 'tribes') of the Noongar are best termed 'groups', and their constituent extended family units referred to as 'families'.

Early writers generally favoured the use of a single name for the people living in the area where they had settled. This may have been because, as I will discuss below, there was a tendency to assume that there was a 'tribal structure' that accorded with their preconceptions. That is to say, there was a discrete community of people, with a classifying name, speaking the same language and with a system of government that included a chief or leader. The use of a name to identify the 'tribe' was then a convenience born of a preconception which obfuscated a more complex reality. Curr (1886–87), for example, employed the term 'tribe' freely throughout his work, and his correspondents used names to identify regional groups[20] without properly understanding what they might mean. However, this was not universally the case, and where correspondents did not have a 'tribal' name they used the local European name instead. Thus, while Curr's sources for the King George Sound region identified the locals as members of the 'Minung tribe' (Curr 1886–87, p. 386), those around Perth are provided with no group name. One of Curr's sources for his Perth account was Armstrong, who appears to

---

19 Berndt does not supply the reference in Moore. However, in Moore's account of the massacre at Pinjarra, Norcott, one of the police, called out on seeing those pursued that they had found the 'old rascal Noonar' whom they sought. The man replied, 'Yes, Noonar me' (Moore 1978b, p. 241). In Moore's *Descriptive vocabulary*, he lists the term 'yung-ar' as 'People. The name by which they designate themselves' (1978a, p. 84). This may be the source of Berndt's reference. Moore was writing in the early 1830s.

20 That is, a group of people who together were associated or identified with a region.

have spoken the language, so the absence of a name may reflect the fact that there was no single name that could identify a 'tribal' entity. Similarly, Salvado, in his contribution to Curr (pp. 318ff) does not identify any name for the New Norcia 'tribe', although Curr employs the term 'tribe' in his account (pp. 318ff). Nor does Salvado use any generic tribal appellation in his memoirs, referring instead to the Aboriginal people he writes about as 'natives' (Stormon 1977).

This is not to say that there were no names used to identify groups associated with particular areas. However, it is evident from the early writers that these names were neither exclusive nor derived from a single mode of identity. The result is that names as recorded are not always consistent, because different terms were recorded according to the context, the perspective of the informant and what was being named. Nind (1979, pp. 44–6) reports that there were regional names for groups living in the vicinity of King George Sound. He records the Meananger around what is now Albany because they ate the *mearn*, a red root (see p. 36), while Collie (1834, p. 91) calls them the Mongalan.[21] To the west of Albany, Nind records the Murram and inland the Yobberore, next to them the Wil, then the Warrangle and to the west of them the Corine (Nind 1979, pp. 44–6). Green (1979, p. 45) has drawn these areas 'vaguely', following Nind, but also reproduces Tindale's (1940) account. A comparison of the two, as set out by Green (1979), shows that different names were recorded at different times. Based on the observations of Hassell, her editor (CW Hassell) has included a map of 'tribes and localities' (Hassell 1975, p. xiii). With the exception of the 'Wheelman' located well to the east of both Nind's and Tindale's accounts, the names are different, while those living around Bremer Bay have no Aboriginal name at all.

Browne (1856, p. 488) describes four tribes for the Albany region: the Murray, Weal, Cockatoo and Kincannup. Again, with the exception of the Weal (Wilmun) these names are not found in the other sources noted above. Browne explains that, in his view, these names relate only to the areas they mostly inhabit, less as a distinct tribe than 'as a combination of many small tribes, inhabiting a territory lying in a certain position' (p. 488). He explains that Kincannup is the area name for Albany, and so the name used for those who live there (p. 488).[22]

21 Keen, reviewing the available literature on the region, concludes that 'there is general agreement in the sources' that the people of the Sound were the Mi<u>n</u>ong, which is the name he adopts for his analyses. Keen cites eight sources, including Nind, but not Collie. See Keen (2004, p. 173, n. 39).

22 The copy of this article viewed was included in the National Native Title Tribunal's research report, *South West Trial Area Two* (NNTT 2001) and is a typescript of the original. Original page numbers are interpolated into the text and these are the references used here.

Hammond (1933, p. 16) considered that the Aboriginal people of the South West of Western Australia comprised one cultural group with three major 'tribes' and similar laws, customs and amusements. He noted a fourth to the east of Albany, 'toward Esperance'. Hammond suggested that the application of numerous names was a result of the fact that Aboriginal people used the term for their birthplace (*boujera*),[23] implying that this resulted in the use of numerous identifying names for groups.

The early writers were not alone in their tribal inclinations. Keen (2004, p. 134) notes that:

> many early ethnographers assumed that Aborigines were divided into relatively large and discrete 'tribes', each of which shared a common language, culture, and territory. This model survived through the first two-thirds of the twentieth century, adhered to, with variations, by Radcliffe-Brown, Elkin, Tindale and Birdsell.

However, he observes that 'the tribal model had begun to unravel more than a decade before Tindale published his book and maps of Aboriginal tribes in 1974' (p. 134). Berndt (1959) had questioned the applicability of this model to the Western Desert. Keen notes that other researchers (in Queensland) had demonstrated that the relationship between language, social identity and community was complex for areas well outside the Western Desert. People tended to be multilingual (or to speak several dialects of the same language); they often married members of other language or dialect groups, so that language, while important, could not be seen alone as a diacritic of group membership. The formation of an identity also involved references to a locality or a relative appellation, like 'northerner' or coastal dweller (Keen 2004, p. 135).

Keen provides more detailed comments relating to the Wilmun and Mirnong,[24] which he develops from the early sources (2004, pp. 155–7). He notes that some terms appear to have been applied more consistently than others: Mirnong, Mirram, Wilmun and Kaninyang.[25] While Keen concludes that 'there

23 Hammond notes that there term also means 'territory . . . dirt or spoil' (Hammond 1933, p. 17).

24 Keen writes 'Wiil', indicating a long i, and Mi<u>n</u>ong, indicating a retroflex n. The suffix '-men' gives a plural (see Douglas 1976, p. 63), and 'wil' means 'north' (see Bindon and Chadwick 1992, p. 336), so 'wilmun' means 'northerners'.

25 Tindale (1974, p. 244) includes references to Nind (1979), Clark (1842), Small in Curr (1886–87) and Hassell (1936), among others, as sources for the Kaninyang, and places them on the Upper Blackwood River. The Mirram were to the west of Albany.

is general agreement' that the Mirnong were people 'between the coast and the ranges, and from Albany east to perhaps Bremer Bay', he further states:

> These were not the names of clearly defined territorial groups or 'tribes', but referred, I think, more loosely to people belonging to a certain general region — hence the relativity of some of the names . . . They were not endogamous groups, especially given the preference for marriage to a distant cousin; consequently, many people probably had parents of different regional identities and their own regional identities would have been ambiguous. (Keen 2004, pp. 156–7)

Early writers were not able to appreciate the complexity and diversity of the nomenclature of identity. My own view concurs broadly with Keen's. Identity was (and is) not necessarily absolute and a person may acquire an attribution of identity depending upon circumstances so identity names may not be exclusive. So, for example, it would be possible to be both a 'coastal dweller' (*waddarndi*) as well as a person from Albany (a Kincannup). It is from the multiple uses of identities that the confusion and inconsistency in the early accounts develops. This does not mean that the terms recorded by the early writers were necessarily wrong. It does, however, mean that they cannot be relied upon as indicators of fixed social groups that have so conveniently and erroneously been understood to constitute 'tribes'.

Language

Anthropologists generally accept that language is one of the unifying cultural traits which can be understood as forming commonalities between groups, resulting in their members being considered part of one society. Moore (1978) provided early evidence of acceptance of this proposition as he presented his 'Descriptive Vocabulary of the language in common use amongst the Aborigines of Western Australia'. Moore distinguishes dialects of the language, since he included in his book words collected from a number of different regions, including King George Sound; however, he considered them dialects of one language (p. v). Salvado records two dialects of the one language, from the east and north of New Norcia (Stormon 1977, pp. 255–66), and he observes that 'the natives of Perth and those of King George Sound, although they are about 300 miles apart, speak practically the same language' (p. 132). Clark disagrees, stating that the King George Sound 'natives' did not understand Grey's vocabulary (Clark 1842, p. 5). Hassell, who collected her information some decades after Moore, identifies a number of groups (which she calls 'tribes'), including the Wheelman (60 miles (100 kilometres) from the coast), Mongup tribe, 'further inland', Caractterup tribe, Kar Kar 'more toward Esperance Bay', Qualup tribe and their coastal neighbours and the 'Bremer Bay tribe'. She states that the language spoken by these various groups was the same as that spoken in the rest of the South West of Western Australia, but with dialect variation (Hassell 1936, p. 680). Hammond considered that the people of the South West spoke mutually intelligible dialects of one language and were 'one big tribe' with similar 'laws, customs and amusements' (Hammond 1933, p. 16). He noted that Armstrong was unable to understand the language spoken 'north' of Moora and 'east' of Meckering (p. 16). It is unclear how far north and east of those places he meant — and, of course, all would depend upon Armstrong's fluency in the language and its dialects.

Inter-group cooperation and movement

I noted above that Tindale, using early sources as well as his own field studies, had differentiated the South West of Western Australia from adjacent cultural groups by reference to the absence of the rituals of circumcision and subincision. However, there is evidence from the early literature that other forms of initiation were practised across the South West. The joint practice of religious observances, including life-stage rituals of induction, requires some commonality of beliefs, at least at an over-arching level, as well as an adherence to a normative system that binds people together as a society. Noongar rituals of induction then indicate that the people of the South West of Western Australia shared laws and customs and constituted a single social and cultural bloc.

With the exception of funeral rites, which appear to have been mostly public affairs, early commentators did not obtain much information about the ritual lives of those they observed. This may be a result of the fact that ritual was regarded by the Noongar people as a private (and possibly secret) matter and they saw no need to divulge details of their rituals to the colonists. For example, Moore passes over the details of initiation rituals, except to comment that they involved the piercing of the nasal septum while noting that the ritual was performed by men from areas other than that to which the initiate belonged (Moore 1978b, p. 281). Curr (1886–87, p. 338) records that people from the York area pierced the nasal septum, as well as practising scarification, as did Salvado for the New Norcia region (Stormon 1977, pp. 142–3). Barker, writing of the Albany area, notes that initiation rituals of nose piercing typically involved cooperation between neighbouring groups, observing that a 'Will's boy' (that is, a member of the Wilmun 'tribe') called

Perityan was to experience ritual induction locally (Barker 1992, p. 359). Barker notes that neighbouring groups performed other rituals together and visited each other peacefully, apparently for non-ritual purposes (pp. 358, 331).[26] Armstrong (1979, p. 204) makes similar observations with respect to the Perth area, as does Hassell for the Jerramungup region, noting that as a result many friendships were made and marriages often contracted (Hassell 1936, p. 684; 1975, pp. 71, 72–3).

Crawford and Crawford (2003, p. 12) also conclude that ritual activity was shared between South West groups and this ensured that individuals built up a network of friends and acquaintances and developed extensive geographic knowledge. There is some evidence from the early literature that people travelled widely over the South West (e.g. see Crawford and Crawford 2003, pp. 16–17), a practice that undoubtedly was facilitated by European settlement. Nind (1979, pp. 46–7) observes that Aboriginal people might travel 'forty or fifty miles' to visit neighbours, while Barker's view was that the Aboriginal people of the Albany region sometimes travelled great distances (see Barker 1992, pp. 302, 310 and 324). On the other hand, Moore states that the Aboriginal people he knew rarely travelled (Moore 1978b, p. 146), while Grey says they were reluctant to do so for fear of 'hostile tribes' (Grey 1841, vol. 1, p. 312). Grey observes, however, that while some Aboriginal people were disinclined to travel with him, they asked him to ensure that he did no hurt to any people within 'ten days' journey to the north' of Perth, and thereafter 'indiscriminately to shoot every body I saw' (p. 293). Grey does not explain what was meant by this. However, one interpretation could be that those with whom he spoke regarded people within 10 days' journey as their friends and therefore not to be harmed, while those beyond were enemies and could be shot.

The extent of inter-group movement probably depended on the state of relations between groups. During times when relations were good, movement expanded; when things got tense, movement contracted. It is evident, however, that both ritual activity and other activity (trade, perhaps) encouraged travel between groups, indicating that practitioners shared common interests and understandings.

There are a number of other cultural indicators of commonality among Aboriginal groups of the South West of Western Australia, and many of these will be considered in the pages that follow. However, for convenience I consider two aspects of Noongar customary activity here: marriage and material culture.

---

26 Both Barker and Salvado note that the practice of piercing the nasal septum was not universal among those with whom they lived.

Marriage

In common with many other areas of Aboriginal Australia, there appears to have been a rule-based system in operation that prohibited marriage between members of the same family. This, in turn, was linked to a categorical system of identifying kin which in this region of Australia took the form of named moieties. I will examine this aspect of social organisation below. Seeking marriageable partners within the same group (dialect unit) appears to have been common, provided they were not of the same family (that is, they could not trace common ancestry). However, there are examples in the early literature of marriages contracted between members of neighbouring groups, indicating further cohesion, cooperation and commonality between the component groups of Noongar society. Barker (1992, p. 391) notes a marriage between an Albany man and a woman from Porongurup. Mokare's niece, Condalyan, was 'engaged to a man a long way off' (cited from Barker by Le Souef 1993, p. 11). Le Souef observes that marriages with members of other groups were arranged 'to reinforce friendly relations or political alliances with other groups' (p. 11). A wife might also be obtained following an initiatory travel to and residence with a neighbouring group (cf. Hassell 1936, p. 684). Nind states that it was considered 'best to procure a wife from the greatest distance possible' (1979, p. 46). Bates (1992, p. 23) confirms that the alliances that resulted from gaining a wife from a group other than the one to which the husband belonged permitted free movement over wide areas (see also pp. 76–7).

Seeking a wife from a group other than the one to which the husband belonged can be seen as a part of the cement that bound the society as a whole together. For marriages to be contracted and for the resultant alliances to be beneficial to the parties involved, there had to be a sense of commonality between the participant groups. It is likely that there were also marriages contracted between Noongars and non-Noongars, particularly where these people lived in relatively close proximity on the border of what is now the application area. Certainly the genealogical data contain examples of such marriages and, with the demographic changes that were a result of colonisation and subsequent settlement of the South West and beyond, the incidence of such marriages probably increased. However, intra-Noongar marriage appears to have been a significant feature of the traditional society, and a means by which the solidarity, cohesion and commonalities of the society were sustained.

Material culture and use of natural resources

The Noongar people have been recorded by the early writers as possessing a singular material culture that differed in some important respects from that of their neighbours. Perhaps most notable was the Noongar use of the kangaroo skin cloak as a form of dress and covering. There are many examples in the literature of this characteristically Noongar garment, but some good pictorial examples are to be found in Tilbrook (1983, pp. 13–14, 17) and Hassell (1975, plates between pp. 114 and 115; see also p. 15). Hassell remarks on the absence of the cloak among *pardook*; that is, 'natives of tribes further inland, language and appearance quite distinct' (Hassell 1975, pp. 151, 233). The Wilmun used bags made of kangaroo skin, which appear to be characteristic of this culture (e.g. see Curr 1886–87, pp. 328, 337). Noongar people used a particular style of axe, called a *kaju*, as well as a saw-like knife, called a *tapa*, each described in detail by Salvado (Stormon 1977, pp. 148–9; Hassell 1975, pp. 14–15 and plates between pp. 34 and 35, and pp. 98 and 99). Curr (1886–87, p. 329) notes the axe as characteristic of the material culture of the Perth area as well as that of York (p. 337), from where he also records the knife (p. 337).[27]

Food preparation constituted a cultural marker of the Noongar people. Salvado records that a kangaroo was first skinned before cooking, either directly on the fire or in an earth oven (Stormon 1977, pp. 154–5). Hammond reports that kangaroos were cut into pieces and then cooked on the fire, although he does not mention whether the animal was first skinned, although presumably it must have been (Hammond 1933, p. 29). Clark records that kangaroos were cut into pieces and roasted (Clark 1842, p. 6, col. 3).[28] Collie records that smaller marsupials were not skinned, but rather cooked directly on the fire (Collie 1834, pp. 66–7). Both Curr and Hammond describe how possums were cooked by first placing their plucked fur into the gutted animal, which was then cooked on the fire; the fur, which had soaked up the excess blood, was then removed. Curr reports that this was then 'sucked with great relish' (Curr 1886–7, p. 329; Hammond 1933, p. 29).

---

27 For other accounts of Noongar material culture contained in early records, see Millett (1872, pp. 72–3); Roth (1902, pp. 47–8, 67–8) and Terry (1994, pp. 1–5).

28 The author viewed this article as a photocopy, provided as Appendix C in the National Native Title Tribunal's research report *South West Trial Area 2* (NNTT, 2001). The photocopied pages of the article are paginated by hand and do not relate to the original pagination of the article. The article is from the newspaper *The Inquirer* of 16 February 1842.

While the methods of cooking smaller marsupials may not be unique to the Noongar, the skinning of kangaroo was not preferred practice in many Aboriginal societies to both the north and east.[29] There is, then, some evidence from the observations of early writers that the members of the constituent groups of the Noongar shared a number of practices and utilised a common material culture, which may have distinguished them from others.

The earliest settlers encountered the Aboriginal people of the South West while they were still following a hunting and gathering lifestyle. There are no exhaustive accounts of their use of natural resources for food, medicines or the manufacture of artefacts, and it is likely that the early settlers regarded the use of 'bush' resources as something from the past. This may have been, in part, a consequence of the reduction of hunting and gathering practices progressively over the region in the wake of European settlement. In contrast, there are references to the use of plants and other materials in the early literature. For example, Grey (1841, p. 58) records the use of the nut of the zamia palm (*Macrozamia riedlei*), along with the *bohn*, a succulent root. Zamia use is recorded by Clark (1842, p. 3) and Millett (1872, p. 99). Millet records the use of ochre (p. 87) and a native cherry (p. 98). Salvado records the eating of wattle gum, *menna*, 'of which they are very fond' (Stormon 1977, p. 149), as well as the use of white clay (p. 173) and *waragn*, a potato-like plant (p. 161). A comprehensive inventory of the natural resources utilised by the Noongar people is found in Meagher (1973) and Meagher and Ride (1979), and see also Meagher (1974). This list of materials is derived from the early sources, and includes animals, insects, fish, reptiles and plants, along with minerals (stone, clay and ochres). A list is provided by Green (1984, p. 13), sourced in part from Meagher but also drawn from early accounts. Obviously, use of natural resources lay at the heart of Noongar economic life, and it represented a vast traditional knowledge base that was handed on from one generation to the next.

Summary

There is substantial evidence from the early writers that there existed a discrete cultural society within the South West of Western Australia. I have reviewed the use of a single term for the members of this cultural bloc and shown that the

29 This statement is based on the author's own experience. In Western Desert cultures, for example, a kangaroo must not be skinned, and a series of normative rules dictate how the animal will be gutted, cooked and subsequently shared. See also Gould (1967); Tonkinson (1978, pp. 35–7); Palmer and Brady (1991, pp. 33–6).

term 'Noongar' (or its variants) has long been employed to identify the members of this society. I have noted that early writers identified a number of other names which identified groups within the larger society. The names were non-exclusive and provided a means of identifying groups in relation to particular characteristics, such as place of normal residence or by reference to their location from the perspective of those who used the name.

The society of the South West was characterised by a preference for seeking a wife who came from that society but from a group other than that to which the man belonged. As a consequence there was a forging of inter-group relationships, social and cultural interactions (including joint ritual activities) that both developed and enhanced social alliances and facilitated economic interdependencies. The occupants of the South West also exhibited a distinct material culture and a detailed knowledge of their natural environment, and they employed domestic customary behaviour that further identified them as a cultural unit. Finally, across the whole region there was a similarity of language that found expression in regional dialects. However, these aspects of Noongar culture do not represent a complete account of the traditional laws and customs as recorded by the early observers. In what follows I will consider others that can conveniently be discussed under separate headings.

Daisy Bates

Bates on the Bibbulmun

Bates used the term 'Bibbulmun' for all the Aborigines of the South West of Western Australia. She considered them to be a single cultural group, having some internal differentiations as a result of dialect and local association. In her descriptions of the 'derelicts' of the Maamba Reserve, at the foot of the Darling Range outside Perth, Bates differentiates people by reference to place of origin and dialect but observes that 'all were Bibbulmun' (Bates n.d.d). She makes this assertion in a number of other places as well, calling the Bibbulmun a single group (Bates 1992, p. 7), while in *The passing of the Aborigines* she defines the Bibbulmun as made up of 'seventy groups', 'linked by one language with local variations' (Bates 1966, pp. 59–60). She states that the 'Bibbulmun Nation . . . had but one fundamental language, and possessed similar customs, laws etc.'[30] (White 1985, p. 46). Bates was also clear as to the boundaries of the Bibbulmun, providing coordinates

30 Bates goes on to discuss the internal differences in the moiety system, which I will discuss below.

that stretched from Jurien Bay in the north to Esperance Bay in the south-east. It was Bates who defined the easternmost extent of this line by reference to the non-practice of circumcision by those living to its west (White 1985, p. 46).

Generally, Bates does not use the word 'tribe', although she is not entirely consistent in this. The first chapter of her book *The native tribes of Western Australia* (published posthumously) includes the term in its title, as does the title of the book itself. However, she did recognise regional groups of the Bibbulmun, which she lists (White 1985, pp. 48–55). She drew these onto a map, where she identifies them as 'tribes' (Bates 1907–09a, 1907–09b).[31] She recognised that there were relative directional terms employed, like 'Gooreenuk', meaning 'eastern people' (Bates n.d.d, p. 103), and 'Meenung', which she perhaps mistook to mean 'inland people', as she placed them on her map on the coast as well as inland (Bates n.d.e, p. 1). Bates collected a number of vocabularies (e.g. Bates n.d.b, n.d.c, n.d.f, n.d.g, n.d.i, n.d.j). She clearly did not collect all these herself and has annotated the last, which was collected by James Whitworth of Busselton, as 'incorrect'. She mapped the dialects (Bates 1907–09b),[32] but the results are confusing. Meenung appears in several places (Beverley, Bannister and Broome Hill) but not at Albany, although it appears at that location on the 'tribal' map just referred to. 'Yabberoo' appears both east of Katanning and just north of New Norcia, it being a term meaning 'north', as Bates herself records (Bates n.d.e, p. 102; see also Douglas 1976, p. 95). It would appear that Bates was as confused as her predecessors in her identification of component groups of the Bibbulmun. However, like them, she did perceive the Aboriginal people of the South West of Western Australia as comprising a single society.

Bates and inter-group cooperation and movement

Bates's informant Yaburgurt told Bates that he could travel 'from Pinjarra and Mandura to . . . Vasse, Busselton on the South and to Karganap near Moore River' (Bates n.d.e). While this indicates that a person could be expected to be able to travel freely over substantial areas, Bates states that, 'His *muart* went eastward to Kugalerap, near Nanap (Lower Blackwood), west of Katanning, to Boginap near

31 Portions of this map were viewed in the National Native Title Tribunal's research reports. A copy of the map, showing the whole of the South West, is to be found in *South West Trial Area 2* (NNTT 2001, Appendix 5).

32 The map, relevant to the whole of the South West of Western Australia, can be found in *South West Trial Area 2* (NNTT 2001, Appendix 7), where the author viewed it. Bates also produced a list of the names on the dialect map (Bates n.d.h).

Kujungap (Kojonup), to Bordaburda and Belgarap, west of Kujungap. His *mangur bujur* and *Nganganjura bujur* were within these places.' This needs some translating. Bates defines *muart* as a person's m, F, MB, mz, FB and fz and their children (White 1985, p. 84).[33] *Mangur* is fz,[34] *bujur* means 'home place' (Hammond 1933, p. 17; Douglas 1976, p. 73; Bindon and Chadwick 1992, p. 277) and *nganganjura* means a person's own mother (White 1985, p. 83). Taken literally, this means that Yaburgurt had close kin, including his mother and paternal aunt, in the places he mentions, so he was free to visit them. The exegesis is required because of Bates's cryptic note-taking. The meaning of the passage is amplified by Bates in her later work:

> Yabburgurt, the last Murray district native, whose father's ground was in the Manjuburdup (Mandurah) district, stated that he could travel to Yunderup (Busselton), and find *mururt* (blood relations) there; he could go to Kugalerup (Blackwood River district) where some of his *nganganjura* (mother's people) lived; to Karrganup near Moore River (Gingin district) where *waiabinuk* (relations-in-law) lived. (White 1985, p. 52)

In short, Yaburgurt had *bujur* (country) from Mandurah down the coast to Busselton, as well as to the east from Moore River to Blackwood River, which he claimed through either matrikin, patrikin or affines. The nature of his rights in this whole area is not spelt out, but it is clear he was free to travel and presumably to use the resources of the country.

Yaburgurt was not alone in his claim to the Busselton area. Bates also lists as an owner of Busselton a man called Woolgurt, whose son was called Boolyen. Woolgurt gained the country from his FB (his son's 'granduncle') (Bates (n.d.d, p. 23). Bates's informants for this information were Baabalgurt and Nilgee, the latter identified by Bates as 'of the kangaroo of Busselton' (Bates 1966, p. 69). She reports Baabalgurt as saying, 'My country extends from Champion Bay to Esperance. I can hunt from Leeuwin, Port Augusta to York and Wagalin, all this is my *kalleep*'[35] (Bates n.d.d, typescript from Notebook 15, p. 41).

---

33 Standard abbreviations for kin relations will be used in this report, thus F = father, m = mother, z = sister, S = son and so on. Capitals indicate male; lower case indicates female.

34 The term is defined in White (1985, p. 82).

35 *Kalleep* is a 'property in land', according to Bindon and Chadwick (1992, p. 79). It also carries the sense of fire (*kal*), hearth and home. See Bates (1992, pp. 22, 187).

Yaburgurt and Baabalgurt were consanguineal kin, and Woolgurt was a putative or consanguineal father to Yaburgurt.[36] Rights to areas of country would appear to have been shared between kin as well as between other families whose original relationship, one to the other, is now lost, as is the case with Nilgee. Bates's data indicate that individuals and families travelled (and had rights to travel) widely over areas of the South West.

Bates's informant Jubyche (Joobaitch, see Hallam and Tilbrook 1990, pp. 170–1) told her that his 'district' included Guildford, Bunbury, Canning, Toodyay, Northam, Dandarragan, Moore River and York (Bates n.d.d, question 84).[37] Baabalgurt (Bates n.d.e, 41) told Bates that his *kalleep* ('homes, hearths, and fires', Bates 1992, p. 187) 'extends from Champion Bay to Esperance' and that he could 'hunt from Leeuwin, Port Augusta to York and Wagalin'. Bates describes how Fanny Balbuk's (see Hallam and Tilbrook 1990, pp. 112–13) 'hunting ground stretched from near Gingin to beyond Fremantle' (Bates 1992, p. 76). She was able to travel more widely than this, however, because of her extensive kinship relationships through both matrikin and patrikin, enabling her to pass 'not only from [one] end of her own people's country to the other, but penetrate through the eastern "hill" side of the river and travel amongst the "relations" that might be found in every camp along the foot of the hills through which she desired to pass' (pp. 76–7). Elsewhere, Bates notes how the Manjugoordup (Mandurah) people 'could travel in safety from Yoonderup (Busselton) to Karrganup (Moore River district) as they had intermarried with the local families in these places, and in the intermediate districts; and their relatives-in-law stretched eastward towards Koogalerup, near Nanup; Boginup, west of Koojingup (Kojonup), and Bordaburda near Bel'garup (ten miles from Koojingup)'. She adds that they did not usually travel 'over the hills', the people there being 'strangers, and consequently enemies . . . except on special occasions where there was a great gathering' (Bates 1992, p. 23).

36 According to one of Bates's genealogies, Yaburgurt was Baabalgurt's FFFSS. Baabalgurt's F was Yungap, his FF Yugul and his FFF Mogam. By a second marriage, Mogan had a son, Winjan, who was the father of Yaburgurt. See Bates (n.d.d, pp. 1–5). However, elsewhere in the same source (p. 25) Bates gives Wulgart as Baabalgurt's father and his FF as Wiritch, who is probably the same man she has in her notes as Wineetch. She does not include Boolyen as the son of Woolgurt. Either Woolgurt or Winjan may have been the social (or adoptive) father of Baabalgurt, but it is evident from these data that the three men Yaburgurt, Woolgurt and Baabalgurt were related.

37 The typescript is not paginated. It includes answers to numerous questions that Bates must have asked her informants. The reference provided is to the question number as set out in the manuscript.

Bates's account of inter-group movements in her *The Native tribes of Western Australia* repeats the emphasis found in her manuscripts on freedom of travel. She considers there to have been 'constant intercourse from time immemorial' between the coastal groups living between Jurien Bay and Augusta (White 1985, p. 48). She is more specific in relation to Yaburgurt and Joobaitch, whose range of travel has already been noted from her manuscripts. However, she adds material about Woolberr from Gingin, who could travel from Jurien Bay, Goomalling and Dowerin to the east and south to the Murray. This was because he had relations (*mururt* and *waiabirding*),[38] who were members of the 'local groups of these areas' (p. 52). Bates notes Monnop from the Victoria Plains, who was free to travel from Jurien Bay in the north to Perth in the south, 'through relationships' (p. 52).

Summary

Bates's accounts demonstrate, in her own words, 'the unity of the Bibbulmun nation' (White 1985, p. 52). In other parts of her material she shows that she collected extensive data on the ritual life, which can be seen as a means by which 'relationships' were developed and sustained. Unlike her predecessors, Bates was interested in understanding something of the social interactions which underpinned the society she studied, as well as demonstrating its practical outcomes. While her observations of endogamy are generalised in these accounts, they provide a helpful insight into the dynamic complexity of the interrelationship of the different parts of Noongar society, as well as providing some explanation for how its members interacted cooperatively.

38 *Mururt* is glossed above as a person's m, F, MB, mz, FB and fz and their children. *Waiabirding* is translated as 'relations-in-law' in White's text, following the word in square brackets. It is unclear whether this is Bates's own interpolation or White's addition.

Chapter 3

RELATIONSHIPS TO LAND

Introduction

Early writers made comments about the relationship which they considered to exist between the original inhabitants of the South West of Western Australia and the land. Many of these related to proprietorial interests in land — that is, how groups of people asserted rights to areas of land and what the implications of this process were. Since the nature of the social units which occupied the South West were not well understood by the early settlers, there is consequently some confusion over the nature of the group whose members asserted rights to country.

Bates's principal interests lay in areas of social organisation, kinship and classification, as well as in totemism and religious observances. However, she does provide some material on local organisation, which I review here. At the time she was writing, however, anthropological understandings of Indigenous Australian relationships to land were still poorly developed. This is a matter I will return to later in this section.

Early sources

Early accounts for the Perth region

Curr (1886–87, p. 325) reports that the country was divided between the few families of the tribe.[39] Salvado stresses that families were an important social unit, but that each was 'independent of the other, governed by the head, the father and families do not interfere with one another' (Stormon 1977, p. 130).[40] However, with

39 The comment is made in relation to Newcastle, an early name for the area round Toodyay and Northam.

40 The comment is made by Salvado generally in relation to the New Norcia area.

respect to rights in country, Salvado notes the importance of the individual, which he conflates with the family:

> every individual has his own territory for hunting, gathering gum and picking up yams, and the rights he has here are respected as sacred . . . each family regards one particular district as belonging exclusively to itself, though the use of it is freely shared by nearby friendly families. But if an enemy or stranger is caught there, he is put to death by the owner. (Stormon 1977, pp. 130–1)

Moore's work (1978a, 1978b) provides historical information on the first 10 years of the colony. It is taken up with his rapid rise to prominence as a public official and his increased capital and landholdings. Much of what he writes concerns his quotidian activities, like planting potatoes and later establishing a large flock of sheep. He probably did not spend much time with Aboriginal people, although he was sympathetic to them (when not angry at the loss of his sheep or pigs). He also became increasingly caught up in administrative and legal matters and was an important man of the time in the region of Guildford, Perth and Fremantle. His comments appear, for the most part, to relate to Aboriginal people of the Guildford region.

Moore identifies the term *kallip* to mean 'property in land', being areas with which a person was familiar (Moore 1978a, p. 39). Moore has parcels of land and 'chiefs', although it appears that he gained at least some of his information about local organisation from Lyon. He notes that, according to a report from Lyon:

> it seems that the land is all parcelled out into districts among themselves, and that they rarely travel far from their own homes. The chief of this district[41] is called 'Worragonga':[42] Yagan is the son of Worragonga. I write this from recollection; but it is not great matter if I should have made a false heraldry in blazoning his pedigree. (Moore 1978b, pp. 146–7)

Lyon associated Worragonga (Midgegooroo) (Hallam and Tilbrook 1990, p. 207) with areas to the south of the Swan River and west of the Helena River (Lyon 1979, p. 177).

Elsewhere, Moore writes that 'each tribe has its distinct ground; and they will, of course, rather adhere to it, dispute its possession, and take their revenge on

41 Presumably the Guildford-Midland area.

42 According to Hallam and Tilbrook (1990, p. 207), this is an alternative name for Midgegooroo.

the intruders, then fall back on other tribes of their own countrymen, and fight their way inch by inch' (Moore 1978b, pp. 199–200). While his meaning here is not altogether clear, it would appear that he understood there to be a landowning unit comprising 'countrymen', which was greater than the 'tribe' or family, implying perhaps that several groups together shared a commonality with respect to areas of land. Elsewhere, he writes that on the death of a person (presumably a man) his land was divided between his children. He writes, 'It appears that among themselves the ground is parcelled out to individuals and passed by inheritance. The country formerly of Midgegooroo, then of his son Yagan, belongs now of right to two young lads (brothers), and sons of Yagan' (p. 259). He adds that there had been a fight because 'some trespassers' had used the land (lighted fires and chased wallabies) and a large meeting resulted in a fight with spears. The trespass was committed by Ningana, along with others. Armstrong (1979) recorded that Ningana was living with Yellowgonga in 1836 (see below), north of the river, where he evidently enjoyed rights, through affinal links, as a member of that group. The nature of his claim to areas south of the Swan River is unclear,[43] as is that of Yellowgonga's children, Googelley and Garbel,[44] who appear to have claimed it. However, the disputes that followed over succession to Midgegooroo's country, after the deaths of his sons Yagan and Narral (who died in 1838), indicate that succession to estates was a part of traditional Noongar law and custom.[45] They indicate that descent was not the only means by which rights to land were gained or claimed, as in this account brothers inherit from brothers (Narral from Yagan) and, potentially, others may do so in the absence of an effective successor. However, Moore's materials are incomplete and conclusions drawn from his observations should be tentative.

Robert Menli Lyon (1979) also reports that the Aborigines of the Perth region comprised a number of 'tribes', each with its own area:

> . . . they are formed into distinct tribes; and that the whole country is divided into districts. But, though they have places to which they are accustomed to report for encampment, they have no fixed habitation, and generally move about from place

43 Hallam and Tilbrook suggest it was a result of Government 'encouragement' (Hallam and Tilbrook 1990, p. 122).

44 Hallam and Tilbrook have Garbel as 'probably' Yellowgonga's son (Hallam and Tilbrook 1990, p. 122).

45 A third son, Willum, was a teenager at this time, so presumably was too young to assert his rights to his father's country (Hallam and Tilbrook 1990, p. 319).

> to place in large bodies. Private property seems to be utterly unknown among them. The game and the fish are considered the common property of the tribe; and as every dispute between the different tribes is decided by the spear, they are utter strangers to the quirks and quibbles of the law. (Lyon 1979, p. 153)

Lyon set out the extent of these 'districts', which he named (pp. 176–8).[46] Yellowgonga's district was called Mooro. Beeloo, the district of Monday, was bounded by the Canning to the south, Melville Water to the west, and Swan and Ellens Brook to the north, while the eastern boundary was not known. Beelair was the name for Midgegooroo's district, bounded by Melville Water and the Canning River to the north, the 'mountains' (the Darling scarp) to the east, with the sea to the west and south to a line from the scarp to Mangles Bay. He described the districts of Banyowla, Dygan and Beenan to the south and Waylo, 'chief of a tribe on the Boora, commonly called Lennard's brook' (p. 177). To the north was a 'chief' called Byerman, whom he remarked was either 'the brother or particular friend of Yellowgonga' (p. 177). East was a man called Dyoolon (a chief), then further east still a chief called Wullabong of the district called Bargo (p. 177).

Lyon gives by far the most complete view of what he considered to be a tribal organisation, where 'chiefs' ruled discrete, named territories, which Green found convenient to map (Green 1979, pp. 174; 1984, p. 50). However, the lack of any ethnographic detail makes it impossible to reconstruct the social, cultural, economic and ritual interrelationships which may have existed between these groups, and to establish how, in practice, rights were realised in relation to areas of land. The only exception is the tantalising comment that Yellowgonga and Byerman enjoyed some sibling-like relationship, which presumably influenced the affections each had for the other and the rights and obligations that existed between them (Lyon 1979, p. 177).

Armstrong (1979, pp. 193–4),[47] writing of the Perth area, states that certain individuals held areas of land and defined them with some exactness. He is less clear about how the system worked in practice, although he does allow that people moved about over other people's land. Overall, however, he appears to take the view that people mostly lived on their own country (p. 199). His account of the areas of residential groups is not altogether consistent with that provided by Lyon.

---

46 See also Green (1979, pp. 174, 180), where he produces maps of the districts based on Lyon.

47 A revised version of these data, derived from Armstrong, formed part of a paper published in 2010 (see Palmer 2010b).

Armstrong notes that trespass was a punishable act. He writes, 'If any native strangers had settled amongst them they would have done all in their power to destroy them' (p. 188). Following his account of the land of different families, he adds:

> These co proprietors appear equally interested in their respective districts, and are equally ready to revenge trespass, which may be committed, not only by unauthorised hunting, but by taking swans' nests etc. Land is beyond doubt an inheritable property amongst them, and they boast of having received it from their fathers' fathers, etc., to an unknown period back. All the sons appear to succeed equally to their fathers' lands. (Armstrong 1979, p. 194)

Like Lyon, Armstrong sets down the areas (he calls it 'territory') owned by different families:

> The land appears to be apportioned to different families, and is not held in common by the tribe. For instance, Nandaree, Elal and Yalgonga[48] claim between them all the land between Mount Eliza and Fremantle, and from the river towards Mr Trigg's limekiln. Bogaberry[49], Meelup and Bonberry, own a tract eastward from Yalgonga's for a considerable distance round the lakes. From near Monger's Lake to as far as Bassindean, and for a breadth of four or five miles inland from the Swan, is Munday's territory.[50] To the north of Munday's, are Warang's, Miago's, and Moorungo's land. (Armstrong 1979, pp. 193–4)

This arrangement of territory has also been mapped by Green (1979, p. 192).

Armstrong was aware that 'tribes' relied upon one another in times of difficulty.

> They say that when a tribe is pressed by a common enemy, they retire, if the pursuit be very hot, to the nearest swamp that offers concealment; otherwise to some neighbouring tribe, in which they have relatives, who are bound to defend them, right or wrong. The latter course has been adopted by the Swan tribe, when pursued by the whites; they have always retreated to a northern tribe, about a day's journey off. Yagan's tribe used always to fall back upon We-up's. [51] But they would

48 That is, Yellowgonga and two sons.

49 Brother to Yellowgonga's wife, Yangan. It is not known what the relationship was between these three (see Hallam and Tilbrook 1990, p. 27).

50 See Hallam and Tilbrook (1990, p. 234) for Symmonds's account of Monday's country, which is not dissimilar.

51 Weeip was head of an inland group, the 'mountain tribe'. See Hallam and Tilbrook (1990, p. 307).

> not, they say, retire upon a tribe in which they have no relatives. They themselves would not afford refuge, or, at least, protection to any stranger fugitives. The Swan tribes are in the habit of communicating with at least ten surrounding tribes, viz, three to the northward, two to the north-east, two to the eastward, beside the Canning, Mangles Bay, and Murray tribes. (Armstrong 1979, pp. 197–8)

Armstrong was clear about how far people travelled, considering that, for the Perth area, people went no more than 100 miles (160 kilometres) or a little less. However, this was a much greater distance than the relatively small 'territories' or 'districts' mapped out by Green (1979, pp. 174, 180, 192), and it is evident that people were free to move across a wider range of country, access being either by virtue of kinship ties (see above) or 'invitation' (see below), or possibly a combination of both.

> A whole tribe does not, as a custom, migrate beyond its own district; but sometimes a whole tribe pays a visit of a few weeks to a neighbouring tribe, but this is always on a previous invitation, which is sometimes sent to its neighbours by a tribe that has had extraordinary good luck in hunting, or has had a whale cast on its coast. There is good reason to believe that few, if any, of the Swan men have been further from the Swan than 80 to 90 miles, unless with settlers. They move about their own districts according to the season and the consequent variety of food. In winter they separate a good deal and live apart by families, and become stationery for a month or six weeks at the place where they have built their huts, provided the food of the season continues plentiful there. (Armstrong 1979, p. 199)

Armstrong collected the names of the members of residential groups, as did Charles Symmons the Aborigines Protector in 1840.[52] Green has reproduced Armstrong's list of the membership of Yellowgonga's group, which Armstrong collected in 1836 (Green 1984, p. 52). An analysis of Armstrong's account of the membership of Yellowgonga's residential groups is instructive, since it allows us to develop an understanding of the dynamics of the relationships which existed between band members, and their attachments and affiliations to a number of different areas of country. A summary of the data Armstrong collected on Yellowgonga's group is set out in Table 3.1.

---

52 Symmons's materials are reviewed by Green (2003, pp. 101–2) and are sourced from the Colonial Secretary's records held in the State Records Office of Western Australia. I did not view these source documents. Green considers that it is likely that Symmons based his report on information supplied by 'more experienced colonists, possibly Moore' (p. 102).

While it would be unwise to push Armstrong's data too far, some general observations are supportable. The relationship between the members of the group is now only partially recoverable and can only be stated for 11 of the 28 cases, as well as for an additional four names through computing affinal links. This means that a little over half of the group can, with some certainty, be defined in terms of their relationship one to the other. Yellowgonga's sons would appear to be unmarried. Two daughters, Daleer and Gargup, were married to Ningana, whose country appears to have been 'Clarence', which is where Rockingham is now (Hallam and Tilbrook 1990, p. 137). Ningana's two brothers, Domera and Edar, also formed a part of Yellowgonga's group, and the three brothers were living outside their own country. Apart from Ningana's affinal links to Yellowgonga through his daughter, Hallam and Tilbrook record that the brothers had a 'close relationship' with Dower, Yellowgonga's son (p. 90). We know nothing of the nature of this relationship but it presumably was the basis of a bond between the men, manifest in the recruitment of the unmarried brothers to Yellowgonga's group and their residence outside of their own father's country. There is, however, an additional affinal tie that influenced residential choice.

Ningana's brother, Domera, had married Yanyup, who was widow to Midgegooroo, executed in 1833. Midgegooroo's teenage son by another marriage, Willum, also lived with his stepmother[53] and Domera as a member of Yellowgonga's group. The relationship that existed between Dower (Yellowgonga's son) and his sister's husband and his brothers extended to the wife of one of those brothers and her son, the child of Midgegooroo. This residential arrangement probably reflects the close relationships that obtained between members of neighbouring groups (Yellowgonga and Midgegooroo, see above). It further strengthens the view that residential groups were closely allied and had interchangeability of membership, depending on circumstance and the realisation of kinship, marriage and other alliances which were the basis of the relationships that underpinned group cohesiveness. In this case, the deaths of Midgegooroo and perhaps Yagan (his son) may well have been a cause for the realisation of these links in practice, evidenced in the composition of 'Yellowgonga's group' as recorded by Armstrong.

The remaining names on the list cannot be related with any certainty to Yellowgonga and his family, and they may or may not have been affinally or

53 The term 'step-mother' is used for the sake of clarity in this exposition. It is unlikely that such a distinction would have been made between a birth mother and a social mother in Noongar society, any more than it is today.

Table 3.1: Members of Yellowgonga's group

Name	Relationship to ego	Sex/age	Other relationship	Other territorial affiliation	Hallam and Tilbrook page ref.
Yellowgonga	Ego	m, adult			348ff
Windan	w	f, adult			320
Yangan	w	f, adult		Brother's country Lake Monger (343)	343
Nander (Nandra)	S	m, adult			253
Elal	S	m, child			109
Dued (Dower)	S	m, adult	'Close relationship' to Ningana, Dommera and Edar; Ningana is his ZH (90)		90
Elup	S	m, adult?			110
Ningana	DH	m, adult	B to Edar and Domera; wives were Daleer and Gayup	'Clarence tribe' (271)	270ff
Daleer	d.	f, adult	w of Ningana		55
Gayup (Gargup)	d.	f, adult	w of Ningana		123
Woobyte	DS	m	son of Gayup		326
Domera	DHB	m, adult	B to Edar and Ningana. Married to Midgegooroo's widow, Yanyup	'Father a Murray man' (73)	73
Edar	DHB	m, adult	Brother to Ningana and Domera	'Father a Murray man'	105
Yangup (Yanyup or Ganiup)	dhbw	f	Midgegooroo's widow; married to Domera		120

Name	Relationship to ego	Sex/age	Other relationship	Other territorial affiliation	Hallam and Tilbrook page ref.
Willum or Dalbur	DHBWS	m, teenager	Son of Midgegooroo	'Monday's tribe', 'First tribe north' (319); F's country 'south of Swan River' (209)	319
Noreup (Ngorap?)	?	?			266
Bindup	?	f, adult?			24
Quebup	?	f, child			285
Beenyup	?	m, child			11
Warup	?	m, teenager			301
Kadjup	?	f, adult?			173
Barbang	?	m, adult		Father from 'South of York' (345)	6
Gooban (Giban) (M)	?	m			132
Goongar	?	m			142
Datlkup (Dakkup)	?	f, adult	wife to Goongar?		55
Ngoogar	?	f ?, adult	wife to Goongar?		264
Dutomerra	?	m, adult		Wiap's tribe (101)	101
Doonmooit	?	f, adult			87

Page references in the two right-hand columns are from Hallam and Tilbrook 1990. The relationship to ego, where known, is indicated by kinship abbreviations, where S = son, d = daughter and so on. A question mark indicates that either information is unavailable or it would appear to be doubtful from the source. I have rearranged Armstrong's original order to place all of Yellowgonga's immediate family together.

consanguineally related. They may represent several families, and it is possible that Goongar was married to Dakkup and Ngoogar, but nothing more is known about these individuals.

From the records, we can learn that the members of Yellowgonga's group represented several different territorial areas. Yellowgonga himself is recorded as regarding the area north of the Swan River as his own (e.g. see Lyon 1979 and maps in Green 1979, pp. 174, 180). His wife was Yangan, and Yangan's brother had the country round Lake Monger. Ningana and his brothers belonged to the area round Rockingham and probably south to the River Murray. Willum, Midgegooroo's son, was associated with the land south of the Swan River, but was also of 'Monday's tribe' (between the Canning and the Swan (Hallam and Tilbrook 1990, p. 319)) as well as 'the first tribe north' (p. 319). A man called Barbang may have been associated with land south of York (p. 345), while Dutomerra was described as a part of 'Wiap's tribe (p. 101), an area in the hills to the east of Perth (p. 307).

The lessons that can be learnt from Armstrong's material are that 'family' groups were founded upon a complex web of relationships and alliances. These brought people together in acceptance of bonds of kinship, affinal relations and other relationship alliances forged through social and ritual processes. Yellowgonga's group had a nuclear family at its core, but included individuals with affinal relations and, as far as can be ascertained from the data, probably others who were quite distantly related or who saw their relationships in classificatory or social terms. Within this group were representatives of a number of different geographic interests. The presence of these different territorial interests and the bonds which bound them together as a living or residential group, probably had an effect on how the members of the group together accessed and exploited the areas which comprised their traditional range.

The accounts here reviewed relating to territorial affiliations are incomplete and, taken together, lack consistency. Green (2003, p. 111) remarks that 'trying to make sense out of the varying and even conflicting statements of metropolitan land and territory in the historical records is not easy.' As an anthropologist, I would go further than Green. It would be an error to attempt to map 'tribes' or 'chiefs' on to country using these data. In the accounts examined here the extent of an individual's country is sometimes ascertained by reference to imprecise geographical features, or is expressed in the vaguest of terms in relation to some indeterminate direction. It is unclear whether rights to the country (however defined) are being ascribed to one individual or to many. Finally, mapping territory hides the complexity of the relationships between individuals and the implications that these relationships might have had for the exercise of rights to country in practice.

Early accounts for the Albany region

The situation at King George Sound was somewhat different from that obtaining in Perth during the first decade of European settlement. The garrison at King George Sound was a contained outpost, and colonial settlers were not able to take up grants of land and so establish themselves on substantial areas of the hinterland, as they had done in Perth. This may have resulted in the traditional system of land utilisation continuing to operate more or less uninterrupted during the first decade or so of settlement. As with the Perth region, early journalists have left a fairly detailed account of what they observed.

Isaac Scott Nind was an Assistant Surgeon who arrived at King George Sound in 1826, staying there until 1829 (Green 1979, p. 9). In his 'Description of the natives of King George's Sound' (1979 [1831]), he described residential groups (he called them 'bands') as typically comprising no more than 50 individuals, made up of 'near relatives, and deserve the name of families rather than tribes' (Nind 1979, p. 23). He concluded that because of their 'vagrant life' they had little in common with each other and led separate lives (p. 34), even though they were known by the same name and district. There was no general camp or meeting place and no general chief (p. 23). Nind (p. 35) reports that they came together in autumn when the fish were in greater numbers at the coast. Despite his assertions that there were no 'chiefs', he subsequently reports how he had initially assumed this to be the case and gives a list of names of those selected as likely candidates for this position (p. 40). One of these was a man called Naikennon (Nakina). His brother was Mawcurrie (Mokare; see Nind 1979, p. 42; Green 1989, p. 31).

Like other early writers, Nind distinguished between 'individual properties' and the 'tribal' range, indicating that people enjoyed rights across the range and well beyond their own 'property':

> Those families who have locations on the sea coast quit it during the winter for the interior; and the natives of the interior, in like manner, pay visits to the coast during the fishing season. Excepting at these times, those natives who live together have the exclusive right of fishing or hunting upon the neighbouring grounds, which are, in fact, divided into individual properties; the quantity of land owned by each individual being very considerable. Yet it is not so exclusively his, but others of his

> family have certain rights over it; so that it may be considered as partly belonging to the tribe. Thus all of them have the right to break down grass trees, kill bandicoots, lizards, and other animals, and dig up roots; but the presence of the owner of the ground is considered necessary when they fire the country for game. As the country does not abound in food, they are seldom stationary, removing, according to the time of year, to those parts which produce the articles of provision that may be in season. During the winter and early spring they are very much scattered; but as summer advances they assemble in greater numbers. (Nind 1979, p. 25)

While Nind reports that there was a preference for obtaining a wife from a distant group, he states that sons had a right to hunt in the country from whence the mother had come (p. 46). Such an arrangement would extend the potential rights which a man could exercise over country. Nind wrote that rights to witchetty grubs rested with he who pushed over the tree (p. 32), without reference to how those rights were established. Nind was unclear about how a system of land tenure could appear to be both exclusive and inclusive:

> They are very jealous as to encroachment on their property, and the land is divided into districts, which is the property of families or individuals. At some particular seasons of the year, however, the young men visit their neighbours in parties, and sometimes travel forty or fifty miles for that purpose. Their stay, which is generally short, is a period of rejoicing and feasting. (Nind 1979, pp. 46–7)

What Nind appears to be indicating is that 'families' had what could be called 'home areas' ('locations' and 'property') but were free to use other areas as well. Thus home areas were not exclusively held but were shared with others 'so that it might be considered as partly belonging to the tribe' (p. 25). However, for firing the country, the 'owner of the ground' should be present (p. 25). In an area where food was limited, or may be so in some seasons, the ability to move freely across different areas would have been an important feature of the traditional economy. Given his ideas about private property, Nind had a problem with reconciling his notions of exclusive private property with the observations that areas of land were shared.

Collet Barker was commandant of the King George Sound garrison from late 1829 until March 1831 (Mulvaney and Green 1992, p. 246) and wrote a detailed journal for much of the time he was there. Barker's account contains an abundance of information about the traditional life and practices of the local Aboriginal people, including some account of their system of local organisation.

Barker possibly indicates that Mokare's sister, Mullet, had different 'territory' to Mokare (Barker 1992, p. 292, n. 57), presumably because she gained rights to her husband's country. Barker partly confirms this when he writes later that 'females never possess ground . . . [being] liable by marriage to part their native place' (p. 383). It was not then the custom to give land to one who married your daughter. Barker stated that the area around the garrison (now the site of Albany) was owned by two brothers, Mokare and Nakina (p. 295), Nakina being regarded as the more senior.

The rights to country, however, were not simply described. Mokare told Barker that some resources were more exclusively owned than others. Barker wrote:

> Mokare brought in a little grass tree resin for boat. Says the provision of Quinene [cycad] is made by everyone, but it is often stolen. Generally speaking the owners are not sulky at this, it not being considered so sacred a property as Spears, Kangaroo, Wallabi etc, or even grass trees, but he recollects hearing of one man speared on account of it. (Barker 1992, p. 309)

Yet, in a cryptic note written a few days later, he reports that Mokare had indicated that a man had the right to the kangaroo he speared, with nothing being recorded about where the spearing had taken place (p. 310), a comment that mirrors that made by Nind with respect to witchetty grubs (see Nind 1979, 46). It would appear that some resources were regarded as being more important than others, but the basis for such differentiations is not clear.

While these accounts are not unproblematic, they are based on an unquestioned appreciation that areas were 'owned' by individuals or groups who were related. The details of the rights of others are also of note. There appears to have been a freedom of access between neighbouring groups and the journal gives an impression that large numbers of broadly related or acquainted people from a similar cultural background freely traversed the region without requiring any sort of permission (e.g. see Barker 1992, pp. 248–9, 267). It is clear that Mokare ranged considerable distances from his own 'home' area (the land surrounding Princess Royal Harbour) without the need to ask permission, travelling to Woollyong[54] to get parrot chicks (p. 368) and requesting that he be taken to the 'opposite' (eastern) side of Oyster Harbour to shoot kangaroo (pp. 248–9). However, he asserted that to burn the country in order to drive out wallaby required the permission (and

54 Woollyong is in the vicinity of King River, approximately 12 kilometres north-west of Albany. See map in Mulvaney and Green 1992, p. 249.

perhaps presence) of an individual who was considered to be responsible for that land (p. 378). Nakina had indicated that prior to burning the land on Bald Head they needed Coolbun to be present:

> . . . whose ground it was, & their starting there without him would be considered stealing, 'Quippel'. They also required his presence or permission now to burn at King George [Sound], as since Dr Uredale's death it had become his property. They might kill Wallabi but not burn for them. They were joking each other on the consequences of having burnt for Wallabi yesterday on some of Maragnan's Ground & talked laughingly of his spearing some of them for it. (Barker 1992, pp. 382–3)

As indicated in this entry, this ideal behaviour relating to burning and permission appears to have been more honoured in its breach than in its observance (e.g. see pp. 285–6, 404). The differentiation of rights between individuals is not set out, and I think Barker's account reflects a system where numbers of people used common country in small bands within a recognised range.[55]

Barker tells us how land changed hands. If there were sons, portions of an area of country would be set out for each son at birth, but a son does 'not enjoy possession until grown up' (p. 383). A younger brother appears to have taken over the role of a deceased older brother as principal representative for an area of country, but this may have depended upon the age (and assertiveness) a son required in order to press his case (see p. 386).[56] Barker writes that in the event that there were no males in a family 'his next neighbours have his ground' (p. 386). Significantly, Barker takes the view that there was a normative system that accommodated death to ensure continuity of responsibility of ownership of estates.

Alexander Collie became the first Government Resident at King George's Sound in 1831, after the military garrison was withdrawn (Green 1979, p. 56). Although Collie knew Mokare, the latter died during his stay at King George's Sound, and Collie was perhaps better acquainted with Nakina, Mokare's brother, whom he described as a 'chief' (Collie 1834, p. 73). Collie states that individuals had areas to which they were much attached, and his account in this regard is consistent with that provided by both Barker and Nind.

---

55 'The range was the tract or orbit over which the group, including its nucleus adherents, ordinarily hunted and foraged to maintain life' (Stanner, 1965a, p. 2). I discuss this aspect of local organisation in a subsequent section of this chapter.

56 Cf. the dispute noted above concerning Midgegooroo's estate, where the rights of his teenage son were disregarded by those with claims to the land (see Hallam and Tilbrook 1990, p. 257).

Collie states that Nakina's and Waiter's[57] 'natal[58] ground has always been understood to be on the shores of Princess Royal Harbour and towards Bald Head' (p. 86). He writes that 'Talmamundy's natal ground was, I understood, on the borders of the King George's Sound' (p. 91). With respect to access rights to Nakina and Waiter's area, he writes that they:

> . . . were, or pretended to be highly offended at some of the tribe, who, in their absence, had fired the best of their wallabee ground. The trespassers, however, did not seem as if they deemed this offence of a very weighty nature, as they neither made a secret of it before hand or endeavoured to conceal the property which they had carried off. They both held a wordy warfare for a time, till I told them to desist or quit the Settlement.
>
> Very soon after this, I understood that formal permission was granted to some of the tribe to clear the preserves by burning; whether this permission was sold for a stipulated price, or whether it was making a virtue of necessity, and if not spontaneously given would have been taken, I did not learn. (Collie 1834, p. 86)

Collie also records that 'Moollungul belongs to the Mongalan or King George's Sound tribe, and his ground lies three or four miles on this side of Mount Barker or Pwakkenbak' (p. 91). Thus it is possible to build up from Collie a general idea of the areas of land associated with each family group, represented by a senior male. However, Collie gives us very little genealogical information apart from the fact that Nakina and Mokare were siblings. Important relationships between others (for example, Nakina, Talmamundy and Moollungul, who are all associated with particular areas) are absent. What is meant by 'natal' ground is equally unclear. Collie's observations must be treated with caution, since he had a tendency to trivialise and denigrate the Aboriginal people he knew. However, it seems reasonable to me to conclude that Collie was probably recording an example of ideal (or normative) behaviour, which was in turn underpinned by recognition of rights to resources and land that went beyond the members of any one single local or patri-group.

57 Waiter was Nakina's brother. See Green (1989, p. 61).

58 'Natal' means either 'native' or of, or pertaining to, one's birth (Oxford English Dictionary). The former sense is more poetic than the latter, though whether Collie distinguished these meanings is unclear from the context.

James Browne grew up in Albany and wrote a paper on the original occupants of the region, which he published in 1856. His account of local organisation is broadly consistent with that provided by the other writers reviewed here:

> I have already stated that each tribe occupies its own separate division of territory. The district thus occupied is again subdivided into vaguely defined portions, every family or individual of the tribe having its or his recognised tract of country. This property descends in the family, from one to another, and is considered in every way private property, and the proprietors of such are boastful and proud of their hunting grounds in proportion to their extent and nature.
>
> But although thus appropriated, it is difficult to say in what the rights of ownership consist, — for agriculture is altogether unknown amongst them, and the various members of the tribe hunt indiscriminately over each other's grounds. The case, however . . . is somewhat different in regard to strangers, for should an enemy, or one from another tribe wilfully trespass on these grounds, such liberty would be immediately noticed, and would in all probability lead to acts of violence and retaliation on both sides. And in this right of taking umbrage when convenient, and in making the subject matter of quarrel, consists, I think, the sole advantage of proprietorship. (Browne 1856, p. 489)

Browne remarks that they had no 'chiefs', but that there were eminent leaders. He reports that there was cooperation between groups for hunting activities (p. 490).

Clark, who published his account of the King George's Sound 'natives' in a Perth newspaper in 1842, remarks that if a group hunted on country 'belonging to another tribe, beyond a line of demarcation which is accurately fixed and well known to them, the party committing the trespass is sure of attack' (Clark 1842, p. 6, col. 1). Clark gives an example of a man called Mopy from King George Sound, who fired land of the Murraymen to drive out kangaroos and was speared badly as a consequence (p. 6, col. 1).

Early accounts: York, Margaret River and Bunbury

Accounts of relationships with land from these areas are broadly consistent with those already provided. Millett (1872), writing about the York area, states that

> Each tribe possesses a territory of its own, and each family of the tribe has its own especial tract of land within that territory, together with the springs of water thereupon; here he can light his fire and build his hut without fear of molestation;

> it is in fact his paternal estate, so that the word 'fire' conveys to an Australian the same meaning of fatherland or birthplace as the European idiom of 'hearth,'[59] and is used by the Aborigines in the same sense. (Millett 1872, p. 77)

It is possible that Millett gained all this information from Salvado, with whom she was acquainted (see pp. 288–9). However, her ethnographic materials are detailed, so it is possible that she based these statements on her own understandings.

Lefroy observes that Aboriginal people 'own hereditary wells or waterholes', adding that they seldom travelled more than 50 miles from them (Lefroy 1934, p. 107). Further south at Margaret River, Terry notes that land passed to a man's sons, or to his daughters' sons:

> They were to a certain extent landed proprietors and although nomadic the law was that they must hunt in their own district, and if a tribe hunted on another tribe's country it was the cause of war.
>
> A district belongs to a male who is head of the family. He may subdivide it amongst his heirs, but if there were no male heirs the sons of his daughters. Close intermarrying is prevented by well understood laws. (Terry 1994, pp. 9–10)

Roth, writing of the Bunbury area and presenting material collected by Austin, provides a detailed account, again consistent with the material already reviewed. He indicates that families owned their own areas, and that entry upon them by others was subject to respect for the property of others. Yet he also notes that people were free to use the resources of other people's country, subject to invitation:

> Each family of the tribe had a more or less defined area of country belonging to it, a kind of heritage: its rights over such track were respected, and any infringements regarded in the light of trespass. Even if an individual of the same tribe, yet of a different family, had occasion to traverse it, he would only, if obliged at all, take just enough to appease his hunger — e.g., one bird, or one egg, from a nest, leaving the remainder for its rightful owners. And it was wonderful to note how these owners knew exactly what was on their piece of land; they were never selfish about its products, but during the superabundance of any food plants, game, fish etc., at any particular season, would send round for neighbouring families to come and make

59 Millett adds a footnote here: 'I am indebted for this information to Bishop Salvado's "Memorie Storiche dell' Australia"'.

> common property of what Nature had so plentifully supplied them with. Thus also, when the swans were nesting, or when a whale was cast ashore, other tribes would come along by invitation. (Roth 1902, p. 50)

Roth notes that there were 'certain rules benefiting the whole community — for example, the respect for each other's property, and the prior right to certain portions of the land which the tribe in general acknowledged to be theirs' (p. 54). Roth's view was then that the system of ownership was underpinned by a system of rules or laws.

Daisy Bates

I noted in the last chapter that Bates documented how individuals had rights to access and use the resources of a range of country. These rights were based on sets of relationships (mostly kin-based, though some may have had developed through ritual activities). It would appear, then, that people exercised rights to these areas of country and they were not restricted to relatively small confined locales. Moreover, several men, as well as the families they represented, were able to use the same areas, or overlapping parts of the same areas, together.

Bates terms the areas a person was free to utilise their 'run' (e.g. see Bates 1992, p. 21; White 1985, pp. 50–1). She considered that the 'run' was developed as a result of marriage and other alliances, ensuring that a person had affinal kin in areas to which he or she travelled (Bates 1992, pp. 23, 76–7). Once again, her fullest account is in *Native tribes of Western Australia*, where she claims that 'runs' had been held since the *nyitting*[60] times (White 1985, pp. 51–2), and a person's run could not be disposed of. Bates provides several examples of a person's range. She concludes that the freedom of movement demonstrates the unity of the Bibbulmun. 'They were one people, speaking one language, and following the same fundamental laws and customs.' (p. 52) Bates also indicates that ritual practice made manifest a freedom of movement across Bibbulmun lands. In her account of the initiation of youths (White 1985, pp. 151–62), she records extensive travel through the lands of the South West (e.g. see p. 159). In this account, those who effected the initiation rite came from a distant area, but were able to traverse country well in excess of their own 'run' or range. Bates also provides a list of a number of people in relation to places in her *The passing of the Aborigines* (Bates 1966, p. 69) and in her essays (Bates 1992, pp. 79–80).

---

60 A term which literally means 'cold' and probably refers to what is more commonly called the Dreaming.

Bates's fullest account of local organisation is to be found in *The native tribes of Western Australia* (White 1985, pp. 48–54). There Bates ignored the complexity of the data she had collected, wishing instead to provide a simpler view of local organisation in her proposed book. She therefore ignores her own data indicating that several families and individuals used country together. She had written that:

> each tribe, or aggregate of local groups, had a definite area over which every individual member had hunting and food rights. Within this area were certain waters, hills, valleys, rivers, estuaries, which were the property of the groups inhabiting that particular part of the country. (Bates 1992, p. 49)

Bates states that it had become difficult to define these territories. She provides an account from Joobaitch, who describes an area that is considerably smaller than that reported by Bates from the same informant above (and amounting to some 268 square miles (almost 700 square kilometres) by her calculations (p. 49; see also Green 2003, pp. 106–7)). In her discussion of local organisation Bates indicates that there were numerous dialect groups within the Bibbulmun nation (see White 1985, p. 29) and that these dialect groups were local groups (see pp. 48, 53–4). My view is that it is unlikely that each 'local group' (however understood) could comprise a distinct dialect group, as such a group would be too small to have unique linguistic integrity. What Bates may have meant is illuminated to some extent by her records set out elsewhere. On a map,[61] Bates notes the dialect groups as she understood them. These would appear to be much larger than localised family groups of the sort that Bates appears to be describing as the minimal land-holding unit of the society.

While Bates understood areas of land to pass in the family, it is a subject to which she devotes little time. She states that the Bibbulmun had 'a sense of hereditary group ownership of their land' (Bates 1966, p. 61), and provides one observation of a person who claimed country that belonged to his father, to whom 'the *demma goomber*' gave it (Bates n.d.d).[62] *Demma* would appear to be a kin term for fm or MF (see White 1985, p. 80), but *goomber* is unexplained. The use of the definite article might possibly imply a deity, but the matter is inconclusive. This lack of attention to descent is surprising, since Bates devotes considerable

61 See National Native Title Tribunal (2001), Map 7: 'Dialect map', approx. 1907–1909 (Bates 1907–09b).

62 Typescript from Notebook 15, p. 54. See also the discussion above in relation to Woolgurt, who derived his country from a patri-filiate.

attention to social categorisation and how it was derived, noting a variation within the cultural group between matrilineal and patrilineal descent with respect to moiety affiliation. For Bates, descent was significant because of its role in the attribution of moiety affiliation. In her account of descent, in this context, she does not equate moiety descent with descent of rights in land (White 1985, pp. 74–7).

Bates was evidently aware that in some circumstances places or areas of country could become 'vacant'; that is, a last surviving owner had died out, leaving the area without a hereditary successor. She noted that the Bibbulmun term for this was *bindardee.* She wrote, 'it is the "Bindardee" country when the nyungar dies who owned it. Nilgee's house is called Bindardee because it has "no father"' (Bates n.d.d, p. 54).

Bates does not explain how orphaned land was acquired by others but she was certainly recording a process where there was a potential for a change to the ownership of land. Her citing of a Noongar word for a 'vacant' area indicates that the concept of such vacancy was a part of traditional Noongar culture.

Summary

Individuals were regarded (and apparently regarded themselves) as having one area of country, however defined and bounded, that was of particular importance and significance to them. They had undisputed rights to this area of land, rights that were of the nature of an ownership in real property. This is evident from all the writers reviewed above, and particularly from Moore, Lyon and Armstrong for the Perth area, and Nind, Barker and Collie for the Albany area. Although it is something about which the early writers remain silent, I consider that this attachment was articulated through spiritual referents, as this was and is the basis of traditional Aboriginal relationships to land throughout Australia.

The early writers record that land passed through the family, implying or stating that descent was an important means of gaining rights to country. The extent to which a person's affiliation with country was singular is unclear; the accounts, as provided here, are not consistent. However, by looking at one particular residence group, the details of which we have from the early record, it is possible to reconstruct the way things may have worked in practice. Yellowgonga's group comprised members with rights in a number of different areas, who apparently were also free to use the country in which they resided. There is evidence from all three writers from the Albany region (Nind, Barker and Collie) that rights to a '"natal" area' (Collie's term) were shared with others. A person's affiliations to country were expressed in relation to a complex web of rights that might be realised in relation to several areas of country by reference to kinship ties or other relationships.

Keen (2004) confirms this view, concluding that people in the Albany region had rights in a number of different countries, including their father's, mother's brother's and spouse's, as well as that of their birth (pp. 285–6, 295). Keen states that land holding 'centred on patri-groups' (p. 285), and I conclude that Keen considered that the primary 'country group' was then a patri-group whose members lived within a residence group that would include members of other patri-groups as well (their wives or perhaps their husbands) (p. 286). However, the rights to the resources of a number of areas, beyond that of an individual's patri-group, appear to have been exercised freely,[63] and the degree to which members of the country group (or patri-group) exercised exclusive rights to their country is, to my mind, much in question. In short, individuals were recognised as 'belonging to' a certain area (perhaps as a result of a spiritual connection or by reference to descent). Their rights to this area were burdened by rights of others, who were generally known to those who belonged to the country in question. Those who were not known were treated with caution as potential trespassers. For most activities, those with common rights did not need to ask each other in order to take resources. For the Albany region at least, it would appear to have been correct protocol to ask permission before undertaking other activity, such as burning the land.[64] However, while desirable, there were cases, as instanced here, where individuals did not consider that it was always necessary to ask first.

The Bates data is not easy to reconcile, as it shows some inconsistency, and her final position as expressed in her proposed book *The native tribes of Western Australia* does not altogether reflect the complexity of her field data. However, several general conclusions can be drawn from these data. First, the Noongar society that Bates observed appears from her data to be one that allowed quite extensive use of country by family groups, while usually associating people with particular home areas. Second, land use and rights to it were not exclusively held, but were shared between several family groups, and these family groups typically were related in some way, including in prior generations. Third, rights to land were gained through descent, although Bates provides very few details on this principle. It is evident from her example of Yabburgurt that people gained rights to their

63 Hallam (1975, p. 42) saw use rights as a series of overlapping mosaics. See also Meagher and Ride (1979, p. 67).

64 For Perth, see Moore (1978b, p. 259).

mother's country and their father's country, as well as that of their spouse. Finally, Bates recognised that areas of land could become 'ownerless' at certain times, but she does not explain the way by which such land was absorbed or taken over by other groups.

'Tribes', bands and local groups

Tribes

As discussed above, many early writers favoured the use of the term 'tribe'. This term was neither appropriate to the local circumstances observed in places like Perth and Albany, nor a useful term to use of Indigenous Australian local organisation as we have come to understand it (see Berndt 1959, p. 104; see also Berndt 1959, pp. 81–95; Peterson 1976, pp. 1–2, 6–10; Sutton 2003, pp. 59–63, 75–8; Howard 1976, pp. 19–20). The early writers observed groups of people moving about the land who were understood to have rights in what was usually a named area of country. The composition of these groups is reasonably clear from the early literature and can be best described as an extended family group.[65] By this I mean that the group typically might have included a nuclear family (a man, his wife or wives and their children), as well as, perhaps, siblings of the man, his spouses and children, as well as members of his first ascending generation. So, generally speaking, members had either consanguineal or affinal ties but could include those who had other alliances which were not necessarily based on consanguineal ties. Such groups are well documented in the anthropological literature (e.g. see Peterson and Long 1986, pp. 74ff) and are generally called 'bands', or sometimes 'hordes', in the anthropological literature. Keen (2004, pp. 314, 427) also calls them 'residence groups', and this is the term I use in this book. At least one of the early writers accepts that the groups observed using the land were extended family units (Nind 1979, p. 23). There is agreement between later commentators for this region on this point (e.g. Howard 1976, p. 18; Keen 2004, p. 314; Brunton 2003, pp. 19–22).

The early writers reviewed here were thus neither consistent nor clear as to the social unit which held rights to land. There was a tendency to assume that the members of the residential group or band, or a significant person within it, owned land. As the band was understood to be a 'tribe', the land was easily understood to be the territory of the 'tribe'. Moreover, the relationship between different

65 I have already discussed in detail above the composition of one group as listed by Armstrong (1979).

social groups and their use of and rights to different areas was not explored. In her accounts, Bates's focus was on individuals; however, she did record important data concerning the rights to use country which were legitimated by reference to inter-group relationships.

Bands and local groups

Early anthropological writers, notably Radcliffe-Brown in Australia, were, like the early observers of South West society, unclear as to which social entity held proprietorial rights to country. Radcliffe-Brown (1930–31, p. 59) distinguishes the 'horde', which is the patrilineal descent group from the 'clan'; it is made up of several (perhaps two) 'hordes', being ideally those of the mother and the father, which together make up the family unit (p. 59).[66] He concludes that it was the 'horde' that owned the horde territory (p. 59). However, later writers were to criticise Radcliffe-Brown for his failure to consistently separate the 'horde' and the 'clan'. There resulted a substantial debate in the anthropological literature as to whether Radcliffe-Brown did confuse the two (Berndt 1959; Hiatt 1962, 1966; Stanner 1965a).[67] Important articles by RM Berndt (1959) and WEH Stanner (1965a) set out what was to become anthropological orthodoxy with respect to a distinction between the band, as the land-using group (that is, Radcliffe-Brown's 'clan'), and the local group, as the land-owning group (Radcliffe-Brown's 'horde'). Stanner establishes the relationship between a local group's home territory (Stanner terms this the 'estate') and the country ('range') its members used, along with others, as members of bands (Stanner 1965a, p. 2). Local groups were exogamous (that is, members did not marry each other), which was a consequence, at least in part, of the fact that membership was through descent, so people would not be expected to marry members of their own family. The defining feature of the local group is its members' common affiliation with an area of country. Following Keen (2004, p. 421), I call this unit a 'country group' in this book.

Despite these understandings, debate did not subside in relation to aspects of land ownership, including the means by which people could legitimate rights to country by reference to descent. This discussion relates to the issue of whether patri-filiation was the only or preferred means of reckoning descent, or

66 Confusingly, later anthropological writing has used the term 'horde' to mean the residential group, or band, and 'clan' is sometimes used of the local group.

67 For a review of this debate, see Peterson and Long (1986, pp. 13–24); Sutton (2003, pp. 38–53).

whether matri-filiation was recognised in a cognatic system. There is no conclusive or agreed view on the nature of filiation with respect to land. Many earlier writers undoubtedly assumed that all local groups were patrilineally recruited. In more recent decades, however, research has shown that this may not have been the case (e.g. see Radcliffe-Brown 1930–31).[68] Any reading of the available anthropological literature makes it clear that rights to country, at least in some areas, can be gained through a number of ways, patri-filiation and matri-filiation being just two of them (Peterson 1983, pp. 137–8). Consequently, rights cannot be understood to reside in just one exclusive country (or local) group, however recruited (e.g. see Hiatt 1968; Berndt 1972; Layton 1983, p. 23; Myers 1986, pp. 78–9).

Finally, some writers have explored the degree to which political alliances and allegiances can be influential in the realisation of rights to country. While based on a normative system of laws, Myers (1986, pp. 73, 79–88) demonstrates how the exercise of choice affected outcomes with respect to rights in land. As a consequence, Myers considers there to be a greater degree of flexibility in traditional land-owning systems than had been contemplated for the more absolute systems described by earlier writers. Keen (1997, p. 73), summarising work by Sutton in areas north of the Western Desert, points to a land-owning system where 'shared rights and interests in patri-countries . . . exist within a wider set of relations' (see Keen 1997, p. 265), over which players exercise some control.

This brief outline of some of the issues raised in the anthropological literature over the last 70 years or so is instructive. While issues remain unresolved, it is evident that there was most probably a degree of regional variation to be found across the continent. First, it would be hard to conclude from the above debate that one model will fit all (Cf. Keen 1997; Sutton 2003, pp. 40–4). Second, for hunter-gatherer societies there is a need for flexibility, both as a result of ecological considerations and because of the exercise of personal choice. Thus it is unlikely that pre-contact systems were as rigid and fixed as may have been supposed. Finally, it is clear that rights to country, as well as their exercise and legitimation, were complex matters that required the exercise of a range of social relationships rather than reliance on a single principle.

---

68 See Sutton (2003, pp. 44–9) for a review. For a general overview of patrilineal origins and assumptions, see Peterson and Long (1986, pp. 2–7). For views developed from land claim literature, see Maddock (1981); Layton (1983); Hamilton (1982); Myers (1986). See also Peterson and Long (1986, pp. 59–61); Shapiro (1981); Keen (1997, pp. 65–6) and Sutton (2003, pp. 196–9).

Amongst hunters and gatherers, residence groups are likely to change over time. This is both a result of the exigencies of living as well as of social interaction (see Peterson and Long 1986, pp. 3–10). Economic activities will require degrees of cooperation, while food availability or scarcity may invite or require that extended family groups split up for shorter or longer periods. Moreover, tensions between individuals, fights and quarrels are likely causes for separation, while strong friendship may bring together members of different families. While the degree to which band membership fluctuated may have depended upon environmental consideration (cf. Keen 1997, p. 66; see also Peterson and Long 1986, p. 48), this alone is unlikely to account for all changes in residence group composition. It did, no doubt, depend upon a variety of factors, personal, environmental and social. Nor do I think, with respect to the Noongar materials, that inquiry after the relative permanence or impermanence of residence groups will be particularly fruitful, given the poor quality of the early accounts.[69] Residence groups were labile, so could not constitute a fixed enough entity to constitute a land-owning body (cf. Peterson and Long 1986, p. 10). As residence group membership fluctuates, the distribution of members of country groups across the countryside will reflect these changes. This both facilitates and is facilitated by a system wherein a person may gain rights in more than one area of country. This would appear to point to a system wherein rights to country were exercised and enjoyed by sets of people comprising a number of different country groups with cultural, social and filiational commonalities.

It is an error to consider the land-holding system, as it is reported, as comprising a series of hermetic and self-contained land units (estates) over which individuals exercised exclusive rights. This does not reflect the traditional situation as it has been reported by early observers discussed here, and as it was most probably found, for both the Perth and Albany regions and elsewhere in the South West of Western Australia.

Brunton (2003, p. 53) provides some support for this view with respect to the Perth area, although I find his account unsatisfactory for a number of reasons. Brunton writes that 'individuals who were not members of the estate group may have held secondary connections to an estate'; he cites non-patrilineal ancestry,

69 Brunton (2003, pp. 20–2), citing Peterson and Long (1986, pp. 26–7), attempts such an analysis, using three 'lines of evidence' suggested by Peterson and Long. In fact, Peterson and Long are discussing whether bands were localised and had bounded ranges, rather than examining matters relating to composition and perdurance, a matter they do consider subsequently.

sharing a Dreaming track, having a common totem or being born in the estate (p. 53). Brunton then uses this (undefined) concept of 'secondary rights' to accommodate what he calls 'usufructory rights', which he appears to distinguish from the rights of owners (pp. 53–4). Analytically, this is unsatisfactory on several grounds. It is unclear whether Brunton regards rights to the estate as residing only with members of the estate group (there are no secondary rights), or whether they are shared, but in a lesser form (there are secondary rights). If the latter is meant, then what are the nature of the secondary rights, and where are these discussed in the literature he reviews? However, Brunton and I evidently agree that rights within an estate were not exclusive to what he calls 'estate group members'.

The accounts provided by early settlers and writers in Western Australia can better be understood in the light of these comments and conclusions. Early observers, when using the term 'tribe', were probably writing of what would now best be termed a band or residence group. Second, the residence group was not itself a land-owning group, but comprised those who, as members of a country group, did exercise proprietorial rights to country, which may or may not have been the country on which they were observed at the time. Third, members of a residence group, if comprising more than one country group (a likely outcome, given local group exogamy) would, between them, have rights to two or more areas of country. Fourth, given that the Noongar people recognised alliances through kin and ritual, it is likely that some rights to country could be gained through the development or forging of social relationships. Finally, if the system is a relatively flexible one, as some writers have suggested for other areas of Australia, rights to country may be gained by means other than descent.

Chapter 4

SOCIAL ORGANISATION AND KINSHIP

Introduction

Early settlers appear to have been aware of the fact that there was a complex system of social organisation among the Noongar people. While there was confusion in the minds of some writers about the details and how the system worked in practice, it was evident to a number of diarists that it represented a means of organising social relationships which was different from anything they had encountered in their own cultures. One common view, prevalent at the beginning of the nineteenth century, was that the categorisation of people into named exogamous sets was a means to avoid incest, thereby ignoring the fact that in small-scale societies, people were acutely aware of their consanguineal relationships with one another.[70]

Some Noongar social categories were exogamous (that is, those of the same social category could not marry) and so were used to establish (or rule out) prospective marriage partners. Kinship relationships were complemented by the system of categorisation, whereby certain kin were classified together, making for a lack of the differentiation between kin which is found in English systems. So, for example, a man's father's brother would be called 'uncle' by the early settlers. The Noongar people, however, would classify him as a 'father', tending to limit any discrimination between a biological father and a person who is classified as such. If a categorical system is used, kinship relationships can be derived by reference to it. This means that heuristically there is a distinction between 'actual' relationships (consanguineal) and putative relationships (classificatory). This has the effect of placing all persons within a community in a relationship one to another. Consanguineal kin have evident relationships; categorical kin have putative relationships. Since the two systems are not differentiated in practice, the network of kin for an individual expands to include all members of his or her community.

70 For a discussion of this and related issues, see Fox (1967, pp. 54–76).

The manner by which a community organises its members with respect to their relationships one to another is an important aspect of the culture and has ramifications for conduct in ritual, exchanges, social interaction and marriage choice.[71]

Social categories

The purpose of this section is to summarise the accounts provided in the early literature of social categorisation amongst Noongar people. This was the focus of particular attention, particularly by Bates, whose account, as I will show, is complex. I will return to this subject later in this book, when I consider contemporary aspects of Noongar culture.

Early sources

For King George Sound, Curr reports a system of 'marriage classes', with each class being associated with a bird (the white cockatoo and the crow; Curr 1886–87, p. 386). Similarly, around Kojonup, Curr reports a patrilineal system of class marriage (p. 348). For northern areas, Salvado reports six matrilineal 'family names' with associated totemic affiliations, and everyone belonged to one of these divisions. He drew a 'tree' showing which categories could marry which (pp. 320–1). Moore (1978a, pp. 3–4) notes that the Perth Aboriginal people were divided into four exogamous 'families', which he named *ballarok, tondarap, ngotak* and *naganok*. He ascribes typical physical characteristics to each. Nind (1979), writing of the Albany region, was unclear as to the social divisions he recorded. He identified *erniung* and *taaman* as exogamous matrilineal moieties (p. 37). These were found 'near the Sound', but he recorded *moncalon* and *torndirrup* elsewhere (p. 44). However, he considered that 'there are a few who are neither' (p. 44) and that there were more *moncalon* to the east and more *torndirrup* to the west. He comments that they intermarried and had subdivisions ('*opperheip, cambien, mahnur* etc.', p. 44). Nind's account lacks sufficient detail to be of much assistance.

Barker, writing of the Albany area, recorded moiety names *mongalan* and *tronderup* (Barker 1992, p. 311), although it is unclear from the context whether he understood what these names meant. Later, he indicates that certain classes were exogamous and marriage between them was prohibited; in this context

71 See Maddock (1974, pp. 72–83) for an introduction to classes in Aboriginal Australia. See Keen (2004, pp. 139–40) on semi-moieties. See Sutton (2003, pp. 173–8) for a brief introduction to this topic. See also Sutton (2003, pp. 201–3).

he records the names *mostye* and *tallima* along with some kin terms (p. 314). Hassell (1975, p. 32) records two exogamous moieties, *nunnich* and *wording*. She considers the terms to relate to 'a particular totem' (*nunnich*) and crow (*wording*, pp. 233, 234).[72]

Bates

These early accounts are far from satisfactory. It was left to Bates to record the social categories of the South West in more detail. However, she too encountered difficulties in doing this, probably because she was searching for a uniformity and consistency where there was regional variation. In a manuscript in which she records data collected from Joobaitch in the South West of Western Australia, Bates identifies groups of persons within a population as belonging to one of four named categories: *ballarruk* (or *nogonyuk*), *tondarup, didaroke* (or *waijuk)* and *nagarnook*. Paired names formed two subdivisions (Bates n.d.h, question 5, p. 36). In Bates's record of Joobaitch's answers, she is unclear as to the nature of moiety and semi-moiety terms, confusing them with 'tribe or family' names. Thus Joobaitch gives '*ballarruk* (or *nogonyuk*)' as his 'tribe' or 'family name' (question 1). He took his mother's semi-moiety name and his father was *tondarup* (question 16). To some extent, membership of a social category determined marriage. Thus *ballarruk* married either *tondarup* or *didaroke*; *nagarnook* married *didaroke*; and *tondarup* married *ballarruk* or *nagarnook*. The account is not complete and presumably *nagarnook* could also marry *tondarup*, and *didaroke* either *ballarruk* or *nagarnook*. Bates concluded that, '*Nagarnook* and *ballaroke* are one tribe and *didaroke* and *tondarup* are also one tribe, so whatever tribe the *ballarruk* can marry into, so also can the *nagarnooks*; also with the *didarruks* and *tondarups*' (question 96). Bates recorded a system where all people are divided between two moieties (unnamed in this account) consisting of paired semi-moieties. While the moieties are exogamous, marriage with either semi-moiety of the opposite moiety is permitted. In summary the moieties are as shown in Table 4.1.

Table 4.1: Moiety terms collected by Bates from Joobaitch

Moiety 1		**Moiety 2**
Semi-moiety name		Semi-moiety name
ballarruk or *nagarnook*	marries	*tondarup* or *didarruk*

72 For a summary of the data relevant to the Albany region, see Keen (2004, pp. 157–9).

Bates does not provide any name for the moieties and records the totemic affiliation as 'cockatoo' although it is unclear to which moiety this relates (question 12). Joobaitch may have been confused over Bates's use of the term *kobong* for totem, which she took from Grey (questions 34, 67). At this time Bates was aware of numerous other moiety or semi-moiety names, and she puts these to Joobaitch (questions 6, 7 and 8).[73] Elsewhere (Bates n.d.a, Dandarragan genealogy) Bates records *rakanook* or *wejuk* along with *tondarup*, apparently considering that the system was one of two social categories (or moieties) without concomitant semi-moiety divisions. In the same manuscript, Bates recorded that the *rakanook* had the *kardan* (gum tree totem), while the *tondarup* had the *mungaitch* (banksia) totem (Bates n.d.a, Dandarragan genealogy). The implication perhaps is that all persons of the same moiety shared the same totemic affiliation. Bates shows in the same place that children took the totem and social category of their mother. I will consider totemic beliefs in a latter section.

In all, Bates canvasses or is told of 15 different moiety or semi-moiety names, including those first supplied by Joobaitch. Three of these are recorded as being equivalent, although they are different terms (*didarruk*, *rakanook* and *wardjuk*). There remain, however, 13 different terms discussed by Bates, which are set out in Table 4.2 (see also Brunton 2003, 98–9).[74]

Bates's account presents some difficulties, which are not resolved by her subsequent inquiries. Joobaitch did not name the moieties. He was aware of some additional semi-moiety names as local terms but was unaware of others. It is likely that Joobaitch's data reflect a system of social organisation that was much less uniform than Bates was to present in her later accounts.

73 Additional names include *erniung* and *taaman*, *ngotak* (Bunbury), *mongalung* (Bunbury) and *narrangur*, which Bates apparently took from Grey. Joobaitch identifies *ngotak* as a Bunbury name and provides, in addition, *jirajiak*, *monderuk* and *wardjuk* (equated above with *didaroke*). Bates inquires in relation to Salvado's six names (*tirarop*, *palarop*, *mondorop*, *noiognok*, *tondorop* and *jiragiok*; Curr 1886–87, p. 321), but Joobaitch states that he does not know 'all of these names'. Later, in the same manuscript (Bates, n.d.a, 'Table of relationships' which is paginated as 'page 29'), Bates records that 'according to Jubyche' Salvado's names for 'tribes' were not correct.

74 I agree with Brunton that Bates sometimes confused terms and that the names she collected as semi-moieties were in some cases regional or other names. However, the list presented here would appear to comprise semi-moiety terms. Brunton considers Salvado's *noiognok* to be the same term as *nagarnook* and his *mondorop* not to be a semi-moiety name, since Bates had recorded it as meaning 'pubic hair' (pp. 97, 100). However, as noted above, Bates's informant Joobaitch considered that all Salvado's terms were wrong.

Bates refined her views in a manuscript in which she sets out what she termed the 'class divisions' of the South West of Western Australia (Bates n.d.e).[75] There she describes the population of the whole of the South West as comprising two exogamous divisions: *Manitchmat* (*manitjmad*; *manitj* means white cockatoo); and *Wordungmat* (*wurdungmad*; *wurdung* means crow (Australian raven)).[76] Bates records no special treatment of the totemic associations of each, with both being eaten, although the crow seldom, except *in extremis* (p. 2). From Jurien Bay to the Donnelly River (west of Pemberton), a child gained the moiety (Bates calls them 'phratries') of their mother; over the rest of the area it was from their father (p. 1). The moieties were exogamous, there being a term for 'wrong marriage' or moiety endogamy (*mootch*) (White 1985, p. 77), and there were egocentric terms for both your own and the opposite moiety (Bates n.d.c. pp. 3–4). Bates was of the view that the members of each moiety had certain physiological characteristics in common, by which they could be recognised (pp. 7–8). This is an insupportable conclusion, given moiety exogamy and the fact that children are likely to inherit characteristics of either parent, or both.[77]

Table 4.2: Semi-moiety names discussed by Bates with Joobaitch

Moiety or semi-moiety name	Alternative name
ballarruk	*palarop*
didarruk	*wardjuk, wejuk, rakanook*
erniung	
jiragiok	*jirajiak*
monderuk	*mondorop*
mongalung	
nagarnook	
narrangur	
ngotak	
noiognok	
taaman	
tirarop	

75 See White (1985, pp. 74ff) for similar material.

76 According to Bates, *mat* means leg, family or stock. Bindon and Chadwick (1992, p. 106) give *mart*, leg bone or shin bone.

77 Bates was much taken with this idea — see Bates (n.d.d). See also White (1985, p. 75), for a comment, including notes on criticisms made by both Radcliffe-Brown and Lang.

Bates mapped these areas, and indicates that matrilineal moieties were found over an area that extended inland a little west of Nannup, north-west of Greenbushes and east of Collie, west of Williams to Beverley before extending east beyond Kellerberrin and thence north to Mt Churchman, which is east of Lake Moore.[78] Over the rest of the South West, moieties were inherited from a person's father.

Bates's brief account of social organisation in *The passing of the Aborigines*, first published in 1938, is consistent with these views that there were moieties divided into four class subdivisions (Bates 1966, p. 60). In *The native tribes of Western Australia*, she reproduces much of the material outlined above from her earlier 'Class divisions, etc southwestern WA' (Bates n.d.e; White 1985, pp. 74–8). Bates restates the distinction between areas where moiety affiliation was matrilineally derived and those where it was patrilineally derived (White 1985, p. 46). She identifies moieties ('phratries'; White 1985, p. 74) with subdivisions, as set out in her earlier paper ('*Wordungmat* and *Manitchmat*'). Bates then provides additional information. 'North of the Warren River [adjacent to Pemberton] the subdivision of the two primary divisions begins and extends northward as far as about Jurien Bay' (p. 74). The 'subdivision' of the moieties is:

> *Wurdungmad*: subdivided into *nagarnook* and *ballarruk*;
> *Manitjmad*: subdivided into *tondarup* and *didarruk*. (p. 74)

Bates then states that the two moiety names 'are principally used in the South although the four subdivisions are certainly known, and the subdivisional names are used along the south-west coast although the two primary divisions are recognised' (p. 74). Consistent with the principles of patri- and matri-moieties, in the south and east a child takes the social category (that is, moiety and semi-moiety) of his or her father. To the west ('from Williams River to Jurien Bay'),[79] a child takes the social category (moiety and semi-moiety, if

78 Bates (1907–09b). Bates's annotations to the northern (matrilineal) area were initially incorrect, since she transposes the subdivision classes assigned to the moieties. Bates adds a note of correction to remedy this.

79 Bates (1907–09b, p. 75). Bates's lack of geographic precision obfuscates her discourse. The Williams River flows west from Williams to become the Murray, reaching the ocean at Mandurah. However, the following text makes it clear that Bates included 'Bunbury etc' and, presumably, the whole of the western areas of the South West in the 'matrilineal' area, consistent with her discussions elsewhere and her map of social organisation, discussed above. It may be that Williams River was an alternative name for the Warren River. See p. 76, where the matter is partially clarified.

applicable) of his or her mother (p. 75). Thus, in the south and west a *wurdungmad* man marries a *manitjmad* woman, who is either a *tondarup* or *didarruk* (and *vice versa*; p. 76). In the south-east, marriage choices are reported to have been more limited (p. 77). Each semi-moiety has a preferred marriage partner found in a semi-moiety of the opposite moiety. This can be summarised as shown in Figure 4.1.

Figure 4.1: Patri-moieties and semi-moieties in the South West of Western Australia (after Bates)

Moiety 1: *manitjmad*							
			Moiety 2: *wurdungmad*				
➛ Semi moiety	1	*tondarup*	=	*ballarruk*	semi moiety	2	⟵
➛ Semi moiety	3	*didarruk*	=	*nagarnook*	semi moiety	4	⟵

Key: = marriage; ➛ off-spring from female

Source: White (1985, p. 77)

In Figure 4.1, a *manitjmad* man of the *tondarup* semi-moiety marries a *wurdungmad* woman of the *ballarruk* semi-moiety, and their child is *manitjmad* moiety and *tondarup* semi-moiety, as is its father.

Bates expresses the view that there was vigorous punishment for breaking the marriage rule of moiety exogamy and suggests that the system became more permissive following the arrival of Europeans (p. 77). Later in the same work, Bates makes clear that by 'descent' she was referring to the attribution of a social category directly from mother (matrilineal) or from father (agnatic or patrilineal; White 1985, p. 75). Whether Bates considered there to be any relationship between social categories and land ownership is not evident anywhere.[80]

80 Matri-filial institutions have social rather than land-owning functions. Sutton (2003) states that, 'neither serial matri-filiation nor matrilineal descent . . . forms the normative basis of any kind of country-holding group in classical or even post-classical Aboriginal Australia at all, as far as I am aware. Radcliffe-Brown, Elkin, the Berndts, Maddock and Peterson came to this conclusion and there is no reliable evidence to call these views into question.' (Sutton 2003, p. 200) Sutton further argues that the function of matri-clans is to balance territorialism by promoting cross-territorial links between uterine (and fictive) kin (p. 203).

Bates's *The native tribes of Western Australia* may represent her final view on social organisation, and it is certainly her most complete.[81] However, when comparing Bates's field data with her final manuscript on social organisation, it is evident that she simplified her data. It is true that she notes that in the south and west the moiety system was dominant, while the semi-moiety system was incorporated within it. By implication it was then subsidiary. However, Bates was faced with greater diversity in the social organisation she recorded than is evident in her recognition of a division between patri- and matri-moieties and the regional occurrence of semi-moieties. The existence of two named moieties (and their totemic affiliations) was not recorded by Bates in all cases. There were a number of different names employed for semi-moiety divisions across the region. Nor does diversity appear to have presented a problem. Bates notes that, in ritual dealings, people whose role was defined by their moiety or semi-moiety affiliations had no difficulty in adapting from matri-filiate to patri-filiate moieties (White 1985, pp. 77, 158). As Bates discovered from Yaburgurt (Bates n.d.f), those with whom she worked had no difficulty in accommodating one system of social categorisation with another, including the section system to the north. It is even possible that Salvado recorded a hybrid version of the six-section system that incorporated names from the New Norcia region and perhaps elsewhere (cf. Berndt and Berndt 1977, p. 48).

It is now impossible to reconstruct the total system of social categorisation over the whole region, except in outline. Later writers were to recognise that there was some diversity within the South West, with Berndt (1979, pp. 82–4) reporting on four different systems. Keen (2004, pp. 158–9), writing specifically about the Albany area, recognises internal diversity across the South West region. What Bates described was both diverse and fluid; that is, the system of social categories was not fixed as immutable, but changing, with systems influenced by neighbouring systems with which they had an easy and recognisable correspondence and compatibility. Such fluidity and change in the adoption of systems of social categorisation are recorded from many other areas of Australia (see Berndt and Berndt 1977, p. 47).

81 This manuscript was probably completed by 1909 (White 1985, p. 6). However, it is possible that she subsequently added to it, and the final manuscript was not retyped until between 1936 and 1940 (p. 16).

Kinship

Early accounts are almost devoid of any reference to kinship, although there was a general recognition of the importance of families (e.g. Nind 1979, pp. 23, 25; Armstrong 1979, p. 194; Hassell 1936, p. 681; Roth 1902, p. 20). Curr (1886–87, e.g. p. 318) provides a few kin terms (F, MB and z), but the information is too limited to be of any use in developing any idea of the kinship system in operation. Barker notes the classificatory system in operation when he writes that 'a man is a father to his brother's children and uncle (*conque*) only to those of his sisters'. He thought it 'very complicated' (Barker 1992, pp. 287, 314). The information supplied by Barker is too limited to lend itself to much analysis (see Le Souef 1993, pp. 15–16).

In an early manuscript, Bates records that the terms for F and FB and m and mz are 'similar' (Bates n.d.g, p. 1). She records that the term for B and z, by which I take her to mean two siblings, are the same as the term for FF and fbz, when ego is a third party. This is made clear in a list which she provides where FF is listed as *ngoont* and so is SS, while fbz and sd are listed as *jook* (pp. 2–4). First cross-cousin marriage was not permitted, which is consistent with matri-filiate moiety exogamy, although Bates does not make this clear (she later appears to be describing a patri-filiate moiety system, since ego has the moiety of her father) but it is likely that close consanguineal kin were not preferred marriage partners (p. 6). Overall, Bates collected numerous lists of kinship terms, providing some analysis of the dialect variations between different areas, and many of these are reproduced in her proposed book, *The native tribes of Western Australia* (see White 1985, pp. 78–82). Here, typically, father and father's brother are called by the same term, as are mother and mother's sister (p. 78). FBS and fbd were not distinguished, with females, at least, all being classified as 'sisters' (*jookan*; p. 79). However, patri-cross cousins were distinguished from patri-parallel cousins. Bates recognised that the system of classificatory kin meant a person could identify putative relationships among non-consanguineal kin that facilitated social interaction when travelling beyond the normal range of a residence group. She implies that this evoked obligations for hospitality, care and protection to be afforded by reference to the kinship system (White 1985, pp. 82–3; see also pp. 143–5). While Bates appears to have had a greater interest in the list of terms rather than how they reflected social interaction, the terms she supplies do serve to demonstrate a system of kin reckoning whereby a number of relations were classed together by use of the same term. This is summarised by Keen for the Albany region (Keen 2004, pp. 188–9).

Overall, the data on kinship terminology are quite limited. It is reasonable to conclude that there operated a classificatory system, which probably relied on the moieties and semi-moieties for its implementation, particularly where the real or consanguineal relationship was not known.

Chapter 5

RELIGIOUS BELIEFS AND PRACTICES IN THE SOUTH WEST

Introduction

The early accounts of Noongar people in the South West of Western Australia provide limited material on spiritual and religious life. First, as is usual in Aboriginal societies, both historically and today, there would have been reluctance on the part of the Aboriginal people to divulge details of their spiritual beliefs to outsiders. Indeed, this sense of secrecy over details of spiritual beliefs is one of the accepted hallmarks of Aboriginal societies. The second factor is that many of the early observers and ethnographers who wrote about Aboriginal people tended to dismiss Aboriginal spiritual beliefs as falling well short of what they considered constituted a religious system. This dismissal of the significance of the Aboriginal spiritual beliefs and practices characterises much of what was written by the early observers of the Aboriginal people.

Despite this, a principal emphasis in the accounts, and one common to most of them, is that Noongar people held strong beliefs about the spirit world, often associated with death or with spirits of the dead. Funereal rites were understood to be particularly important and were significant public events. In addition, there is material (but very little detail) available on the initiatory ritual life and on the relationship between people and the natural world, a concept often conveyed through the use of the term 'totemism'. There are also collections of narratives (sometimes called 'myths') which relate to the creative period of the Dreaming, a concept that Noongar people shared with other Aboriginal cultures elsewhere.

Spirits and the spirit world

There appears to have been a common belief on the part of the Aboriginal people of the South West that the European settlers were the spirits of their deceased ancestors (Green 1984, pp. 33–4; see also Armstrong 1979, pp. 187–8; Grey 1841, pp. 301–2; Curr 1886–87, p. 339; Roth 1902, pp. 51–2).[82] This probably reflects a complex set of beliefs about spirits, which many early observes did not fully appreciate or analyse. One of Curr's correspondents simply states that 'The Whajook [Aboriginal people in the York area] believe in evil spirits and ghosts' (Curr 1886–87, p. 339). He goes on to report that 'widows and mothers always fear that the lately dead may visit their camps at night to warm themselves'. In consequence 'they make a fire a little distance from their own for the special use of the departed'.[83] Similar fears of the return of the dead are recorded for the Perth area by the same writer, along with the steps taken to attempt to ensure unwanted visits did not eventuate (p. 330). Salvado confirms the belief in a spirit after death (Stormon 1977, pp. 61, 127–8), together with the understanding that actions taken after a death were to assist the departed spirit to leave the area, or to become more comfortable, particularly with respect to keeping warm. He makes reference to a belief that supernatural powers could be responsible for a death initiated by human agency. Thus a cause and effect system was in operation, and Noongar people consequently were acutely aware of the circumstances surrounding a death and their likely consequences (p. 128).

Barker, writing of the Albany region, provides an early account of the belief in spirits of the dead. In particular, Barker notes that the Aborigines had a system of beliefs that focused on spirits and what he calls 'ghosts' (Barker 1992, pp. 281, 283, 286, 293, 323, 345, 351). He was led to ask himself questions as to what this meant for the status of these beliefs with respect to a religion. This was a significant philosophical and theological point of debate at the time.[84] In particular, Barker reports that there was fear of the actions of the returning dead (p. 281) or that they boded ill, being harbingers of death. Their appearance generally was associated with night and occasioned great fear (pp. 283, 286, 293, 323). Barker provides a detailed account of the belief in the origins of spirits:

> Ghosts of deceased blacks, men women and children wander about at night in the bush, does not know what becomes of them in the day. Formerly a great number used to be seen, now it is not the case often. (Barker 1992, p. 345)

---

82 For more general references to ghosts and spirits, see Moore (1978b, p. 194; Nind 1979, p. 50; Grey 1841, p. 323).
83 See Millett (1872, p. 76) for another example of this belief; see also Hassell (1975, p. 60).
84 See Barker 1992, p. 345, n. 30 by the editors.

Hammond, writing some time later, provides a more generalised account of spirits but sees them as an important component of Noongar beliefs (Hammond 1933, pp. 63–4). Hassell reports that people were reluctant to speak too openly of the spirits for fear of offending them (Hassell 1936, p. 680; 1975, p. 141). She notes that spirits were associated with certain places where it was too dangerous to go at night for fear of harm (1975, p. 31)[85] and confirms the belief that spirits were considered to be abroad at night, and that it consequently was a dangerous time to leave your camp (p. 44). Hassell provides her own inventory of spirits (pp. 59–64), which are all named.[86] Roth, using data collected by Austin in the nineteenth century, remarks that:

> . . . the earth was permeated with evil spirits, whom they feared. Such spirits could be checked or repelled by means of fire, and this was one of the chief reasons why, in the dark, they would never leave their camps without taking a lighted fire stick with them. (Roth 1902, p. 52)

The themes noted above are echoed by Bates, particularly with respect to the spirits of the dead (White 1985, pp. 222–5). Bates states that the spirits of the dead went to a place called Koorannup or Woordanung, which was 'far beyond the sea' (p. 222). They sometimes showed a reluctance to go, or for some reason returned, living in caves or other parts of their own country. A departing spirit might take one of the living it loved with it, unless steps were taken to prevent this (p. 223). Bates provides information about some regional variation with regard to the beliefs surrounding the passage of the spirit to the spirit land (pp. 223–5).

Funereal practices

Funereal practices figure prominently in the early literature, showing that funerals were significant public affairs and an important part of Noongar culture. Curr, for example, provides details from the York area about steps taken to limit the movement of the spirit after death by removing the fingernails and securing the forefingers together (Curr 1886–87, p. 324). In the Perth area, 'limbs' were tied together for a similar reason, since people were fearful of the return of the dead (p. 330). Moore (1978b, pp. 345–47) provides more detail, it being clear

85 This is a reference to a place called Twertup which is some distance south-east from Jerramungup.

86 Hassell lists 'jannocks', mischievous spirits; 'coombar jannock'; the 'big spirit'; 'noitch', 'the supreme evil one'; 'marghet', an inland water spirit; and 'gnolum', who abducts young boys.

from the context that he witnessed the event he subsequently described. He notes that the grave was dug north to south, with the earth mounded on the western side. Prior to interment, legs were folded back, hair was singed and the nail of the little finger was removed by burning and that finger then tied to the thumb. The grave was then burnt with brushwood, with people being careful to avoid the smoke. Following the application of white ochre to the corpse's face, it was placed in the grave on its right side, head to the south, face to the east. Moore notes that he was advised that some groups buried their dead east–west, with their faces to the north.[87] After the grave was filled in, a man's spear, broken for the purpose, was placed on the grave along with other effects, and a small fire was made before the mound (p. 347).

Nind provides a similar account for the Albany region (1979, pp. 49–50), adding the detail that the grave site was marked with circles cut in the bark of trees growing near the grave. Collie describes in detail the burial of Mokare (Collie 1834, pp. 73–5). The oval grave was dug east–west, with earth thrown up on the south side, while the grave was filled with material from the north side, thus leaving the piled crescent-shaped earth to the south intact. Grave goods were left on the grave and a fire lit close by. Lyon (1979, p. 166) provides a more biblical account, which is of limited value, while Armstrong (1979, p. 200) gives a brief description that lacks Moore's detail, perhaps revealing that he did not himself attend a funeral. Barker reports that 'resurrections' after burial were not unknown because, in that area, burial was preferred to follow closely upon the death, which was sometimes misdiagnosed (Barker 1992, p. 392; see also Clark 1842, p. 4, col. 2). Hassell reports that the Wilmun expressed a preference for being buried in their own country (Hassell 1936, p. 708). She provides a detailed account of the burial of Winmar (pp. 708–10),[88] which is the most thorough account in the early literature and is broadly consistent with the descriptions discussed so far. In this case, however, the arm, leg and thigh bones were broken to prevent the 'dead from jumping about until after the bones had knitted together, thus ensuring him of a long rest' (p. 710). Personal effects were left on the grave, food and water provided as grave goods, and two fires lit and subsequently maintained. Trees were marked

---

87 See Moore (1978a, pp. 11–128), where he explains that the 'mountain tribes' bury the body north to south, the lowland tribes east to west. The account provided by Moore here provides more detail than the one cited above, but is substantially the same regarding detail. See also Roth (1902, p. 53), who states for the Bunbury region that the 'corpse ... was invariably toward the east'. The meaning is unclear.

88 See also Hassell (1975, pp. 51–4) for a similar account.

close to the grave. Hassell describes a fire ritual, which was designed to ensure that there were no spirits in the vicinity of the grave (p. 709).[89] Hassell also remarks on the difference in the grave's orientation between 'Hill tribes' and 'Plains tribes' (p. 710).

Bates was aware of the importance of burial rituals to the Noongar people, observing that they were 'in most cases scrupulously carried out' (White 1985, p. 298). Her accounts of burials, including one that she evidently observed (pp. 299–300), are generally consistent with those already considered and reflect the regional variations recorded by other writers. These include the orientation of the grave, the tying of limbs and burning off of fingernails, the placement of grave goods, the lighting of fires, marking of trees and disposal of personal effects of the deceased (pp. 298–303). Bates provides an account of post-mortem sorcery to establish the perpetrator of the death, which was an important part of the funereal rite (p. 299).

Spirits and death: summary remarks

The accounts of early writers present a picture of South West Aboriginal society that was deeply informed by reference to spirits, death and the afterlife of the departed. This typifies a society that made of the spirit world a preoccupation that informed much belief, action, opinion and emotion. Several consequences flowed from this. First, there existed in parallel with the physical world of people and things, a spirit world that had to be accommodated, placated and negotiated. This meant that certain things could not be done, particularly travel at night and to certain places known to be the resort of spiritual entities. Certain things also had to be done, typified by the lighting of fires or the provision of grave goods. The known world was resonant with spiritual presences, many of which were at best ambiguous, and most dangerous. Activity in country needed to accommodate the eventualities of the spirit world, and people had to be on guard to ensure their safety.

Second, the event of death had repercussions beyond bereavement. Death released into the world spirits that had to be understood and encouraged to go on their way peacefully, leaving the living to their own devices. This meant that funereal practices were important public rituals, which served not merely to dispose of the dead and farewell a loved one but to enter into and manage a

89 This may, in fact, have been a divination to establish the person responsible for the death. Cf. White 1985, p. 299.

relationship with the spirit world. Added to this was the importance, recorded in some accounts discussed here, of establishing the cause of death, usually attributable to a person.

Some writers reviewed here regarded the belief in spirits and the spirit world as 'superstition'. They equated it with a belief in 'ghosts', which was familiar to them from their own culture. However, these beliefs in the spirit world constitute a more substantial body of belief and its management practices represent a system of rules and laws. Following these rules was considered to be essential for maintenance of peaceful relationships between the living and the dead, constituting a significant aspect of Noongar culture. It was a culture that reverberated with spiritual reference, and this was a notable feature of its manifestation.

Noongar doctors or 'clever men'

Some early writers were aware of people within Noongar society who were credited with extraordinary spiritual powers (Stormon 1977, pp. 170–2; Nind 1979, pp. 42–4; Armstrong 1979, p. 189; Barker 1992, p. 290; Hammond 1933, pp. 58–9; Millett 1872, p. 79; White 1985, pp. 227–37). These powers included an ability to foretell the future and practise divination, particularly with respect to establishing the cause of death of a person and being able to cure illness or injury. Popular English terms for a person with these skills are unsatisfactory, carrying with them ethnocentric assumptions about the role of these spiritually gifted people in Noongar society. 'Witch doctor', 'sorcerer' and 'medicine man' are three examples. Noongar people have their own words for these men (and women), notably *bulya* and *mulgarradock*, as well as *mubarn*. In this account, I term these people 'Noongar doctors', although 'clever men' would serve as well. The equivalents of Noongar doctors are recorded for many other areas of Aboriginal Australia, and this is well documented in the literature (e.g. see Elkin 1977).

Salvado identifies Noongar doctors as *boylya* and describes with some cynicism their attempts at effecting a cure for certain illnesses (Stormon 1977, pp. 170–2). Nind, writing about the Albany region, identifies Noongar doctors as *mulgarradock* and states that they were considered to have power over the natural elements, to be able to confer strength and dexterity on others and to effect cures, sometimes with the help of herbs (Nind 1979, pp. 42–4). Armstrong, who calls them 'sorcerers', indicates that their powers included curing illness and wounds, controlling natural elements and an ability to kill another through the exercise of their supernatural powers (Armstrong 1979, p. 189). Barker provides a brief account of how doctors acquired their skills (Barker 1992, p. 290). Hammond (1933, pp. 58–9) provides an account of Noongar doctors treating illness. Millett identifies a doctor as *bollia*; she considers this role comprised 'a faint type of priesthood' (1872, p. 79). A *bollia* was able to see spirits and practise divination after a death (pp. 79–80), a function I noted in the section above dealing with funereal practices.

Bates identifies Noongar doctors as *boylyaguttuk* (Bates n.d.d, p. 108) and *mulgarguttuk*, which she distinguishes (White 1985, p. 231). Bates gives a comprehensive account of the skills and abilities of doctors (pp. 227–33, 237), including the ability to shape change (p. 232). She notes that the term used in the neighbouring Murchison region was *mobarn* (p. 234).

Narratives, places and the Dreaming

The early writers record that Noongar people, in common with Aboriginal people in other areas of Australia, believed in a supernatural time, which had occurred in the distant past. During this time, often termed the 'Dreaming' or 'Dreamtime', extraordinary metaphysical events happened, which are now recounted as narratives. In some cases, the events of this time were responsible for natural phenomena evident today, like stars, hills and rivers. The concept is well known elsewhere in Aboriginal Australia and has been documented copiously by researchers.[90] The effects of the Dreaming are carried into the present by both the recounting of narratives and reference to Dreaming-derived phenomena, which typically are believed to carry Dreaming spirituality. The early writers did not readily identify the details of the belief system that encapsulated the concept of the Dreaming. Moore regarded the narrative he recorded as a 'fable' (Moore 1978b, pp. 387–8). Barker recognised that the events related in the narratives that he came to hear told of an extraordinary time before the present, but he gives it no name (Barker 1992, pp. 289, 308, 361). Hassell, who provides a number of narratives (1934–35) recognised that the stories were told of a period a long time in the past (e.g. 1975, pp. 81, 124, 212). They are mostly aetiological but also associate particular places with spiritual beings (e.g. pp. 31–3). Terry (1994) collected numerous narratives of events, which she indicates happened in the distant past.

Bates (1992, pp. 95, 147; White 1985, p. 51) was the only writer to identify the Dreaming as *nyitting*, which she guesses translates as 'cold, ice age' or 'ancestral

90 See, for example, Stanner (1979, pp. 23–40); Berndt and Berndt (1977, pp. 228–30); Myers (1986, pp. 47–51).

times'.[91] Bates was aware of the substantial corpus of narratives of this creative period, and some of these are reproduced in Bates (1992).

On the whole, the early sources, including Bates, provide us with very little information about the Dreaming, apart from the numerous narratives. This is explicable by reference to a general view, prevalent at the time, that Aboriginal spiritual beliefs fell well short of a structured religious system.[92] As a consequence, narratives generally were viewed as 'fables' or 'fairy stories', and the centrality of the Dreaming, evident in other Aboriginal cultures, was lost upon the early writers. From the evidence available, it seems that the Noongar people encountered by the early writers believed in a creative period that may have been called *nyitting*. During this time numerous extraordinary things happened, recounted in narrative. The consequences of these actions were evident in the physical world, and natural phenomena were explained by reference to the events of this extraordinary time.

Totemism

Totemism is a concept founded upon a belief of equivalence and a commonality between an individual and a natural species or object. Sometimes this results in a socially articulated set of behaviours required or expected of the individual in relation to the species, but not invariably so.[93] A number of early writers were aware of this concept and recorded it for the Noongar people with whom they were acquainted; however, on the whole the system was poorly understood in their accounts. Some seem to have been unaware of the term 'totem'[94] but nevertheless recorded the belief. Salvado notes that a child might be associated with a particular natural species, which was evident at the time of his or her birth (Stormon

91 Bates's reference to *nyitting* in her early manuscript 'The native tribes of Western Australia' indicates some doubt about the specific meaning of *nyitting*, although the general meaning, 'ancestral times', is clear (White 1985, p. 51). Several decades later, when Bates wrote the newspaper articles subsequently edited by Bridge, she translated the same word without qualification as 'cold times' (Bates 1992, pp. 95, 147; the newspaper articles were published in 1927 and 1932). Bindon and Chadwick (1992, p. 137) give both *nyetting* (cold) and *nyettin-ngal* (ancestors), citing Grey (1840) for the former and Symmons (1841) for the latter. I have not been able to check either reference. Armstrong gives *ngitding* as 'cold' (Curr 1886–87, p. 335).

92 For a brief overview, see Charlesworth (1984, pp. 1–3).

93 See, for example, Elkin (1933; 1945, pp. 182–5); Stanner (1965b, pp. 225–6).

94 The *Shorter Oxford English dictionary* gives the date for the word 'totem' as 1760, but its use by anthropologists, according to this source, is 1874. It was originally an American Indian term.

1977, p. 136). Roth, writing at the turn of the century, records belief in the totemic principle, reporting that at birth a child might be named after 'a particular animal, some circumstances in connection with which may have impressed the mind of the mother either during pregnancy or confinement' (1902, p. 53). In this observation he comes close to Salvado's account. Hassell was familiar with the word 'totem' but in her published work provides an incomplete account of the belief, stating simply that a particular individual had a wild dog as his 'totem' (Hassell 1975, p. 32). Davidson provides additional details taken from Hassell's original manuscript (Hassell 1936, p. 684), in which she states that each person had one or more totems, which were called *couburne*. A person should not harm or eat his or her totem. Totems were ranked, with flying things being the highest and ground-dwelling animals and plants (grass) the lowest. Marriage was prohibited with a person of a superior totem to your own (Hassell 1975, p. 32). Hassell's data as it relates to totemic ranking is not corroborated by any other source.

Bates devotes a chapter to totems in her proposed book on the South West. White demonstrates that she developed her ideas about totemism cognisant of (if not in agreement with) anthropological thinking of the times (White 1985, p. 191). Bates links the totemic principle to that of a means of effecting a social organisation through the allocation of all persons to one of two (or sometimes more) social classes or categories, a system of social organisation discussed in Chapter 4 of this book.

Bates's accounts of the operation of totemic principle contain inconsistencies.[95] For example, in one manuscript she identifies a set of people with honeysuckle.[96] She then allocates the plant to two social categories (*tondarup* and *didarruk*), possibly indicating that this was a moiety totem (that is, belonging to two of four social categories). This is in contradistinction to her view expressed elsewhere that the moieties related to the crow and white cockatoo (White 1985, p. 192). Either Bates was recording a regional variation in the moiety totemic system or she was recording some other form of totemism which was associated with two of four social categories. In her account of her discussions with Baabalgurt (Bates n.d.d, p. 43), she records the attribution of a personal totem that would appear to represent a different

95 Bates uses the term *borungur* for 'totem'. She notes that Grey had recorded the term *kobong*, which she says is reserved for a special relationship between brothers-in-law (White 1985, pp. 191–2).

96 Bates (n.d.d, p. 76). The note does not indicate where this group was, but presumably it was from the Busselton–Capel area, given that her informants were Baabalgurt and Nilgee and the notes relate 'mostly' to the Vasse District.

type of totemic belief altogether. In another manuscript, Bates records the totem of a number of individuals, and shows them to be inherited, for the most part, from the mother (Bates, n.d.a see Genealogies, from Gingin).[97] Class totems went with the social category of the individual; district totems derived from the place of birth and were recorded by Bates on a map (Bates 1909).

Bates refined her views on totemism elsewhere in her notes (Bates n.d.e). Here, she describes the whole of the South West as comprising two exogamous divisions called *Manitchmat* and *Wordungmat*, being either patrilineally or matrilineally inherited and each associated with the white cockatoo or crow respectively. These were ideas that she was to reproduce in her proposed book on the Aboriginal people of the South West (see White 1985, pp. 74, 191–3). Bates reports that some trees were associated with moieties (p. 193) and that there were 'class totems, district or local totems, hereditary totems and personal totems' (p. 193). Hereditary totems could be quite recent in origin (White 1985, pp. 194–5) but were passed on to the children and the children's children. Bates then amplifies these categories in her text (pp. 195–202).

Bates's final account of totemism in her proposed book is more satisfactory than her earlier notes. Initially, Bates did not provide a systematic or analytical account of totemism. Consequently, she undoubtedly confused a number of different ways of associating people with the natural world. Use of the single term 'totemism' masks a complex system of associations which takes a number of different forms and shows some variation. Thus Bates's early accounts undoubtedly conflate different manifestations of the totemic principle. Her final position, in which she was able to differentiate the several forms of association with natural species, shows that there was a complex and variable system in operation. It is evident that it formed an important part of the belief system of those with whom she worked. It was a system that was laden with intricacy and detail, so did not lend itself to uniformity and consistency. In short, this was probably not a neat system that was uniformly in evidence.[98]

Ritual

Accounts of ritual in South Western Australia in the early literature lack detail. Moore (1978b, p. 281) notes that the nasal septum of youths was pierced, as does

97 Bates collected a large number of genealogies from all over the South West.

98 Rose, writing of a matrilineal totemic system in the Northern Territory, describes it as 'untidy' (Rose 1992, p. 83).

Armstrong (1979, p. 204), adding that the operation was conducted by the neighbours of a 'tribe'. Barker provides a somewhat cryptic account of rituals, which he identifies by name but not content. One involved nose piercing (Barker 1992, pp. 358–9). Barker notes that ritual activity brought different groups together (pp. 306, 359). Consistent with these accounts, Curr reports that the Mi_n_ong did not practise either circumcision or subincision (Curr 1886–87, p. 386). Hassell admits that she was unable to find out very much about ritual activity (1975, p. 78). Despite this qualification, she provides some details of the piercing of the nasal septum, evidently a public ritual (pp. 71–2). She was aware that boys underwent a form of initiation involving being sent away to live with a neighbouring group for a period of time (Hassell 1936, p. 684; 1975, p. 78). She describes a ritual where boys of different groups were made 'blood brothers' (Hassell 1975, pp. 72–3). She records a public ritual that she and her brother attended, which was probably not an age grade ritual but a ceremony, often called a 'corroboree', a term Hassell herself employs (pp. 111–13).

Bates's account of rituals is more comprehensive. In her published works she provides a detailed account of a public ritual or corroboree (Bates 1992, pp. 30–7),[99] as well as of a friendship ritual of the sort described by Hassell and noted above (pp. 28–30). In her proposed book, Bates provides a detailed account of an initiation ritual (White 1985, pp. 150–61). Unlike Moore and Barker, Bates understood the piercing of the nasal septum to be a major life stage ritual involving inter-group cooperation. The boy was sent away to live with his mother's brother (a member of a different country group, since the groups were exogamous). There he was looked after by young men of his opposite moiety, who consequently were his prospective wife's brothers. This provided opportunity for the development of a special relationship with these men as close lifelong friend or *babbin*, a relationship established through the ritual noted above. He was taught many skills and sacred knowledge (p. 152). One of his carers was responsible for the piercing of his nasal septum, pushing the bone though his nose. Finally, he returned to his parents' camp, where presents were given and then redistributed to the assembled group, there being a desire to ensure that everyone was content. Cicatrisation may occur at any time during this period (p. 153). Bates provides variations of these rituals, which she collected from the Capel and Swan River areas (pp. 158–61).

White (1985) considers that Bates collected these data from old men who themselves had been initiated about the time of first European settlement in Perth.

99 See also Bates (n.d.h, answer to questions 79 and 80).

White concludes that by the early 1900s these traditional customs had lapsed (p. 150). Consequently, it is unlikely that Bates herself observed any of the rituals she describes. White notes that while cicatrisation and nose piercing were the only bodily operations that marked initiation into manhood among the Noongar people, circumcision was not unknown where the influence of northern and north-eastern groups was apparent (p. 150).[100]

Taken as a whole, these early accounts of Noongar ritual life reveal rich cultural activity that must have been an important feature of both social interaction and the forging of alliances. It is evident that ritual activity must have been a significant preoccupation for people, influencing where they travelled and how they developed relationships with their neighbours. It is likely that initiation rituals had ceased by the time Bates worked in the South West. The same was evidently not true for other ceremonies, generally public in nature and often referred to as 'corroborees'. These appear to have continued as a part of cultural observances up to (and presumably beyond) Bates's time in the region.

100 Curr (1886–87, pp. 367–8) reports that inland groups (he calls them 'Minung'), for the most part did practise circumcision. He postulates the demographic changes that might have led to this state of affairs. Curr would appear to have placed the 'circumcision line' further to the west than later writers. Hammond (1933, p. 63) states that circumcision may not have been unknown in the South West.

Chapter 6

AUTHORITY AND DISPUTES

Introduction

We can gain a general idea of aspects of the nature of Noongar society from the early writers by looking at how they understood that society to be regulated by the imposition of authority. An earlier chapter noted that some writers, in seeking to find 'tribes', also looked without success for 'chiefs'. The early writers mostly recognised that an extended family group (or residence group) formed the basis of Noongar social organisation. This residence group exhibited a clear structure, with a senior male at its head, and each residence group operated more or less autonomously and was not subject to a centralised authority. Together, all residence groups lived subject to common cultural precepts, while interaction between them was common and expected. In this chapter I outline what the early sources have to say about Noongar social structures, authority and disputes, fights and other breaches of the peace.

Authority

Writing about land ownership, Moore reports that the land was divided up between families, and that the chief of Guildford was a man called Warragonga, Yagan's father (Moore 1978b, pp. 146–7).[101] While he appears to have a limited understanding of the authority structure of the society he studied, he does note the term for 'one having authority' as *wurdagaderak* (p. 379), even though he used it in reference to himself.[102] Clark (1842, p. 5, col. 1) reports that the Noongar people had a patriarchal form of government:

101 See Hallam and Tilbrook (1990, inside back cover) for a genealogy of Yellowgonga and Midgegooroo.

102 Moore (1978a, p. 73) translates the term as, 'a hero; a great warrior; a man of renown, or authority'. Bindon and Chadwick (1992, p. 172) also record the term from Grey, who may have learnt it from Moore (Binder and Chadwick 1992, p. ii).

> They are divided into families forming a tribe, each tribe having a chief or head authority to whom obedience is paid in all matters of internal government, and who leads them into battle. These tribes are however entirely independent of one another.

Similar misunderstandings in relation to 'chiefs' are to be found in Collie (1834, p. 73) and Lyon (1979, p. 177), although both recognised that certain individuals had authority in the community. Browne is more explicit, stating that there were no chiefs or rulers. There were, however, influential and powerful men who Browne considered had attained their status through acts of violence and a forceful personality (Browne 1856, pp. 9–10). Hassell (1936, p. 681), with the assistance of Davidson, provides a short section on 'political organisation', dismissing the idea that there were 'chiefs'. Instead, she concludes that there were heads of families who governed their family, each being independent of the other. In fights, a man would be selected as a leader, presumably because of his skills and prior success in this regard. Community decisions were made only after the matter 'had been thoroughly discussed by all' (Hassell 1975, p. 140). Those with particular spiritual gifts (*mulgars* — men and women with healing and divinational abilities) could exercise considerable influence over events by virtue of their supposed supernatural abilities (pp. 140–1).

It is likely that authority within residence groups rested in senior males but that authority did not extend outside of the residence group. Authority was acquired by others (according to Hassell), including women (according to Bates, see p. 79) for specific purposes (e.g. religious activities and resolution of disputes). In this, it is likely that religious knowledge and experience equipped people to take leading roles in community discussion as well as ritual activities, as this has been recorded for other areas, while kinship obligations mediated relationships between roles assumed in any particular interchange (cf. Berndt 1965). This is consistent with the operations of a community comprising a number of autonomous residence groups, but who came together on occasions for joint activity (exchanges, seeking marriage partners, warfare, rituals). In such a system there is a lack of centralised authority beyond the residence or family group, and no office of chief or leader; rather, leadership roles are taken by those with the necessary qualifications for the duration of an event. Implicit in all the above accounts, however, is that age was an important qualification for the legitimate exercise of authority, but this had to be backed up with ability.[103]

---

103 See Howard (1976, pp. 71–5, 142–5) for an overview of the early material on leadership in the South West.

Bates does not provide much information on authority, although she recognised that there were knowledgeable and senior men and women, with whom she worked. She also provides us with little information about their role as leaders within the community. In an early manuscript she makes brief reference to the fact that authority was not hereditary (Bates n.d.d, p. 108). She identifies the term *bideer*[104] to identify a person who has respect and authority, indicating that this must be gained through 'personal prowess' and skill in boomerang and spear throwing (p. 108). In this account she appears to associate *bedeer* and a native doctor (*boylyaguttuk*). In her proposed book, Bates provides more details (White 1985, pp. 145–6). This account relates specifically to women, who, having gained seniority through age and childbirth, 'became of influence in their tribe' (p. 145). They were called *yogga biderr*, which Bates glosses as 'strong' or 'great women', from *beedee*, meaning vein or strength. Bates describes a ritual that served to confer this status upon a woman; thereafter she was immune from revenge attacks, could intercede in fights without fear of being injured and was listened to and respected in disputes. She was considered to have 'magic power', and the account implies a relationship between the status of being a 'powerful woman' and that of being a native doctor or *boylyaguttuk*. Bates describes one of her informants, Balbuk, as a *yogga biderr*.

The early accounts pay scant attention to the relationship between young and old. Only Barker notes that the elderly were afforded respect (Barker 1992, p. 354). However, from the material already considered on age-grade rituals of initiation, it is reasonable to conclude that Noongar society was characterised by a process whereby the young learnt under instruction from the old and older people were respected and treated accordingly. Bates (White 1985, pp. 151–62) shows that youths were subjected to a series of ritual relationships which involved their submitting to instruction by their elders. In this society, as in many other areas of Aboriginal Australia, older persons were afforded respect in social dealings by younger men and women, who were expected to learn from them. Kinship relationships between generations articulated behaviour that required respect for older people and an acquiescence to instruction (cf. Berndt 1965, pp. 168–9).

Disputes

Despite the authority of certain people within Noongar society, many of the early accounts indicate that fighting and disputes were common. This appears to have

104 Bindon and Chadwick (1992, p. 10) give *beedee-eer* as 'old man, large family, having some influence' which they source from Grey.

Table 6.1: Some references to spearing in the early literature

Author	Pages	Reason	Comment
Armstrong 1979	193	Trespass	
Armstrong 1979	194	Revenge for death	
Armstrong 1979	196–7	General; revenge	
Barker 1992	254	Revenge	
Barker 1992	277	Trespass	Fear that neighbouring group would arrive and a spear fight would result
Barker 1992	278–9	General	Women and a child speared
Barker 1992	313	General	Spear fight involving a number of individuals
Barker 1992	314	Elopement	Unclear whether an actual incident
Barker 1992	326	Infidelity	Woman speared
Clark 1842	4, col. 3	Revenge for death	
Clark 1842	6, col. 1	Trespass	
Collie 1834	82	Revenge for death	
Collie 1834	89–91	Revenge for death	
Grey 1841	304–6	General	
Hassell 1936	711	Revenge for death	To provide company for deceased journey to land of the dead
Hassell 1975	57–8	Revenge for death	
Hassell 1975	99–105	Over a woman; subsequent escalation	
Lyon 1979	152	Revenge for death	
Lyon 1979	153	General	
Millett 1872	78	Spearing a woman	
Moore 1978b	199–200	Trespass	
Moore 1978b	259–60	Succession to land	Fires lit without permission. Attempts to spear women.
Nind 1979	47–9	Revenge for death	
Roth 1902	55–6	General	For 'wilful murder, incest, etc.'; manslaughter
Stormon 1977	173	Revenge for a death	

been a result of a tradition that required revenge, in the form of a spearing, for certain actions. These included infidelity and death, the latter being understood to be caused by others upon whom revenge was required. No doubt there were many other forms of dispute that were not identified as to their cause by the early writers. Where a spearing was seen to be a legitimate punishment or revenge, dispute resolution by a senior person would have been inappropriate.

The early literature offers copious examples of spearing, and the prevalence of the practice was apparent to the settlers.[105] Table 6.1 sets out some of the relevant references, along with the main reason given in the account cited for the spearing. Where a general observation is made as to the incidence of spearing, the comment is simply, 'General'.

Not all these references were to a spearing witnessed by the writer of the account; some are statements of the principle understood to be in operation. However, it is reasonable to conclude that spearing was a common feature of the society. Of the 25 cases cited, revenge for death comprises the largest group (44 per cent), with 20 per cent for trespass and only 16 per cent for disputes concerning women. Some 20 per cent were unidentified. However, the figures are too small and the data too unreliable to draw any firm conclusions.[106]

105 See Green (1984, pp. 226–31) for a comprehensive account taken from early sources of conflict between Aboriginal people of the South West. Green reports 58 separate incidents.

106 Bates does not recount any spear fights, as far as I am aware. However, she notes that revenge for a death was expected following divination (White 1985, pp. 199–300).

Chapter 7

EARLY ACCOUNTS OF NOONGAR CULTURE: CONCLUSION

The early literature on the Aboriginal people of the South West is diverse and voluminous. It provides a wide range of ethnographic data. The accounts discussed furnish a view of how some aspects of Noongar culture may have been before European settlement, since most early accounts record what the observers assumed to have been customary behaviour. That said, the early ethnography should be read in the context of its collection. Some accounts contain limited data, and all were recorded through a lens. While relative refraction varied, the prejudicial views of a number of observers limit the usefulness of their material. The understandings of the social and cultural institutions which the early settlers observed were limited. Many of the accounts were written from second-hand observations and reports. All accounts were made after initial European settlement, some many decades after it, so the degree to which these practices had been subject to change is not known. Daisy Bates's accounts, which provide a substantial contribution to our ethnographic knowledge of the South West, should be viewed in their totality. Her clearest accounts are to be found in her proposed book, *The native tribes of Western Australia*. However, in preparing her often complex and sometimes perplexing material for publication she simplified some of her data, indicating a uniformity and consistency in customary belief and practice not evident in her earlier manuscripts.

The South West appears to have constituted a single cultural bloc, with dialects of a single language spoken by people who shared laws and customs in common. Those who lived in the South West recognised local and regional names, but appear to have shared a commonality of beliefs, customs and material culture which distinguished them from their neighbours to the north and east.

Groups of people had rights to areas of land, which were gained principally by descent. A family was generally associated with a particular area. These rights were articulated as ownership of relatively well-defined areas of country. The exclusivity of rights to country was mediated by a complex set of relationships developed through kinship, consanguinity, affinality and other alliances. As a consequence, rights in land were not hermetically or exclusively bounded, and more than one country group had rights to use country beyond their own. The exercise of such joint or shared rights was tempered by a requirement to follow protocols requiring the seeking of permission for some activities, although this was not an invariable rule. People who were not known and with whom no alliances were recognised always required permission if seeking to visit unfamiliar country, and trespass was regarded as a serious offence.

There operated within Noongar society a system of social categories, complemented by the use of kinship terms, whereby all people within a known social universe were classified as kin. Certain behaviours and obligations were required, reflecting the relevant kin classification.

In religious thinking, there was a strong emphasis on the importance and influence of the spirit world, and funereal rites were particularly important. Divination was a part of these rites, and the Noongar doctor, or 'clever man', had a key role here, as in other activities which involved sorcery. The culture was marked by the telling of narratives of place, relating the here and now to the creative period of the Dreaming, and explaining how places in the landscape were imbued with spiritual potency. Other relationships with the natural world were expressed through a number of forms of totemism, although these appear to have been variable and not uniform across the region. There was also a rich ritual life, which was marked for the Noongar people by the absence of circumcision and subincision.

Finally, there was a structure to the society, which rested on an acceptance of the seniority of older people and that young men (and, presumably, women) must learn from them and respect them. Authority was not centralised, but rested within the family groups, usually with a senior male, although women could be recognised as having authority through their seniority. Other leadership roles probably depended upon circumstance and individual ability, and were tempered by kinship requirements. The society was marked by some acts of violence, which developed from a desire to revenge death as well as punishment for transgressions of Noongar social rules, which were understood to constitute a law by which people lived and acted.

The early accounts tell us very little about the economy of Noongar people prior to settlement of the region by Europeans. Nor do we learn much about political relationships between groups and individuals. The accounts of the religious life lack firsthand detail and much must have been left unrecorded. Finally, we learn little or nothing about art and aesthetic expression. Despite these significant gaps, the accounts of the early settlers and those who followed soon afterwards provide a basis for understanding Noongar culture. They provide a point of departure for forming a view as to whether contemporary Noongar culture is founded on traditional and customary practices and rules.

Chapter 8

OVERVIEW OF CONTEMPORARY ACCOUNTS OF NOONGAR SOCIETY

Introduction

The classic Australian ethnographies which marked the flowering of anthropology in this country were based on material collected from northern or central parts of the continent. Phyllis Kaberry worked in the Kimberley region, Lloyd Warner in Arnhem Land, Mervin Meggitt in Central Australia. The Berndts had worked in the southern parts of South Australia, but the majority of their publications were based on materials collected from Arnhem Land or the northern desert regions. There were many others — Strehlow, Stanner, Hiatt, Munn and Peterson, to name a few — who worked, for the most part, in northern and remote areas; none worked in the South West of Western Australia. This inclination to work away from 'settled' areas reflected a view that remote ethnography would yield better results, as the object of study was, ideally, to gain an understanding of a 'complete' Indigenous culture. While an appreciation of the process of change was not necessarily absent from this account, settled areas of Australia were considered to be too altered to have much to contribute. It was not until the last quarter of the twentieth century that this approach to anthropological inquiry began to change as the result of a view that what may be termed 'urban anthropology' was a subject worthy of study. For this reason, after Bates's work there is a substantial silence in the account of the ethnography of the South West. Gerhardt Laves undertook some linguistic fieldwork in Albany in about 1930 (Laves n.d.). Radcliffe-Brown (1930) wrote a brief note on the 'former number and distribution' of Australian Aborigines, which included a population estimate for the South West. However, it was not until later in the century that any new anthropological fieldwork was to be reported upon.

Birdsall (1990, pp. 54–87) traces intellectual thinking in some Australian anthropology over the middle decades of the last century, showing how the government policy of assimilation affected writing on Aboriginal people. The concept of assimilation rested on a fundamental acceptance that those from non-mainstream Australian cultures (including Aboriginal cultures) would, over time, see their own culture dissolve and be replaced by that of the dominant culture.[107] During this process, which might take several generations, remnants of the old culture would be found, but as diluted or bastardised parts of the original. Acculturation models, as Birdsall calls them (p. 55) tended to see urban Aboriginal people in transition:

> Aborigines of the towns and cities continue to be characterised in negative terms. Socially they were 'detribalised', 'acculturated' and 'remnant'. Ethnically they were 'half-caste', 'coloured', 'the dark people' and 'black' as often and more as they were Aborigines, or Koori, or Nyungar, or Yamadji. (Birdsall 1990, p. 92)

While these prejudices remain, at least to some extent, in the general population today, they certainly informed some of the early anthropological writing on Noongar people of the South West.[108] I agree with Birdsall's analysis. This understanding is relevant to the way in which those few anthropological studies of the South West that are available from the period 1960–80 should be understood.

Assimilationist influences

Brunton (2003, pp. 133–6), reviews BA theses by both Katrin Wilson and John Wilson, written in 1958 (J Wilson 1958; K Wilson 1958). He notes that John Wilson is open to the possibility that 'more elements of traditional beliefs might have come to light [in his research]' had he spent longer than three weeks in the field (Brunton 2003, p. 134). Brunton concludes that 'nothing the Wilsons wrote could be taken as evidence for the acknowledgment and observance of traditional laws and customs' (p. 136). This is an unsurprising conclusion, given the focus of their inquiry (a cooperative Aboriginal settlement), the scope of their research (three weeks at undergraduate level) and the preoccupations of the times (assimilation and acculturation). Despite the limitations of the Wilsons' work, Brunton acknowledges that they did find evidence of language use, attachment to country, beliefs in spirits and sorcery, as well as a general interest in traditional matters

107 It also involved biological engineering and was one of the bases for the removal of Aboriginal children from their parents. See Haebich (1988, pp. 315–21); see also Rowley (1972, pp. 383–403).

108 Cf. Howard (1976, p. 58; 1981, p. 35).

(pp. 133–5).[109] Katrin Wilson, writing in 1964, saw acculturation as an inevitable, if problematic, process (K Wilson 1964). Her short essay looks at how cooperative ventures might aid the process and so provide a better life for Aboriginal people. She is silent on the customary practices of those she studied in the Perth region, but it seems reasonable to conclude, given the context of her discussion, that she considered them to reside in the past. The Wilsons' work provides no assistance in determining the incidence of customary laws in the Perth community they studied because this was something with which they did not concern themselves. In any event, what may or may not have been the case in 1964 with respect to one small settlement does not assist me in reaching a conclusion as to what might be the situation with respect to the whole of the South West today.

RM Berndt reflected a view that Noongar culture was beyond recovery when, in 1979,[110] he wrote in a paper that the only source of information on traditional Aboriginal life in the South West was 'early records', which were 'anthropologically unsatisfactory' (Berndt 1979, p. 81). His account relies on these accounts, however, and the paper attempts a brief reconstruction of the culture. He concludes that by the third decade or so of the twentieth century, the Aboriginal people of the South West 'possess[ed] little or nothing of their traditional heritage', and most of them were 'of considerably mixed Aboriginal affinity' (p. 87). He states that Aboriginal people of mixed descent were culturally 'European-Australians', implying that their Indigenous culture was lost to them (p. 87). He cites Hasluck and Neville in support of these conclusions, and it is evident that his views were not based on any field studies, although he would have been aware of the Wilsons' work.

Ken Colbung (1979), writing in the same volume, takes a rather different view. While he considers there to be a 'paucity' of traditional heritage (p. 100), he states that land remained central to belief, emotion and practice (pp. 100–1) and was integral to Noongar culture (p. 103). He recognised that there were older people alive who were 'heritage-bearers' (p. 105). While Colbung does not provide a complete rejoinder to Berndt, the two pieces do not sit comfortably together. My view is that Berndt's prejudicial view was to conclude that Noongar culture was lost, while having no firsthand experience or data upon which to base this. Colbung (whose paper was 'revised and edited by Berndt': p. 100) was less sure,

---

109 I have not viewed the original theses discussed here. Brunton also cites a thesis by Makin from 1970, noting the author had concluded that little [traditional] knowledge was being handed on (Brunton 2003, p. 136).

110 The paper actually dates back to 1973.

understanding himself to be 'an Aboriginal' (the title of his paper) and to have retained a land-based culture.

Howard (1979) also has a paper in this volume. It reports data he collected for his PhD thesis, under the supervision of Berndt. In his thesis Howard acknowledges John Wilson (Howard 1976, 'Acknowledgments'). The paper covers in an abbreviated form issues similar to those found in his thesis (1979, pp. 16–61), while some of the original headings have been preserved. Howard also reproduced parts of his thesis in a 1978 paper that examined 'Aboriginal leadership' (Howard 1978),[111] and substantial parts of the original thesis were published as a book in 1981 (Howard 1981). In all accounts Howard reconstructs pre-contact Noongar society as a backdrop to his main purpose: a study of Noongar leadership. He concludes that by the end of the nineteenth century 'traditional Aboriginal culture and social life had changed greatly' (p. 9). He paints a picture of the abandonment of some practices and phenomena altogether (bands and clans; ties with totemic sites; use of artefacts for pre-contact purposes; religious, curative and ritual knowledge). However, he states that some traditional institutions and customs were retained but had been 'transformed'. Locality remained important for social identity, as did kinship, and some ceremonies were performed in the early part of the twentieth century (p. 9). Much knowledge continued to be passed on, 'in less institutionalised fashion through stories'. He concludes that there was 'considerable social and cultural breakdown during the first seventy-five years after the conquest . . . but there was some continuity and syncretic transformation' (p. 11; see also Howard 1976, p. 31). Howard states his appreciation of the fact that Noongar culture must have changed prior to European settlement of the region (Howard 1976, p. 61). Howard based his thesis on substantial periods of field research, mostly in the Perth region, but also some visits to other areas of the South West. He was an experienced researcher (Howard 1976, pp. 7–8).

Howard should be understood both in the context of his research aims and of the academic environment in which he undertook his research. First, Howard did not seek to study Noongar culture with respect to the incidence of traditional laws and customs *per se*. His initial purpose was to reconstruct them from early sources, with particular reference to issues of governance, leadership and authority. This, in turn, was a backdrop to the main purpose of his study, which was a description and analysis of the political relationship between Noongars and the state, articulated though the activities of emergent leaders (pp. 143–9). In these

111 Compare Howard (1978, p. 21) and Howard (1976, p. 158).

analyses, Howard is somewhat ambiguous about the changes he observed. He saw some things as remaining, some things as altogether gone, and others as again changed or transformed, while seeing change, quite reasonably, as a part of pre-contact cultural processes. So to what extent were the changes he recorded consistent with alterations and adaptations that would have been found, to a greater or lesser degree, in pre-contact Noongar society? And which of them were 'transformations' and which wholly new cultural phenomena? These are questions that Howard does not purport to either ask or answer. His interests lay elsewhere.

Like many other writers reviewed here, Howard was aware of the undeniable, rapid and often devastating changes that had affected Noongar people and their culture in the South West. However, there may have been a too-ready assumption that these changes had resulted in the almost total destruction or abandonment of Noongar culture. Consequently, Howard viewed assimilation as both inevitable and largely accomplished in the South West by the time he worked there (Howard 1981, p. 36). Later researchers (discussed in the section 'Later ethnographies of Noongar society', below) were to cast doubt on the validity of such an assumption by showing that much of Noongar culture remained, unknown to the general public but still vital.

Linguistic research

Gerhardt Laves carried out linguistic and anthropological fieldwork in Australia between 1929 and 1931, supervised by Radcliffe-Brown. His papers[112] contain some genealogical material, but are mostly narrative texts. He recorded the name of the Albany language as 'Mi<u>n</u>ong' (e.g. notebooks, p. 5073; Notebook 21, text 208). He collected details of the moiety system (pp. 5627–79) and material that showed the importance of seeking a marriage partner from afar (p. 5828). A more thorough examination of the Laves material, following the development of a key to his phonetic transcription, might add to our knowledge of the ethnography of the Albany region at this time. However, Laves's principal concern was with language. Since his material is in cryptic note form, he provides no analysis or statements as to his views on the culture he studied or its state at that time.

112 Copies of some of these are held by the South West Aboriginal Land and Sea Council. They consist of undated paginated notebooks. He used phonetic script to record the many texts that comprise his Albany material, which makes the material particularly difficult to read. Time did not permit a thorough examination of these materials. Laves also worked in northern New South Wales, Broome, Cape Leveque, Cape York and on the Victoria and Daly Rivers in the Northern Territory.

Douglas, who undertook pioneering linguistic research in the South West, considered that, despite changes, the Noongar language he recorded remained viable, if somewhat altered (Douglas 1976, pp. 5–8). He indicated that changes to the language were tempered, to some extent, by a restoration of language and its use to express traditional aspects of the culture (pp. 8–24). Brandenstein viewed Noongar culture as something that 'once flourished' (Brandenstein, 1977, p. 169), but he was able to collect language data from informants along with matri- and patri-moiety totems. Much of this was recorded from a Noongar man who lived in Esperance (Brandenstein 1977).[113]

Later ethnographies of Noongar society

Toussaint (1987) wrote an account of Noongar people's interface with the dominant European society, particularly in relation to the state, and more particularly in relation to the custody of children and the allocation of housing. Throughout, Toussaint makes it clear that there is a Noongar identity which is a significant factor in these interactions. Such identity is founded upon traditional Noongar cultural beliefs and practices. Like some of her predecessors, Toussaint relies on the early literature to provide a reconstruction of pre-contact Noongar society (pp. 47–54). In providing a definition of Noongar identity, Toussaint refers to the importance of birth (pp. 78–9) and association with place (pp. 81–2). She comments on a number of cultural contemporary practices which typified the society. These include the importance of kinship and the obligations implied in the operation of the system (pp. 84–9), seniority and the role of grandparents (p. 86), the 'family' as a key element in social action (p. 92) and that feuding may have been a feature of traditional Noongar life (p. 90). She notes the importance of funerals (p. 93) and that the use of the Noongar language was a distinctive mode of establishing an identity (pp. 94–7). She provides comment on the importance of spirituality (p. 97) and notes that while religious beliefs had been much influenced by missionaries at settlements there remained a fear of spirits (pp. 101–2). She states that totemism was an important belief in the community (p. 103) and that narratives about supernatural beings continued to have currency (p. 104). While Toussaint accepts that Noongar culture had changed, her account does not characterise Noongar culture as one that had

113 Brandenstein (1988) produced 'an artificially re-created Aboriginal language of the south-west of Australia'. In this he seeks to redress what he conjectures to have been the creation of the Noongar language, before the arrivals of Europeans, by 'clever men' or a 'single individual'. My view is that such speculation does not assist this current inquiry. See also Brandenstein (1986).

become a dim or poor shadow of the original. It was strongly marked by cultural practices that, according to this account, were traditionally based.

Brunton (2003, pp. 137–9) dismisses some of Toussaint's assertions that Noongar culture continued to exhibit traditional elements. He states that the Noongar language she describes 'does not seem very different' to that discussed by the Wilsons, and so is of no account because it was mostly English (p. 136). Such a comment would indicate that the author does not recognise either creole or distinctive styles of English (for example, American or Australian English) as means by which a distinguishing cultural identity is maintained. Brunton dismisses beliefs about spirits because 'the information she presents seems to indicate views and reactions that appear somewhat idiosyncratic' (p. 137), although he has no comparable data available upon which to base such a conclusion. Brunton dismisses a belief in a totem because Toussaint's references to elderly Noongars 'would seem to imply that totemic affiliations were no longer relevant to the younger generations' (p. 138). The implication is Brunton's, not Toussaint's. Finally, he dismisses storytelling as being 'not particularly strong' on the ground that this is implied in one of her comments. Toussaint in fact states that, '"story telling" is the major means by which Nyungar spiritual beliefs are passed from generation to generation' (Toussaint 1987, p. 104). My reading of Toussaint's comments is that the activity of storytelling was generally the responsibility of older people, and she had collected stories from older Noongar people elsewhere. In her Perth study, however, she had worked mainly with younger people.[114] Overall, my view is that Brunton has been unfair to Toussaint. A reading of her thesis makes her position quite clear: the Noongar people with whom she worked exhibited a distinctive culture. She accepts that there had been a loss of aspects of it; however, she also indicates that elements of it were based upon what might be considered to be pre-contact elements of Noongar culture.

Patricia Baines wrote her PhD thesis on the 'intergenerational transmission of knowledge among Nyungars' (Baines 1987). She sought to show not only that the Noongar people had a distinctive culture but that 'culturally informed understandings which constitute Nyungar traditions' had been handed on from previous generations (Baines 1987, p. 1). She notes that 'anthropologists have, in the main, heretofore denied the survival of culture to those Aboriginal people who live in the settled areas of Australia' (p. 1). The thesis consists of a series of reported

114 Only 5.4 per cent of her study population was over the age of 50 years. The majority (58.9 per cent) were aged between 21 and 40. See Toussaint (1987, p. 19).

incidents, which constitute a narrative of the research. These are variously interpreted. The style is reflexive, positioning the author prominently in the exegesis. However, the text contains a large number of references to what the author implies are traditional Noongar beliefs and customs. The following list is not complete, but it is indicative. Baines discusses the importance of spirits (pp. 106–21, 139, 254), funerals (p. 102), relationships to country through birth and the spirit returning there after death (p. 77). She examines narratives as a means of relating people to country and providing identity (p. 95) and the fact that visits to country must be accompanied by proper greetings and ritual action (pp. 102, 196). Baines notes the importance of kinship (pp. 127, 278), discusses traditional cures (pp. 131–2) and writes of the need to gain permission when visiting someone else's country (pp. 136, 196). She notes the importance of language (pp. 147–8) and provides a detailed account of continuity and transmission of narratives, concluding that traditions have not disappeared but have been remodelled into something else (pp. 175–7). She notes signs and portents (p. 161), prohibitions (p. 231), a belief in sorcery (pp. 240, 267), the operation of marriage rules (p. 242) and affiliation with specific areas of country (p. 239).

The thesis is a rich compilation of ethnographic materials, which provides a corrective to earlier accounts that had seen Noongar culture as bereft of traditional content. Baines provides detailed accounts of Noongar laws and customs that challenge this view. She gained insights into Noongar culture that other researchers did not achieve and consequently presents us with a rich culture that is in no way bankrupt or degraded.

In 1990, Christina Birdsall completed a thesis about Noongar family and social identity. She paid particular attention to the role of women in urban Noongar society. Birdsall identifies the relationships between women, particularly between mothers (and those who are mother equivalents in Noongar kinship thinking), as fundamental to the structure of Noongar social life, identity and continuity (1990, pp. i–ii). She identifies kinship as a fundamental operating principle in Noongar society, understanding that it extends relationships beyond consanguineal links and that it is (and is assumed by Noongars to be) the basis of interactions (p. 148). She relates this account to people's ties to their country through birth or descent (pp. 149–51) and identifies kin groups as those whose members trace common descent bilaterally (by cognatic reckoning: p. 153). The kin groups comprise numerous sub-groups (p. 155),[115] each of them identified with a particular region.

115 Birdsall also called them 'kindreds'. See Birdsall (1990, p. 182).

Consequently, members of sub-groups are related by place as well as kin group affiliation (see Birdsall 1987, p. 141). In Noongar terminology the kin sub-group is called a 'family' (Birdsall 1990, p. 152), the kin group 'all-one-family' (p. 153). The kin group come together only for major events like funerals. They do not hold property in common and they have no common authority (p. 153).

In her thesis Birdsall identifies a strong matrilineal bias at work in the Noongar society in which she worked. This she relates to a strong matri-focal emphasis of contemporary Noongar society (Birdsall 1990, p. 158), presumably as a result of the marginalisation of Noongar men (Birdsall 1987, pp. 138–9). She states that the strongest claims to country were through the mother (1990, p. 154), but that a person was also able to gain rights to father's country since the system was cognatic (p. 153). Elsewhere, however, she states that while there is an evident matrilineal bias (which she identifies as being expressed in the phrase 'fall on the mother's side') this is a 'trend rather than a proclivity'. Some groups are recruited matrilineally, others patrilineally (Birdsall 1990, p. 133). Birdsall provides detail about the relationship between families (or kin sub-groups) and country (pp. 182–6). Members have knowledge of and attachment to a set of towns with which they often identify.[116] The term 'run' is used to identify the set of towns inhabited or identified by members of a kin sub-group (p. 182) and the runs of kindred within an 'all-one-family' overlap, as do the runs of unrelated kin sub-groups (i.e. a sub-group of another 'all-one-family': pp. 182–3). However, some kindred may have runs that are geographically separate, a result of forced demographic changes (p. 183). In any cognatic system, some choice must be exercised by children in stating a preference for territorial affiliation (p. 185). Attachment must be attested by lived action; that is, you must live in or visit the towns frequently. If this does not occur, the attachment is seen to diminish (p. 186).

Generally, Birdsall does not enter into any debate about the traditional — that is, pre-contact — foundation for Noongar cultural beliefs and practices. Birdsall sets out in her thesis the difficulties that assimilationist writers posed for anthropology. She notes that there had been an inclination by some anthropologists in the past to view urbanised peoples as somehow living in a culturally diminished state (Birdsall 1990, pp. 54–86). It is likely that Birdsall wished to present Noongar society and culture as she recorded it, without the prejudice of any judgments made with respect to its so-called 'authenticity'. It is evident from her account that she sees Noongar culture as distinctive and as showing a continuity with the

116 See Birdsall (1988, pp. 138–45) for a more succinct account of these principles.

past. At the end of her thesis she remarks of Noongar funerals that 'the beliefs surrounding the action of providing the dead with such a service are not Christian, but Nyungar. They remain Nyungar, in their outlook, their system of social organisation, and in the bases and construction of their identity, both social and personal' (p. 388). Birdsall shows that relationships to country were important for the people with whom she worked, and that the family (a group of peoples related by descent) was a fundamental social unit in the representation and perpetuation of attachment to country.[117] She shows that kinship was a primary means of articulating relationships and enunciating obligations. There is abundant evidence that these represent aspects of a pre-contact Noongar society, as well as we can understand it. However, this is not a relationship that she chooses to explore.

Brunton makes no comment on Birdsall's thesis, or her related publications, in that section of his report where he examines the anthropological literature on cultural continuity in Perth (Brunton 2003, pp. 132–40). This is despite the fact that he does discuss Toussaint, the Wilsons, Makin and a more recent report by O'Connor in this chapter. Nor does he discuss Baines' work. He does, however, list one of Birdsall's articles in his bibliography as well as Baines' thesis (Brunton 2003, pp. 141, 142). In this regard, his account must be considered incomplete.

Taken together, the detailed ethnographic accounts of Toussaint, Birdsall and Baines provide an important corrective to the earlier writers, who characterised Noongar culture as remnant and decayed. All three researchers undertook extensive field research, and came to the field without the prejudices which, with the benefit of hindsight, it is evident that some of their predecessors exhibited. These three later accounts challenge the earlier conclusions which diminished the worth and existence of Noongar culture. The research reflects a success in gaining information from Noongar people that may have been denied to earlier researchers, either due to the limited scale of their research or because they were not interested in traditional aspects of the culture they studied. In some cases this was because they wrongly assumed that it had all gone. While the three pieces of research reported here are quite different, they all lend support to each other. It would be difficult to dismiss all three as aberrations or fancy.

Recent reconstructions

For the sake of completeness there are several other accounts that can be considered here. The first is an essay by Ian Crawford, which forms the first chapter of a book

117 'The all-one-family' is an exogamous cognatic descent group: Birdsall (1987, p. 131).

on the South West forests (Crawford and Crawford 2003). Crawford describes the original Aboriginal inhabitants of the Northcliffe area, in the far South West of Western Australia. He does this by relying on historical sources, particularly those written for the Albany area, which have been reviewed above (pp. 9–11). Crawford was unable to locate any reliable early sources for the Northcliffe area itself. Keen (2004) has written a comprehensive comparative account of seven areas of Aboriginal Australia, compiled from historical sources, which includes material derived from early sources from the Albany area. Keen's principal purpose in writing this book was to explore the nature of Aboriginal economy and society, 'at the threshold of colonisation' (p. 1). The book is a useful and helpful reference for any consideration of the Albany materials, and I have already referred to it on a number of occasions in my discussions of the early material collected from that area.

Also in the nature of a review, but dating from the 1970s, is work by Meagher on the material culture and use of resources by Noongar people in the South West. Again, these accounts (Meagher 1973, 1974; Meagher and Ride 1979) are based on sources found in the available literature, but provide a useful reference in relation to material culture and resource utilisation. Finally, Hallam (1975) wrote a book on the use of fire by Noongar people, again constructed from archival and other historical sources. While this is primarily a work of prehistory in the sense that it relies on at least some archaeological data, it provides a clear account of how the Noongar people utilised their country and modified it for their benefit through the use of fire. The book includes many extracts from the early literature and also provides some more general ethnographic data.

Conclusion

In this account I have not considered the substantial contribution that has been made by historians to our knowledge of the Noongar people of the South West. This is not because I consider them to be unimportant, but because I think their insights are beyond the scope of this book. Nor is this account of the twentieth-century research exhaustive. However, from the material reviewed I think it reasonable to conclude as follows.

First, there has been a general acceptance by all that Noongar culture has been heavily impacted by European settlement of the region, by subsequent acts of alienation of land, by economic dependency and by government policies and actions. Noongar culture suffered under these onslaughts.

Second, I have outlined how government policies, prevailing paradigms of the anthropology profession and even popular thinking have influenced researchers.

The priorities and interest of some anthropologists predisposed them to a view that the South West had little to offer in the way of traditional Aboriginal culture or as a fertile field for classic anthropological research. This was principally a result of their preconceptions, and the focus and scope of their research. It may have been a product, to some extent, of working with Aboriginal people who were inculcated with a view that cultural matters were best suppressed, eschewed or devalued in any discussions with non-Noongars, consistent with the assimilationist views of the time. Consequently, researchers in the period 1960 to 1980 did not provide much evidence of an enduring Noongar culture. This was an understandable but not necessary corollary of an acceptance of the conclusion that Noongar culture had been heavily impacted. Impacts on culture do not automatically mean their extinction, nor are consequential changes necessarily productive of novelty rather than modification and adaptations of traditional formations.

Finally, I have examined later research that seems to me to throw doubt on the findings of earlier researchers. The works of Toussaint, Baines and Birdsall represent a significant corpus and together share commonalities. In all three cases we are presented with a view of Noongar culture that shows it to have survived remarkably, though not unaltered. None of these studies provides any detailed analysis of the extent or nature of change, which is accepted by all three writers. If the work of these three writers is accepted in this regard, the question relevant to this inquiry is not whether there is a discrete and recognisable Noongar culture, however developed and changed over time. This has been demonstrated. Rather, the matter to be explored is whether these changes reflect radical departures from traditional practices that yield cultural novelty, or whether they reflect contemporary laws and customs that are founded upon and have developed from those that obtained in the South West prior to European sovereignty of the region.

PART II

NOONGAR LAWS AND CUSTOMS AND RIGHTS TO COUNTRY

Chapter 9

THE CLAIMANT COMMUNITY

Introduction

In this chapter I identify and characterise the claimant community. In order to do this, it is necessary to distinguish its constituent parts. I explore how it may properly be called a 'community', by which I mean a social unit whose members understand themselves as having cultural similarities and who are either actually or potentially consociates or kinsmen and women. Relatedness may be classificatory or consanguineal. The members of a community recognise others who are not of their community as being different because of their culture and identity or the country with which they identify, or because they do not share kin. The recognition of difference is reciprocal: those others, not members of the community in question, in turn recognise members of a different community as distinctive from themselves.

I provide material drawn from the research data to support the following propositions. A principal means of establishing and perpetuating membership of a community is through the recognition and exhibition of a clear identity. For members of the claimant community, identity is forged through the practice of cultural ways of behaving, associations with areas of country and adherence to beliefs and mores, as well as the use of a name or names. It is usually ultimately derived from parents, since descent is understood to be of consequence. It is then possible to characterise the rules for recruitment to the claimant community. The claimant community exhibits its own structure, with members accepting principles of authority and instruction. Authority relates not only to the governance of activity, action and behaviour but also to property. Finally, there are a number of cultural aspects which might be considered as typifying the Noongar community. While many of these will be discussed in the next chapter, language remains an important identifier of the whole community, so is considered here.

The name

The name 'Noongar' has a very wide acceptance among Aboriginal people in the South West. In the course of my research I came across no one who did not use the term as a fundamental means of identification. While there was a widespread use of local names as well, for the most part there was no suggestion that the name Noongar was either new or imposed. From the data, it appears to be both widely accepted and considered as a term that has been used as long as anyone can recall.

One claimant explained that he identified himself as a Noongar person. He remarked that years ago 'Noongar' meant a man or male person in the Noongar language, whereas now it meant being an Indigenous person. However, others considered it to be a unique term for the Aboriginal people of the South West. One claimant (who is 60 years old) said that when she was young the old people used the word 'Noongar', and another man a decade older stated the same thing. One group of claimants said that they preferred to be called Noongar rather than 'Indigenous'. This was because the term Noongar made them feel proud. A number of others, however, simply stated that for them being Noongar was a fact of life, and it was a name that they commonly used to refer to themselves and that others used to refer to them.

Claimants also recognise a variety of names which can all be subsumed under the heading Noongar. For example, one claimant stated that he recognised a group called Namankannyaki as a sub-group of the Noongar. Others recognised local names like Ballardong (York) and Pinjarub (Pinjarra). There were local names for 'salt river people', and three names for coastal people (Wadangara, west of New Norcia; 'Shell people', east of Albany; Wardandi, west of Busselton). There were regional names, including Wilmun (east of Albany), Minong (round Albany), Bibbulmun (Bunbury area and south) and Yued (Moore River and North). These names remain important as local identifiers, but are not understood to mean that members of the groups are not Noongar. Indeed, several claimants stressed that all were Noongar but named for different areas or because they were seen to be associated with particular natural features.

The use of these names would lead to the following conclusion. First, there is an overall identity forged by reference to the use of the term 'Noongar'. The term appears to have wide currency and is used by members of the claimant community. Second, within the Noongar community there are a number of named constituent groups. These names are not definitively referenced, nor do all people identify with a regional or area name. These names, where they are found, are a means by which people identify themselves as being a component part of the Noongar community and a subset of it.

Recruitment

Being Noongar is a matter of descent. I was told on a number of occasions that being Noongar is a matter of 'blood': you become a Noongar person because either or both of your parents are Noongar. In cases where one parent is Noongar and the other comes from another cultural group, the child can exercise choice over his or her identity. While descent was cited as the most usual way by which a person can become a Noongar, and the most important, there were other ways put forward by which a person can become a member of the Noongar community.

One is through marriage. If a person marries a Noongar spouse there is a general view that they can, over time, become accepted as a Noongar person. However, according to at least one claimant, acceptance is a matter of becoming assimilated into Noongar culture. The claimant gave an example of an American woman who had married a Noongar man. She had been accepted by the community, but in order for this to happen she had to give up her American identity and adopt a Noongar way of life. Another claimant talked of a non-Noongar woman marrying into a Noongar family, living on Noongar country for a long time and raising Noongar children. As a result, she achieved significant Noongar status. Other claimants, however, were less sure about the situation with respect to marriage. One stated that a person could not become a Noongar by marrying a Noongar. However, she did indicate that she herself had a role 'behind her husband' (who was Yamaji) in Yamaji country. Presumably, then, she understood marriage as providing some means of recruitment to the Yamaji community. Another claimant stated that a person could not become a Noongar by marrying a Noongar, but the children of the marriage would be Noongar.

There were also views expressed about whether birth in Noongar country made a person a Noongar. Birthplace in Noongar country is considered to be very important in relation to a Noongar person's affiliations to land, and I will discuss this in greater detail in Chapter 11. However, few statements were collected that reflected a view that being born on Noongar country was sufficient in and of itself to make the child a Noongar person, and then with the qualification that the person must be bought up on Noongar country to realise status as a Noongar. One claimant considered that birth gave a non-Noongar no recognition as a Noongar, but if they subsequently married a Noongar person and their children were brought up as Noongars, then those children would be accepted as Noongar people. Others saw place of birth as often being the result of demographic movements and therefore of no real consequence. Birthplace did not affect who your ancestors were, which was the key factor in determining who you were. A claimant's mother, who was born in Onslow, stated that she always felt a stranger in her place of birth because she was uninformed about the country there.

Children adopted into a Noongar family were considered by one claimant to have rights equal to those of natural children. It was a view shared by others but not without qualification. For example, one claimant said that if a person were adopted as a baby by Noongar parents and brought up as a Noongar person then that person would be considered to be a Noongar person. But if they were adopted as an older child or adult then they would not be considered to be a Noongar. Another stated that a person who was not Noongar by biological descent may be adopted and brought up by Noongar parents. Over time, that person may come to be regarded as a Noongar and accepted as such by the community. However, they should not speak for country as a general rule unless they were the only surviving child of the family. Another again stated that adoption was a traditional practice and an adopted child had the same rights as a natural child. Others spoke of children whose parents came from an area other than that in which their children were born being 'adopted', over time, into the community as a consequence of their birth.

Conclusion

Based upon these research data it is reasonable to conclude that recruitment to the Noongar community is considered to be primarily by descent. This represents a normative system, which underpins much acceptance of membership of the community: if your father or mother was Noongar, so are you. In turn, parents are understood to have gained their Noongar identity from their parents on either side, so there is perceived to be a lineage extending back to Noongar ancestors in a time beyond memory. This cornerstone of Noongar identity is fundamental to Noongar relationships to land, and I will examine this in due course.

With respect to gaining membership of the community through affinal, putative or natal relationships, situational circumstances, over time, appear to be determinants. Recognition requires enactment to be realised, and therefore these means are not sufficient in themselves to effect membership of the community. As acts of incorporation, they require that those who undertake the incorporation yield recognition of the outcome of their actions. They are then socially negotiated, the product of interrelationships. They thus remain possibilities that, if given sufficient collateral support, may be effective, but probably always to a lesser extent than by reference to the principle of descent. In particular this may be the case with respect to the exercise of rights that are a concomitant of community membership. Contestation is a feature of a dynamic community, whose members seek to negotiate or position themselves in relation to others. While recruitment is founded upon clear principles (descent, ancestral connection and in some cases adoption or incorporation), these will always be subject to debate and challenge. This reflects a social process that nevertheless is underpinned by reference to a system of rules.

Sentiment

Sentiment is an important part of Noongar identity. By sentiment I mean the feeling, emotions and ideas a person has about who they are. It is also based on a recognition that there is a distinctive Noongar identity, manifest in particular ways of behaving, cultural practices, ways of speaking and affiliations with country that are unique. It is a concept summed up in the phrase 'Noongar way' (cf. Toussaint 1987, p. 3), meaning archetypical enactments that embody an essentiality of being Noongar.

Consistent with the primacy afforded to descent, a number of claimants saw identity as fundamentally derived from their forebears. One man explained that his sense of Noongar identity was instilled mainly through his mother, his mother's brother and his mother's mother and mother's mother's brother. Another claimant emphasised the importance of coming to know and learn about Noongar land, traditions and families from a young age. Those who actively and consciously participated in Noongar society become more deeply entrenched in that society. Another stated that being Noongar was 'the cultural things like what [my] Mother handed down'. It was a matter of respecting 'the cultural parts of yourself' and feeling a pride in your family. There was a sense of commonality gained through an acceptance of having family members in common, as well as an appreciation that Noongar culture and beliefs could be clearly differentiated from those of others. Together, this feeling of being a part of a bounded community finds its expression in a belief that, for example, Noongars readily recognised other Noongars, and non-Noongars readily recognised Noongars. Noongar people will 'yarn' (that is, talk casually) with each other because they recognise commonalities. This is understood to be the result of the belief that all Noongars share a common identity and that this is expressed in their language and the types of foods Noongars enjoy from their country. This identity is also recognised by other cultural groups.

Noongar identity, then, is a lived experience that derives recognition from defined commonalities. The community is formed from those who consider themselves to be consociates and kinsmen, and to share a common culture that provides for a strong emotional bond between them. In its totality, the Noongar community becomes an entity that represents something greater than the sum of its parts. People who regard themselves as a part of this community feel proud of this association. It provides a means by which people can situate themselves, both in relation to other Indigenous cultural groups and to the wider Australian population. It provides an identity by reference to a defined geographical area.

Community structure

Authority

There is no indication from the data that there is any centralised authority within the Noongar community. Rather, the community is structured along lines that are defined by reference to age, knowledge and experience. A person recognised as having authority is respected by all others, including members of other families, according to the customary laws in operation.

The English term 'elder' is widely used by Noongars and other Aboriginal people to identify a person with authority within the family and commanding respect in the community. One claimant identifies *birdiya* as a name for a 'boss' or senior person, but the term 'elder' has wide currency throughout for those with whom I worked and appears to be a favoured term. The term 'elder', however, has a range of different meanings, depending on circumstances. The different meanings reflect the degree of authority that can be commanded. However, all uses have in common a recognition that an 'elder' is of a certain age. According to one claimant, an elder is a person over 55 years and experienced in Aboriginal ways. Another claimant put the age a little lower, at 50. Others described an elder as 'an older person', meaning that they were of some age or older than those who must respect them. Being of a certain age earns respect in Noongar thinking, and this appears to be a fundamental principle of Noongar social organisation. One man told me that if young people broke this rule, they would 'get bad feet' as a result. Respect means listening to the older person, taking note of what they say and not interrupting them, and addressing them appropriately. All older Noongar people are 'elders' in this limited sense and are ideally treated accordingly.

Authority is not institutionalised in an office. Rather, for authority to be effective there must be recognition among those upon whom it is exercised that he or she who seeks to commands that authority has certain qualifications. These include knowledge and wisdom as well as personal qualities necessary for interventions in disputes or in influencing decision making. Not all older people have these qualities. In cases where these are judged to be lacking, there is a potential conflict between the rule of respect and the requirements for the recognition of authority. However, from my experience, it is generally not the case that older people are criticised (at least publicly or before strangers), either for their lack of knowledge or their personal qualities. One claimant remarked that not all 'elders' spoke up, but they would still reprimand you if you did wrong. Elders with authority based on their age and standing are expected to command members of the community. In this, they are expected to intervene in fights or other disputes. They may also be required to prevent wrong-doing, either with respect to traditional Noongar laws or in relation to European law. Elders are the principal and first point of contact in any matter that relates to land, and in this are recognised as having an authority over a particular area, but not over others. As I have stated above, elders are recognised for their knowledge of many aspects of Noongar culture, including history and their own family relationships, so are expected to provide definitive views on these matters as well and to settle disputes should they occur in this regard.

The family

The family forms a fundamental building block of the Noongar community. Two claimants, for example, told me that it is families which make up the Noongar community. It is necessary, then, to consider what is meant by the term 'family', although it is a subject to which I will return, in more detail, in the next chapter. As with 'elder', the term 'family' has a range of referents, depending on the context. Noongar people trace their ancestry to forebears, who were either given family names by Europeans or used and adapted their own Noongar names to serve this purpose. Today, families are initially identified by reference to their family name. However, this is often qualified by reference to the family names of matri-filiates, whose family name generally is different. Reference is also made to place, since a particular family is identified in relation to an area, in contradistinction, say, to one with the same family name (and perhaps sharing common ancestry) but associated with another area. This family referencing process has been well documented for Noongar people by Birdsall (1990, pp. 151–2). I encountered it in casual conversation with the claimants with whom I worked.

Birdsall states that those with whom she worked called the set of family relations which could be traced through the genealogical account and common descent 'all-one-family' (1990, p. 153). Noongar people recognise consanguineality as the key characteristic of the 'all-one-family'. Claimants sometimes referred to it as 'family' or 'extended family'. For clarity I will refer to this, the largest family group, as the 'greater family'. The greater family, composed of many different branches, probably does not come together often, except perhaps for big meetings and funerals. Constituent family groups, each with their own non-exclusive family name, are characteristically larger than a nuclear family (husband, wife and children), and members of the first and third ascending and descending generation level may be included in the one household. Relations of affines of children may also be present. Different households of the same family characteristically have close social contact, share material items and assist each other as required. For this reason, such families can be considered as 'social families' in the sense that their members are likely to interact. However, circumstances, spatial distance and personal inclinations will affect the degree to which this takes place in practice. I will call these families which are subsets of the Noongar greater family, 'extended families'. The extended family is regarded as being of the utmost importance to a Noongar person. One man told me, 'Your family is always together. A Noongar family is closer than a *wajala* [European Australian] family. The family extends a long way and are all recognised as a part of the family, even if they have a different name.'

The authority of elders or older people is recognised within these extended families. This is generally manifest in the expectation that the oldest family member will be the spokesperson for affairs that directly affect the family or in which the family has an interest. In some cases being the eldest was not stipulated, but in at least one case the physical absence of older siblings was seen as a reason why a younger sibling should take the role, with due deference to those older, in the absence of the older brother or sister. There is some evidence, then, that a senior (if not the most senior) family member takes a leadership role in all matters which relate to the family.

Language

Those with whom I worked were not only aware of their Noongar language but held views about its importance as a determining aspect of their culture. A number of claimants stated that they continued to speak the Noongar language and that its use was common among the Noongar population. Some stated that they had learnt the Noongar language from their parents or older relatives. Noongar words were used during interviews and site visits. Those with whom I worked regarded the use of the Noongar language and styles of speaking as a means of establishing their identity. This was because the language was different from those used by neighbours belonging to different cultural groups to the north and east. One man told me that when Noongar language words were used they provided a means by which non-Noongar people recognised you. It was a widely held view. Use of the Noongar language was seen to provide a ready means by which people could be identified as being Noongar. Noongar language was a means of identifying yourself to other Noongar people, with whom you were not personally acquainted. In addition, the use of the language was seen as a source of pride, even if it was others who spoke it and therefore made you 'feel good'.

Others recognised that there were regional differences within the Noongar language, characterised by differences in the pronunciation of words. It appears that at least some claimants continue to teach their children Noongar words, and Noongar is taught in some schools in the region. I was told that while young people speak a form of standard English this frequently utilises Noongar words, creating a distinctive style.

In relation to these data I make the following observations. Given the scope of my research, I cannot make any definitive comment on the degree of fluency with which Noongar is currently spoken. It would appear to me, however, that the language is used by the majority of the claimants as a form of what one linguist, Wilf Douglas, calls 'Neo-Nyungar' (Douglas 1976, pp. 9–14). Douglas does, however, state that Noongar continues to be spoken by some middle-aged and 'elderly folk' (p. 9), and I would expect that there do remain some fluent speakers of the Noongar language.[118] Neo-Nyungar is characterised by Douglas as a development from Noongar, influenced by English, and sharing semantic, phonemic and grammatical aspects of both languages (p. 14). Neo-Nyungar is, according to Douglas, 'a unit in the continuum of language change' (p. 14). My view is that most claimants are referring to Douglas's 'Neo-Nyungar' in the discussions referenced above. This does not diminish its social and cultural importance, nor the evident role it plays in the maintenance and establishment of a distinctive Noongar identity. The language, as used, has a distinctive style, which means that its use is an ideal vehicle for establishing identity with outsiders, as well as with insiders, both known and unknown. In this sense it is the phenomenon of the language (or language style) that is important rather than any debate about whether the language is original Noongar or some modern-day adaptation that also incorpo-

118 Dench (1994, p. 174) states that there 'are now very few speakers of Nyungar'.

rates English. The language used is a development of Noongar, not a departure from it (see Douglas 1976, p. 14), and it continues to be used, as it presumably always was, as both a means of communication and a statement of identity.

The data presented above indicate that regional variations in the Noongar language remain. These dialect differences were noted in present-day Noongar by Douglas (1976, p. 8). Douglas identifies six regional dialects of Noongar (pp. 5–6). Dench recognises only three dialects, but lists words as belonging to six regions (Dench 1994, pp. 174–5). These regional variations in speaking are understood to be in evidence today, as used by the claimants. They are seen to be markers of regional difference within the single Noongar language.

Finally, my view is that the Noongar language, however typified in practice, is considered by many claimants to be an important part of their culture and has value to them. Language is an important aspect of any culture, since it may encapsulate concepts, beliefs and ways of thinking. Its use provides a clear statement about the speaker's geographic origins and territorial affiliations, their ancestry and their cultural heritage. Noongar language would appear to me to be used by many of the claimants to enunciate these aspects of their identity. The fact that Noongar is taught in schools, and that some of those with whom I worked stressed that they taught their children the Noongar language at home, further supports the conclusion that Noongar language use remains important.

Conclusion

In this chapter I have set out to characterise the claimant community and to explain how it can be considered as a social unit, with constituent parts. I have shown how the use of the name 'Noongar' has widespread currency through the South West and is used to identify the claimants as a social unit. Regional groups are identified by the use of a number of other names, but all members of these groups are understood to be Noongar. I noted in Chapter 2 that the term Noongar was recorded in the 1840s as being used by the Aboriginal people of the South West to identify themselves. I also demonstrated in Chapter 2 how the regional names recorded in the early decades of European settlement can be understood to be regional subsets of a single cultural society. The use of the name to refer to a cultural community today is consistent with the views of earlier writers, including Bates, who saw the Aboriginal people of the South West as forming a single cultural unit or community (again, see discussion in Chapter 2).

Membership of the Noongar community is prescribed, and descent is the principal means by which a person comes to be Noongar. While adoption and other means of incorporation may provide possible means of recruitment, they are heavily dependent upon circumstances and social acceptance. The early literature, which I reviewed in Chapter 3, has many references to the principle of descent, although these were given in relation to the recruitment to what was probably a country group, rather than to the community. However, if descent is the principal means for recruitment to a country group, this must hold true for recruitment to a larger social unit, comprising a number of country groups.

I have set out that members of the Noongar community maintain that there are strong bonds of commonality between members, based on their shared culture, language, experience, attachment to land and common ancestry, real or supposed. The sentiment that forms a strong bond between members is manifest as an ideology of shared cultural understandings and mutual support and assistance, particularly between consociates. This represents the social and lived reality of community members' interaction. Within this operates a socially sanctioned authority structure, evident across the community by reference to age, knowledge and experience. I have set out that the family is an important structural element in Noongar society, manifest in different forms. Authority is evident within the family, represented by a senior person who is recognised as being responsible for decisions and actions made by family members. There are substantial parallels between these accounts and those found in the early literature (and reviewed above), particularly relating to the role of senior family members and families, which I discuss in Chapter 6.

Finally, I have reviewed data on language use and its role in sustaining a distinctive Noongar identity. Through its use, the Noongar language, or its contemporary manifestation, provides a means for people to demonstrate their membership of a single cultural community. It provides for a unique identity. The language as it is used, according to Douglas (1976), is based upon a language form that would have been spoken in the South West prior to sovereignty. Consistent with that language as recorded at that time, Neo-Nyungar continues to exhibit regional variations (see Chapter 2).

In this, it seems reasonable to conclude that the claimants together can properly be understood as a single community, with constituent parts. They exhibit homogeneity, so members show an appreciation of sameness by reference to shared cultural precepts, use of a single name, language and attachment to the South West of the state. I have shown in the preceding four paragraphs that many aspects of Noongar culture which are relevant to this discussion can be found in early accounts of the Aboriginal people of the South West. Many of these accounts were written close to the time when the region was first settled by Europeans.

Chapter 10

NOONGAR CULTURE

Introduction

In the last chapter I examined some aspects of Noongar culture which are important to an understanding of the nature and structure of the Noongar community and how members variously identify as Noongar people. However, Noongar culture is both diverse and complex, and it has many aspects.

One of the characteristics of people who consider that they form a part of a community is that they have commonalities with others of that community. These commonalities provide for a shared set of understandings that relate to core values, beliefs, ways of doing things, customs and activities. They are elemental in the sense that, while people may hold different personal views and emotions, there is a set of values and beliefs that are considered to be quintessentially of their common culture. This means that they cannot be altered — or so it is believed — and they provide a reference for how action should be initiated. This gives them the status of rules within the culture. Of course, some aspects of Noongar culture are not unique to Noongar people, as there is some consistency in Australian Indigenous culture across the continent. However, Noongar people regard their culture as fundamentally Noongar. It then becomes a ready point of reference for any discussion about Noongar culture or Noongar ways of doing things. Through the maintenance of its integrity by adherence to customary ways of doing things, it is regarded by members of the culture as being of central importance to their lives. Any disregard for these cultural precepts is seen as breaking customary practice and therefore is censured and greeted with opprobrium.

In this chapter I explore these issues while describing some of the more common or noticeable aspects of Noongar culture that came to my attention during my research. In the process I provide data to support these preliminary statements.

Kinship and social organisation

Kinship

Noongar people recognise a system of classificatory kinship reckoning, which combines both English and Noongar terms.[119] According to this system, parallel and cross-cousins can be classified as siblings, although they may be distinguished in some instances by the use of alternative terms. Members of the first ascending generation who are related to ego as FB, fz, MB and mz (see Table 10.1 below) are usually called by the English term 'aunty' and 'uncle', but some claimants expressed the view that they were regarded as equivalents to parents. There is a single term for each sex for members of the second ascending generation, FF and FFB not being distinguished. Ego's chch also have the distinctive name 'grannies', which has wide currency. The terms 'uncle' and 'aunty' may be extended to any older Noongar person, as a sign of respect. Ego can call a close male friend 'brother' even though they are not related. These kinship terms are supplemented by Noongar terms, some of which are remembered and used.

These data are set out in summary form in Table 10.1. The Noongar kinship system is typified by the use of English terms with culturally specific meanings. Members of ego's second ascending generation level are called 'Nanna' and 'Pop' (female and male), which terms are sometimes found as reciprocals, in place of the more common 'granny' or 'grannies' for grandchildren. The siblings of parents are sometimes categorised as 'Father' or 'Mother', or as 'Old Mum' (presumably of a mother's elder sibling), 'Second Mum' or 'Second Dad'. Cousins are sometimes classified as siblings, or distinguished to some degree by the use of terms like 'cousin sister/brother' or 'coz'. With both cousins and the siblings of parents, the choice of kin terms would appear to reflect the degree of intimacy and familiarity with the kin. Thus a FB who is very close to a family might be a 'father', but a more distant mz might be an 'aunty', and so on.

The kinship system set out in Table 10.1 indicates that there is a classificatory nomenclature that operates to bring certain relatives together, which is distinct from standard Australian English usage. Moreover, the terminology, while representing a form of English, is distinctive, particularly with respect to the Noongar use of the term 'granny' (which is very common) and 'sis' and 'coz'. While in this account original Noongar terms have been replaced by terms derived from

119 An account of the characteristics of a classificatory system was set out in Chapter 4. Classificatory systems are common throughout Aboriginal Australia. See Sutton (2003, pp. 175–7).

Table 10.1: Noongar kinship terms

Relation to ego*	Ego calls	Ego is called
FF, FFB	Granny, Pop	Pop, Old Pop
fm, fmz	Nan, Old Nan, Nanna	Granny
MF	Pop	Granny
[mm], mmz, [fm]	Nana	[Granny] Nana
chch, zchch, bchch	Grannies, Gran Niece, Nanna	Nanna, Pop, Granny
FB	Father	
FB	Uncle (Second Father)	
FB, fz, MB, mz	Mum, Dad	
FB	Uncle, Second Dad	
FFBS	Uncle	
mz	Aunty, Second Mum	
mz, fz	Old Mum (Aunty)	
mz	Mother	
cousins (male)	Brother Boy, Coz, Cousin Brother	Brother Boy, Coz, Cousin Brother, Bro
cousin (male)	Brother	Brother
cousins (female)	Cousin Sister	Cousin Sister
cousin (female)	Sister, Sis, Sister Girl	Sister, Sis, Sister Girl
zch, bch		Aunty, Old Mum

* Square brackets indicate relationships and terms supplied by the author, where these can reasonably be deduced.

English, the classificatory system as recorded shows preservation of a number of features of the kinship system as recorded by Bates (White 1985). This includes the classification of ego's parents' siblings as 'parents', and the classification of cousins with siblings and reciprocal terms for grandparents/grandchildren (see White 1985, pp. 78–9). Some of the claimants indicated that traditional Noongar words continue to be used for relationship terms. These terms are set out in Table 10.2.

Several of these terms were recorded by Bates, and these have been noted in the right-hand column with the relevant page number. These terms would appear to be known and used by some claimants, and constitute a distinctive Noongar kinship vocabulary, which is used to complement the Neo-Nyungar terms outlined above.

Claimants made statements about the behaviour expected between certain categories of kin. In this, they provided additional evidence of the operation of a classificatory system as specific ways of behaving were equated with classes

Table 10.2: Noongar language kinship terms collected during the research

Noongar term	English	White 1985
ngulja	brother-in-law	*ngooljar*; p. 79
guda	brother	
ngarni	brother	
ngorn	brother	*ngoont*, brother; p. 81
nuurut	brother	
kwiniyard	children	
kwulanga	children	*koolong*, son; p. 79
namba	cousin	
kubany	family and friends	
budong	family, blood relations	
moort	family, blood relations	*murart*, family relations; p. 84
konjul	father	
jugun	sister	*jook*, sister; p. 81
kong	uncle	mother's brother, *konkan*; p. 81

of relationship, however internally differentiated. For example, cousins were 'treated as brothers and sisters', and those who grew up together subsequently would 'stick together'. Siblings' children should be cared for in the same way as your own children, while a brother's wife becomes a part of the family and should be treated accordingly. A father's brother is like a father and accepts the role of a father. Grandparents have a duty to bring up their 'grannies' should circumstances require it. More generally, any close friend can be called a 'brother' to a man, and older people should be called 'uncle' or 'aunty', regardless of consanguineal ties, as a sign of respect.

Social organisation

The family is an important concept in Noongar thinking. In Chapter 9 I differentiated the 'greater family' from the 'extended family'. During the research reported here, many comments were made about the centrality of the family (in either or both manifestations) to Noongar thinking. One claimant stated, 'Family is first for Noongar; it's all that matters,' and another said, 'Family makes up the Noongar community.' The family is seen as an important means of locating an individual in both time and place. The history of the family is considered to provide the basis by which a person can understand their heritage and culture.

The attachment of that family to areas of country is the principal means by which an individual comes to know of their own affiliation to country. One man said that Noongar country was divided up between family groups and different family groups looked after each area with which they were affiliated. The members of different extended families that are affiliated with common country are called *moort*. Noongar people acknowledge that their greater family consists of a number of extended families, many with their own family name. It is accepted that relationships between far-flung parts of the greater family are discoverable as discussions and inquiry uncover relationships in the distant past that reveal such links. This is understood to be important, since it provides a bond between individuals through consanguineal or affinal ties. A Noongar person talking to another Noongar person for the first time is likely to be able to discover some common ancestry, thus cementing their commonality as Noongar people. This commonality of identity, by reference to both being Noongar and of the same extended or greater family, provides for an ethos of mutual support and interdependency. Family members, according to this cultural precept, are obliged to help one another, to share material goods and to support each other in adversity. One claimant commented, 'Noongar families always want to be close.'

Knowledge of the moiety system appears to be limited, and there were only two instances in the data sets where claimants commented on this. Bill Webb stated that he learnt from his father about two groups and that a person would belong to one or the other. These he identified as *manatjmut* (white cockatoo) and *wardangmut* (black crow). He considered that membership also related to marriage and that you would marry into the group that was not your own. Another claimant stated that he was told about 'marriage laws' by the old people in 'hand down' stories. He was told about the cockatoo and crow groups by the old people, but he could not recall whether he was told the group to which he belonged.

Another claimant stated that her family had the *wardang* (crow) totem, something that was given to her by her mother and had been handed down traditionally for many generations. This may have developed from the moiety system, it may have been solely a totemic reference, or it could have been a combination of both, as totemic belief appears to remain strong (as I discuss below).

Notwithstanding the lack of information regarding a moiety system, there was a strong view that there were rules about marriage. These arise mainly from the view that marriage of cousins or other family members is prohibited. Some claimants told me that you could not marry 'close-up family' and that this was a rule. Another stated that 'close-up marriage', particularly with a cousin, was not approved, though they conceded that it did happen. Some claimants set out families with whom their children should not seek marriage partners, because of consanguineal links in higher generations. I was told of two trees, which were believed to be the representation of a couple who married 'too close' and had been turned into trees as a consequence, entwined together. Marriage with a person ego calls *muart* (or *moort*) is forbidden. *Muart* comprise extended families with affiliation to common tracts of country.

Noongar rules, laws and customs

My research leads me to conclude that there are numerous rules, laws and customs that are evident among the claimants. These aspects of Noongar culture are too diverse to set out definitively in this book. However, in what follows I will consider some of the more common aspects of customary belief and behaviour, and provide examples where I have sourced these from the data sets and my own field notes. For convenience I divide this corpus of beliefs and customs into headings and will include under each heading those rules, laws or customs that appear to have some commonality. Fundamental to many beliefs and practices is an enduring conviction that there are spiritual forces and beings whose presence informs daily experience. All these rules, laws and customs are distinctively Noongar, and their practice and observance distinguish Noongar people from others who live in the same region of Australia.

The Noongar spirit world

Noongar people hold fast to the belief that the physical world is powerfully informed by a metaphysical presence which manifests as spirits. These may be encountered directly or indirectly. Such meetings require management and right practice to ameliorate or deflect untoward consequences. The spirit world is unpredictable and potentially dangerous, a concept expressed in the Noongar term *wara*. Spirits can be categorised. Some are merely malevolent, residing at known places in the countryside, particularly caves. Others are spirits of animals, in particular a kangaroo, which is sometimes reported as being white. There are also many spirits of deceased people, often referred to as 'the old people' or the 'ancestors'. These can be found almost anywhere in Noongar country, but are particularly populous close to places which are known to have been favoured camping places. Government House on St Georges Terrace, Perth is believed to be the home of many spirits, as are the old camping areas round Albany and many other places across the claim area. Yagan's spirit is believed to dwell both round the area where he was murdered in the Swan Valley and on Heirisson Island, Perth. As spirits of the deceased may wish to follow you from the place where they dwell, steps have to be taken to ensure that this does not happen. Mentioning the name of the dead may be enough to evoke the presence of the spirits, so the practice is discouraged. Not all spirits of the deceased are shunned, however, and some claimants explained how the spirits of loved ones remained with them, or had visited them, an incident that was remembered by the lingering smell of the liniment that the deceased had habitually used when alive. In another case, the spirit of a loved relative was recognised by the smell of the tobacco they had always smoked.

Other spirits have specific names and physical characteristics, like the *bulyip*, which was described as being like a 'big monkey', while a narrative was told of an encounter with it. Two other important Noongar spirits are *wutaji* and *mumari*. *Mundung* or *janark* are other spirits, which may be encountered in the countryside. There are very large spirits, which are described as being 'like giants', and these will steal children. Both *mumari* and the giant spirits are believed to have been seen in the Midland area. One claimant stated that he was unwilling to give their name, as even mentioning them would potentially summon them. Another claimant explained how a certain cave was imbued with much spiritual significance, as it formerly had been inhabited by a *malarka* man, a real man with six fingers and six toes who had been ostracised by his community. The *malarka* man committed terrible atrocities, including killing and eating children and his own mother. This cave still harboured the spirits of this man, and was approached only with the utmost caution. Another spirit was called a *jimbar* and was described as being big and hairy, half-man and half-ape. He and other spirits were like 'policemen', and regulated people's behaviour in the countryside and town. Also mentioned were two spirits of the earth, *wiyarn* (or *wiirn*) and *winitj*, and a spirit that lived inside a person, called *marlgi*. *Jinagabi* are known as 'featherfoots' and are characterised as part-human, but having supernatural qualities. They are sent or commissioned by a person who wishes to exact revenge or punishment, and are a common part of Noongar belief. A summary of these data is set out in Table 10.3.

All spirits are associated with the dark, and dusk is considered a dangerous time when spirits may be encountered. For this reason children are told to return to the safety of their homes well before dusk. Adults, too, exercise caution and avoid known spirit places at dusk or after dark. Camping in a place that has many spirits can result in disastrous consequences, and there were accounts of disturbed sleep and upset resulting from camping too close to spirits.

Table 10.3: Noongar spirits

Noongar name or reference	Characteristic
mumari	Little hairy men
wutaji, mundung, janark	Spirit
balyit, balyip	Ape-like
jimbar	Big and hairy, ape-like
winitj	Spirit of the earth
wiyarn, wiirn	Spirit of the earth
marlgi	Person's spirit
malarka	Man with six fingers and six toes
wara (dangerous) spirits	Spirit of caves and dark places
jinagabi	'Featherfoot' dangerous avenger
Animal spirits	Kangaroo, dog, horse
Giants	Large, child-stealing
Spirit of deceased person	Familiar presence, familiar smell

The Noongar spirit world is diverse, complex and often dangerous. The data set out here provide just some examples from the copious material collected. It is evident that a belief in spirits, in their various manifestations, represents an important and substantial part of Noongar religious belief.

One way to manage the spirits is to provide them with food. This practice appears to be, in part, a consequence of an understanding that the spirits play an active role in the success of the hunt. Some claimants stated that a little bird (unidentified) should always be left a small piece of meat after a successful kangaroo shoot, since it had shown you where the kangaroo was, while another claimant stated that you should leave behind a portion of the kangaroo you did not need, but was less certain as to why this was the rule. Others considered that leaving a part of the kangaroo behind as an offering was essential to prevent the spirits (*wutaji* or *mumari*) from following you home and stealing your children. This custom is observed round the Perth area, where spirits are to be found, particularly in the hills. Another claimant stated that you should leave the intestines and the top part of any kangaroo behind for the *wutaji*, as a sign of respect for the kangaroo and to ensure that the spirits do not follow you home. In the Moora region, one claimant stated that it was important to shoot two kangaroos and leave one for the *wutaji*. This is an act of reciprocation, since it is believed that the spirits frightened the kangaroos and drove them towards the hunters. One should then be left for the *wutaji* to eat.

Dangerous places

The data collected demonstrate that some places in the countryside are regarded as dangerous (*wara*) because of their association with spirits. Moreover, some Noongar people believe that the whole countryside is potentially hazardous, particularly to those who are not familiar with its spiritual potentialities. The concept of 'danger' is complemented by that of *winitj* (also *wunarj*), which carries the sense of a special or sacred place. A *winitj* place must be treated with care. One claimant stated that one strategy used to protect oneself from dangerous places is to boil muddy water and then place ashes in the water overnight. You then drink the water in the morning. Another precaution involves the use of smoke (see below) or taking the leaves from locally growing trees and waving them over your head, which will ward off hostile spirits. Failure to take heed of a dangerous place, or simple ignorance of its situation, will result in sickness. As a consequence, it is essential to know the country and to understand where it is you are travelling and to avoid those places of which you are ignorant. Some places are dangerous to women and not to men; some are dangerous to men but not to women. Massacre sites or other places where people have been killed should be avoided, and sites of this sort were reported through the Walpole and Denmark area, as well as in Ravensthorpe and Narrogin. Similarly, places where people had died as a result of an accident were considered to be best avoided. There were places that marked the beginning of dangerous country, so it was unwise to pass them.

Unnecessary interference with a site may result in dire, or at least unfortunate, consequences. One Noongar man told of how the rocks placed on top of a rock hole had been removed from the site by a man who promptly became ill. At the same time, the weather turned unseasonably hot. The rocks were returned to the site and comments were addressed to the country (see below) to make amends, and things went back to normal. A rock known as Coffin Rock, close to a rock art site called Shark's Mouth outside Kellerberrin, is another example of the danger that may be encountered by the unwary. At some time in the past, a local farmer moved this rock from the granite outcrop and not long afterwards death and illness dogged his family. He returned the rock. Today, no one must touch the rock for fear of illness or even death. Other examples were collected of the disturbance of sites and unwelcome consequences, including from the Mt Stirling (Quairading) area. In a more general sense, any area of spiritual importance is understood to exhibit spiritual danger, and interference with it will have calamitous consequences.

The data presented here indicate that, in Noongar belief, the known country is redolent with ambiguous spirituality. This has important implications for travel and excursions into country, since ignorance of the spirituality of an area of country is understood to result, potentially, in illness, misfortune or death. Country must be negotiated, and the spirituality it contains must be managed and treated according to Noongar ways of doing things. Much of the danger associated with places is directly attributable to a belief in a spirit or spirits that are associated with the place. The manner by which this spirituality can be mediated by those who understand both its location and its nature constitutes an important part of how Noongar people relate to their country.

Greeting and managing spirits of the country

There is a range of actions that Noongar people customarily adopt in order to safeguard against the potency of spirits when visiting their country. One common Noongar rule that relates to the spirituality of the countryside and its dangers requires the greeting of the country and its spirits, to ensure spiritual beings are cognisant that visitors are friendly and have no hostile intentions. This is effected by calling to the spirits of the country when visiting, both to ask for the spirits to provide food and to seek permission to enter what is regarded as their domain. Joe Northover explained how, when visiting country that is not his own, he calls out to his father and to the wind to send his spirit home to his own country. Another man described the ritual adopted when approaching a waterhole. He stressed that you must not drink from the *gnamma* hole without first asking permission from the spirits of the country. This should be done by speaking in the Noongar language, before throwing a stone or some sand into the water. If the water is clear then you can proceed. It is necessary to identify oneself in front of the *gnamma* hole, stating who you are and to which group and family you belong. Yet another man, when visiting a site on Noongar country, said he calls out to country and a wedgetail eagle there. Angus Wallam stated that when he visits Martup Pool (adjacent to the Albany Highway near the road to Woodanilling), he sings out to the country to let the spirits know that he is there visiting and to stop the *mumari* bothering him. I observed Joe Northover calling out to the spirits of the country at a place called Gibraltar Rock, near Collie. He threw sand in the air as we left in order to stop the spirits from following us. One senior Noongar man greeted the spirits at a proposed camping place to ensure a good night's sleep. Lomas Roberts reported that he conducts a ritual of introduction in relation to the ocean.

Greeting the country should involve the introduction of both babies and strangers. Joe Walley stated that when he was born, his uncle had rubbed mud on him and tossed him into the Murray River, so that the scent from Joe's body would reach the spirit being (in this case the Wagarl) that inhabited the river. The Wagarl would thus get his scent and know and recognise him in future as belonging to that area. Today, when a child is born belonging to Joe Northover's family, the infant is brought to the Collie River and ashes are rubbed on to its face from a tree that grows at the place. This tree was planted by Joe's grandmother. This is done to introduce the baby's spirit to the spirits of the place.

Adults who are strangers should also be introduced to the country. Glen Kelly instructed the author and a co-researcher to introduce themselves to the country. He lit a small fire and picked a branch with leaves off a nearby tree, and instructed that we do the same. He then brushed the branch against his body and placed it on the fire. He explained that the leaves have your body smell on them and then the smoke carries your smell to the country. This, he said, was a mark of respect and a way of saying 'hello' to the old people (the spirits of the ancestors) and of telling them why you are there. Provided your intentions are good, you will be safe. However, if your intentions are not good, you might suffer illness or misfortune. Glen explained that he sometimes leaves fish or tobacco, or pours water on the ground for the old people, as a sign of respect. At a site we had visited earlier in the day, he asked that we leave a pastry, one excess to our requirements, for the spirits of the country. This we did.

It appears to be common Noongar practice to perform a short ritual as acknowledgment of the spirits of the country. This normally involves taking a small quantity of sand from the edge of a creek, pool or lake in one's hand, and throwing it into the water. For example, Joe Northover stated that it was important to go down to the water's edge and throw a handful of sand into the water to let the spirits know that you were visiting and who you were. This should be done when a stranger first came into an area of Noongar country, and visits to other places in the area could then be undertaken in the knowledge that the spirits of the country would know and recognise you. This would also ensure a good night's sleep and one's general safety. Joe called the ritual of throwing sand into the water *dugabarnin*. He threw sand into the water, and called out to the spirit of the place in the Noongar language, in order to let the spirit know who we were and what we were doing on this trip around his country. This ritual was observed on a number of occasions during the research reported here. Another claimant, Angus Wallam, stated that before swimming in the river a person should throw a handful of sand in the water to the spirit inhabiting the water to let it know who you were and that you were there visiting. Angus said he had learnt this from the old people when he saw them do it. Other claimants provided similar accounts. One senior Noongar man told me that you should throw sand into the water before swimming in a pool, or before drinking from a rock hole or a pool. This was to let the spirits and (in the case of a pool) the Wagarl know that you were visiting. He said that during the Avon Descent boat race competitors did this as a sign of respect because the Noongar people had told them they should do so.

Noongar people believe that smoke can be used to discourage the spirits. One senior Noongar man explained that smoke was produced by burning a bush called *moorok*. Standing in the smoke, a person would be freed from any evil spirits. The ritual had been done in the past to reverse bad luck in a kangaroo hunt. Charlie Shaw stated that places were smoked on a regular basis to free them of bad spirits. Smoke was cited by one claimant to be particularly effective against *mumari* spirits, while children playing with lighted sticks will attract them so the practice is forbidden. Sitting near a smoky fire would protect a child from the powerful spirituality of an important Noongar place. Other claimants explained how smoking freed a person of a bad spirit and so helped to heal them, and said it was done at funerals to enable the spirit of the dead person to leave the grave site. Houses were also smoked to free them of a spirit after a death. However, this was not always regarded as a good thing, sincc thc spirits of loved ones were sometimes encouraged to stay. One claimant complained that White people had lit fires in the old homestead, 'Ellensbrook', at Margaret River, and so had driven out the spirits of her ancestors, which she now regarded as her loss. There was the memory of burning the camp of a deceased person in the past.

Some Noongar people believe they have a particular relationship with the natural world, and in particular with specific animals, birds and reptiles. I will return to a more detailed examination of this aspect of Noongar culture when I consider 'totemism' below. However, I here examine how Noongar people characterise interactions with the natural world as providing portents and signs of things which have happened but of which they have yet to be advised.

A senior Noongar man talked about the signals Noongars received from the land and animals. In his account, three animals were important: the frog, the willy wagtail (*jitijiti*) and the curlew (*wirlu*). The frog, which was associated with one side of his family, would appear when a member of that part of the family had died. The appearance of a willy wagtail or curlew, acting in a strange or particular manner, also meant that a relative had died. The same man gave accounts to illustrate the veracity of this belief. He stated that when people die, the activity of these animals serves to inform the spirits of other deceased people of the death. They assist, in some way, to help the return of the deceased person's spirit to his or her own country. This spirit is called *wiyarn* (see above). Other claimants identified the magpie as well as a small brown bird, the size of a sparrow, which appears only when there has been a death, called *kwirdling*, as death messengers. A bird called a *daran* was similarly identified for the Perth metropolitan region. Pink and grey cockatoos were cited as messenger birds, although in this case not always bringing news of a death.

Other portents from the natural world involve the falling of a branch from a tree, unexpectedly, which indicates that someone has died. This is called in Noongar *winitj*, which means that something untoward has happened. Similarly, a dog calling out in the middle of the day bodes no good, this being related to a narrative told of the Stirling Ranges.

Domestic and social customs

Food

A number of Noongar laws and customs relating to hunting, food and food preparation were collected during the research reported here. Some accounts provide details of customs and practices that are beyond the scope of this book to document. Consequently, the customs, as recorded, are set out in summary form in Table 10.4. Since the research on which this book is based did not focus specifically on issues of domestic production and consumption, it is likely that there remain numerous other customs and practices which have not been recorded.

Sharing

Sharing is a central tenet of Noongar thinking and is regarded as being particularly important within both the social and the extended family. A part of being together is that material resources, including food, are shared. A senior Noongar woman said, 'It's a help to be with one another because you get to share.' For one claimant it is regarded as not only a very Noongar characteristic, but an obligation. This view is echoed in the accounts of other claimants. For example, Lomas Roberts talked about the continuing Noongar tradition of distributing resources widely to many relations, and of being constantly available to assist people in need. He further explained that if these obligations are ignored, then there can be negative consequences. For those unable to attend family outings to such places as Bremer Bay or Cape Riche, it was expected that some of the bounty of the trip would be brought back to those who remained at home. Others characterised

Table 10.4: Some Noongar customs and practices relating to food

Food or plant	Custom
Christmas tree (*mujar*)	Prohibition on women picking flowers
Goanna	Prohibition on killing close to waterhole
Goanna, black	Killing will cause rain
Goanna, black	Prohibition on eating
Goanna, yellow	Correct way to carry, prepare and cook
Goanna	Correct way to gut
Kangaroo and other game	Treat with respect and take only sufficient for immediate needs
Lizard, Blue Tongue	Correct way to cook
Marron	Correct way to cook
Porcupine (echidna)	Correct way to cook
Porcupine (echidna)	Shows on death where to cut to extract intestine
Snake	Prohibition on cooking close to waterhole
Swan, black	Correct way to prepare and cook
Turtle, liver	Will cause pregnancy if eaten by a woman
Turtle, long neck	Correct way to cook in the ashes. Prohibition on use of steel implements
Turtle, long neck	Correct way to locate
Wallaby, brush	Unlucky to kill

sharing as a part of tradition ('the old way') and said that when you shot a kangaroo you were expected to share it with others and that this was a part of the rules. As one man put it, 'You can't say no.'

Names

Field data was collected relating to the use of Noongar customary naming practices. These can best be understood as being of two sorts: naming after a family member, including an ancestor, and a nickname. A nickname is a term which characterises the individual consistent with Noongar terminology and conceptualisation. Lomas Roberts explained how Noongar nicknames are used. His father's Noongar name was Jinjil, meaning 'good man'. His own Noongar name is Hibit, meaning 'good boy'. He said that his son, Geoffrey, also has a Noongar name. Another claimant said his Noongar name was Big Eagle, a name that was given to him by his parents in consideration of his personal characteristics. Other examples of Noongar names were Ilaran (meaning not recorded), Jitijiti (willy wagtail), Ningi ('not afraid, strong'), Walitj ('like an eagle'), Watj (emu), Numbert (perhaps 'numbat') and 'froggy', after a frog which is considered to be particularly important to the family. Others again stated that Noongar names were given to children, but the names were not provided.

A number of other claimants stated that it accorded with Noongar tradition to give a child the name of an mm, or fm and other family member in the second ascending generation. The practice appears to provide a means of honouring the elderly, consistent with Noongar practice, as well as providing for continuity of both the family unit and the culture over successive generations.

Learning

Continuity of Noongar tradition is accomplished, according to the views of many claimants, by the emphasis that is placed on the importance of learning and instruction from older members of the community. Grandparents are often cited as being the primary teachers, but parents also play an important role. So, for example, for one family traditional hunting practices were learnt from 'the old people' or from parents, uncles and aunts. Glen Kelly said that he had learnt about burning the country from his MF. There would appear to be an expectation that knowledge is passed on within the family. Bill Webb said that the 'family line' was 'tradition and law'. Joe Walley indicated that he would pass his knowledge on to his cousin's child, Richard Walley, as he has no children of his own. In some cases, a mother was cited as being particularly knowledgeable and as the person who provided much traditional knowledge. Parents are considered to have a duty to pass on information to their children, particularly with respect to how to keep themselves safe from harm in the bush. However, this should always be limited to information and cultural aspects which relate to country with which your family is affiliated, and not to other areas. Knowledge that has been handed down to you from your parents or grandparents will always be respected in Noongar thinking, because it is regarded as being true to Noongar tradition.

Based on these data, I make the following observations. Noongar social arrangements, particularly the close ties which exist within the extended family, provide ample opportunity for the transmission of traditional knowledge. The culture is one that is marked by a strong respect for the members of ascending generations, as I have already outlined. Consequently, opportunities for transmission are maximised through a culture that privileges the knowledge of seniors. The transmission I have here characterised is largely oral and is often learnt through practice. Those with whom I worked placed great value on Noongar teachings and knowledge and expressed the view that its continuance was of the utmost importance to all Noongar people.

Other customs

A number of additional customs, beliefs and practices were noted during the research. As these do not fit readily into one of the above categories, they are listed in Table 10.5.

Table 10.5: Miscellaneous Noongar customs, practices and beliefs

Effect or implication	Custom
Stop rain	Make smoke with a wet kangaroo skin
Make rain	Bleed a turtle into water
Avoid bad luck or ill-fortune (?)	Prohibition on camping in the same place twice
Men are leaders	Prohibition on women walking in front of men
Women are influential in Noongar dealings	Men should respect women
Respect for a person's fire or hearth	Prohibition on interfering with another person's fire; permission required to sit at another person's fire
Successful childbirth	Aunty should be present at birth
Cure for a stutter in a small boy	Place a small lizard on the boy's tongue
Avoid encounters with spirits	Prohibition on playing with fire after dark
Correct interpersonal skills	Prohibition on talking or looking too directly at a person
Protect trees	Prohibition on cutting trees unnecessarily
Respect for water and pools	Prohibition on unnecessary interference with water (especially for children)
Avoid encounters with *wutaji*	Prohibition on camping close to creeks
Protection of significant birds	Prohibition on killing swans and wedge-tailed eagles

In this section, I have set out some of the available data constituting a part of a large corpus of beliefs, practices and customs which characterise Noongar society. While some practices noted above were recorded from only one informant, many have multiple citations. It is not possible to provide a definitive view on the extent of these beliefs and practices, but it is most likely that the beliefs and practices outlined above would be shared by others within the Noongar community.

Noongar rules, laws and customs: conclusion

Essential and fundamental to much of the above discussion has been a belief that the natural world is replete with a variety of spirit beings. Some are named and have specific characteristics. Others are generic. There are also those that are understood to be the spirits of Noongar ancestors who have died over the years. Many of the customs I have described are ways by which humans can mediate between their own lived experiences and the spirit world. This provides a means to control or limit uncertainty in what otherwise is a highly unpredictable spiritual and physical environment. Noongar culture is strongly informed by a diverse set of beliefs in a pantheon of beings which comprise the spirit world. Customary action, framed by reference to rules, is required to manage the potentialities of this spiritual domain.

These beliefs and customs relate, in many instances, to Noongar country and to places within it that have a special significance as a result of their spiritual potentialities. These I have described as 'dangerous' places, a concept well understood in the literature on Aboriginal Australia (e.g. see Berndt 1969, pp. 8–9; Biernoff 1978). Any interaction with the spiritual actualities found in country which develops from physical use or occupation must be negotiated by recourse to special knowledge. This special knowledge is an attribute of older, experienced men and women who have affiliations with the area in question. For those who lack this knowledge there is continuing danger and jeopardy.

In my account I have shown how domestic activity is underpinned by customary behaviour, some of which relates to the spirit world while some is understood to represent more generally expected practice for Noongar people. I have, finally, set out some more general examples of Noongar customs that have come to my attention in the course of my fieldwork and data analysis.

Taken together, this corpus represents a substantial account. As practised and observed, these examples constitute a distinctive cultural milieu, which it is reasonable to characterise as a system of culturally specific rules that govern, or are ideally said to govern, action. In this, their observance and enactment are of particular importance, since I have attempted to choose as my examples those practices which appear to me to be current and enduring.

With respect to ritual practices, I have indicated those I have actually observed or that were observed by my co-researchers. However, in many cases I have only been told of their currency. It would not be likely, in the fieldwork described here, for me (or the other researchers) to have sufficient exposure to the culture over a long enough period of time to experience all of these practices firsthand. In short, just because a practice was not observed by the researchers does not indicate that it is not a part of contemporary Noongar practice.

Regarding cultural practices, I consider the following conclusions are reasonable. It seems to me likely that the various practices relating to the greeting of country are widespread, although the use of fire in this regard may be less so, for practical reasons. The use of fire (or smoke) in relation to spirits of the dead would appear to be a practice that is current. The use of Noongar names appears to be fairly widespread, but it is not universal. Many of the miscellaneous customs appear to be ideas about beliefs, rather than necessarily observable in practice. However, those who provided the information would appear to hold to the view that the practices ideally constitute Noongar customary practice.

Beliefs about spirits are particularly strong, as are concomitant beliefs about dangerous places, and the relationships with animals and what they may portend. Transmission of cultural knowledge by intergenerational exchanges remains a significant part of Noongar culture. Of course, not all Noongar people will share these beliefs and practices. There will be some who doubt aspects of traditional thinking and avoid observances. However, based on my exposure to the data collected, I am of the view that these beliefs and practices are widespread, have currency and constitute a substantial body of lore which reflects jural-like qualities. In conjunction with other aspects of customary belief and practice, these characterise Noongar culture.

Bases for spiritual beliefs

Fundamentals

Joe Northover understands the origins of all things to reside in a period that he identifies as *kura*, which he translated into English as 'a long time ago'. This was the period when all things were made or fashioned. It was a time before the present, when the world was more spiritual. Joe told me that he did not favour the use of the term 'Dreamtime' or 'Dreaming', since he regarded these (English) terms as recent expressions. Lomas Roberts provided the following account of the Noongar creative period:

> In the long past there was a spirit, *wiyarn*. The whole earth was rock and it was dark. *Wiyarn* came and he made it light and he made everything else, the trees and plants and everything. He gave it all to the Noongar to look after. Of all the things he gave them, the tree was the most important, for out of that he could make all he needed; fire for warmth and cooking, shelter, weapons and even his food came from the trees. Noongars were already in the country when it was dark.
>
> This was a story told by the old people.

Lomas said that the Noongar people had originally been blind, and the *wiyarn* had opened their eyes. *Wiyarn* also granted a particular animal to each group, the swan being given to Lomas's family.

Glen Kelly recounted how he had been told stories relating to the stars and creation by a man called Noel Nannup. Glen reported that during the *nyiting* or 'cold time' the great serpent or Wagarl was in command of everything, and he gave humans custodianship of the country. Joe Walley stated that it was the Wagarl that wrought creative acts, being responsible for bringing water to the land, which in turn brought life to the land and the people. A Noongar person's connection to the land brought connection to the spiritual beings associated with it. In most cases, however, claimants did not identify the creative period by any name, either Noongar or English, but situated their narratives within an indeterminate period that, while not solely of the present, cannot be comprehended as being entirely in the past either. Its past temporal component is characterised by the manifestation of extraordinary spirituality. As a contemporary spirituality, the force of its supernatural presence is very much considered to be a part of the here and now. Moreover, spirituality is ubiquitous and takes many forms, the world of spirits being just one, as I have already outlined in some detail above. Accounts that give credence to this proposition are a significant part of oral testimony.

Narratives

The research data and my own observations support the conclusion that Noongar people entertain an oral tradition that represents the spirituality of the past in the present. This often takes the form of narratives which relate to specific sites within the country. Narratives may also describe marking the journey of a supernatural being across the countryside leaving behind an extensive track marked by significant sites visited. These narratives provide both an explanatory text and an exegesis on the origins and ramifications of the spiritual entity associated with the places where they are believed to have travelled. I will consider these narratives in Chapter 13, when I consider Noongar spiritual relationships to country in detail.

Another set of narratives forms a part of a body of traditions that tell of generalised creative activities, some time in the past, but that generally do not relate to a specific place. A most significant supernatural creature in Noongar belief is the Wagarl, a being like a huge snake, associated with water, pools and waterways. It is sometimes said to be hairy or bearded. The name has become well known generally in Western Australia following widespread media coverage of the disputes over the development of the Wagarl site at the Old Brewery at the foot of Mt Eliza, Kings Park (Vinnicombe 1989). In the north of the application area, the snake is sometimes referred to as the Beemula or Bumara, which may be a Yamaji word. While the Wagarl is identified with many specific sites (usually springs, waterholes or pools in rivers), it is believed to be ubiquitous and pervasive in Noongar country and would appear to be a fundamental spiritual concept in Noongar belief. One claimant stated that he believed that the Wagarl was inextricably linked to all waterways on Noongar country. If these waterways are disturbed or interfered with, the Wagarl is disturbed, and could cause damage in return. The Wagarl is then a principal player in the ambiguous spiritual potency of the countryside, since for the most part the South West is well watered and the Wagarl is consequently widely distributed. Fred Pickett stated that the Wagarl is associated with waterholes and had made the *gnamma* holes when he emerged from the ground while pursuing a personal quest that remains incomplete to this day. He stated that the Wagarl is the keeper of Noongar law. If incorrect action takes place close to rock holes, or they are disturbed or destroyed, those associated with the sites will become sick and may even die. Fred commented that his son, Shane Pickett, includes images of the Wagarl in his art, a motif that is common in Noongar art generally. Similar beliefs about the widespread incidence of the Wagarl were expressed by other claimants, while others simply stated that the tracks of spiritual beings were found all over the South West.

Another spirit being recorded is called Wardan. Bill Webb stated that Wardan, who is characterised as an old man, is the protector of the spirit trails. The trails are related to the rivers and they follow their course to the sea. Bill recounted how the spirits of dead people travel down these trails and encounter guardians who have been placed there by Wardan. A man had built his house on Wardan's area and had experienced nothing but bad luck since he had done so.

Narratives are told which provide evidence of the existence of supernatural beings. They form a part of a discourse that places supernatural beings and the consequences of their potency within contemporary experience. Joe Northover called the Wagarl Ngarngungudditj Walgu. Joe related how he saw the Wagarl when he was a child about six years old. Bill Webb reported that his mother's father saw the Wagarl in Perth, in the Swan River at Pyrton. He accidentally stood on him and saw his head and hairy face. There were other incidents recounted of people who had seen the Wagarl. Encounters with the Wagarl are not to be welcomed, as they are potentially dangerous, and one claimant considered that such a meeting might result in your death.

Finally, there are narratives which relate events to the supernatural and thereby illustrate the metaphysical and spiritual dimension of everyday living. For example, some tell of encounters they or others have had with spirits of the country, some of which have already been discussed above. Others are what could be called 'moral tales'. One such story related to a greedy boy and his encounters with the spirit world. Another warned of the dangers of taking a stone or rock from a pool that typically was guarded by the Wagarl. There were narratives expressed as songs and a story that related to the winds. I recorded two examples of stories about the notorious Noongar character Alec (or Alex) Bibbarn. He is reputed, at some indeterminate time in the past, to have killed 99 people, Noongar and White, and, although he was eventually caught, he was able to escape (in most accounts from Rottnest Island prison) by shape changing, and then is believed to have disappeared. Several versions of these narratives have been collected and analysed by Baines (1987, pp. 240–9).

The research data developed for the preparation of this book are likely to represent only a small portion of the totality of the narratives available throughout the Noongar population. Consequently, what is set out here should be regarded as a sample of the total corpus of narratives, in their various forms, current at the time of writing.

Totemic beliefs

Noongar traditional belief accommodates a close relationship between a person and the natural world. In particular, this is manifested in a belief that a person has a relationship with a natural species, and that this relationship is passed on through descent to subsequent generations. While the English term 'totem' is sometimes used to identify this relationship, Noongar words are also used. These include *burungu* and *mulurp*.

A number of claimants provided the names of their totems, with some stating that they had more than one. Some made only general comments about having an association with the natural world, and did not name a particular species. Others stated that a person should not kill their own totem, and that they were required to protect it. A summary of these data is set out in Table 10.6.

Since not all claimants interviewed were asked whether they had a particular association with an animal or natural species, this list as set out in Table 10.6 should not be regarded as definitive. From the data available, however, the following tentative conclusions can be drawn. Birds are the most common totem (17 of the 44 identified species, or 39 per cent),[120] and animals and reptiles are next, with 11 and 10 (25 per cent and 23 per cent) respectively. The Wagarl is recorded in three instances (7 per cent), with insects, sea creatures and non-animate things

120 The emu is here counted as an animal.

Table 10.6: Noongar species associations

Species	Descent	Other attribute
Crow		
Crow	F	
Crow	m and mm	Exogamous
Crow, goanna, spear	F?	Must look after, gives special powers
Curlew, wagtail, frog, ant	mm?	Frog must not be disturbed
Currawong, bullfrog, kangaroo	m and MF; 'grandparents'	Must not kill
Dingo	m	Belongs to area
Dingo and crow	F and m	Exogamous?
Dolphin	'given'	Dolphins meet up to have corroborees
Eagle		Belongs to ego's region
Emu		Must not eat
Frog		Messenger
Frog	F	Linked to country
Frog	m	Must not touch
Frog	m	
Galah		
Galah	m	
Kangaroo		
Kangaroo, emu		
Kangaroo, *kwulyung* (unidentified)	m, F	
Kangaroo, Wagarl, three others	F and FF	
Racehorse goanna		
Red dog		
Small kangaroo	WF, F and FF	Treat with respect; must not kill
Swan	F	Must not kill
Swan	MF	Must not kill; must respect
Swan, curlew	F	Exogamous, linked to country; must not kill
Turtle		Result of incident
Turtle		Treat with respect, it is 'very special'
Wagarl		Belongs to Swan River
Wagarl, currawong		
Wedge-tailed eagle	m, F	

making up the rest at only one instance each (2.3 per cent each). In the 18 cases where derivation by descent was specified (and permitting some interpretation, shown by a question mark in Table 10.6), there is an almost equal allocation to matrifiliation and patrifiliation. Seven of the 18 cases (39 per cent) are cited as derived from the father and 44 per cent from the mother, while one of these is presumptively patrilineal, since inheritance is cited as being through MF. Some 17 per cent (three cases) were cited as being acquired from both mother and father. Of the 19 cases where comment was made, six totems were described specifically as belonging to an area of country. There is a lack of any fundamental distinction between crow and white cockatoo, although crow figures as a totem in five cases. The idea that totemic exogamy was a rule was present in only three cases of the 19 where comment was provided (16 per cent).

Totemic beliefs are an important part of contemporary Noongar beliefs. While the distinction Bates drew between two moieties (crow and white cockatoo) appears to be absent, other aspects of the beliefs she described remain. There would appear to be a mixture, in the contemporary account, of what might be called personal totems, the acquisition of which may develop from a number of different circumstances and those acquired by descent, some of which attach to country. Some again relate to the supernatural Wagarl, as well as to an area of country. Totems gained through inheritance are divided almost equally by reference to matri- and patri-filiation. I am not in a position to state for certain whether this reflects a geographic pattern, as Bates considered it did, but my general impression is that it does not. In my discussion of Bates's analyses of totems (see Chapter 5), I conclude that she sought to characterise totemic beliefs as constituting a more orderly system than her earlier ethnography supports. I therefore conclude that, while aspects of totemic belief are absent from the contemporary account, I do not see the totemic beliefs now as merely a chaotic shadow of what was once a neat and ordered set of beliefs. Rather, totemic belief reflects a complex and diverse set of relationships that Noongar people claim exist between themselves and the natural world. This is consistent with at least some of the ethnographic data which was reported by Bates at the turn of the last century. This does not mean that totemic beliefs have not changed. The moiety system and its totemic attachments are little in evidence, and consequently totemic exogamy, while not absent, has perhaps been replaced by a reckoning whereby close family are prohibited marriage partners, a customary rule I have already discussed above. Despite these changes, totemic affiliations continue to constitute a part of contemporary Noongar spiritual belief.

Noongar doctors, or clever men, and revenge activity

There exists within the Noongar community a belief that there are those who have supernatural powers, which enable them to exercise control over the spirit world, heal sickness, foresee events and understand phenomena which may be beyond the ken of ordinary people. The term commonly used for these people is *mubarn*, which is also understood to be a word used by groups living to the north and east of Noongar country. This term appears to have wide currency now and may have replaced the Noongar terms *bulya* and *mulgarradock*, which I noted above as having been recorded by earlier writers.

The term *mubarn* may be used to refer to supernatural power exercised by a person, as well as of the person themselves. *Mubarn* is thus both a spiritual quality and the person who exhibits or exercises this quality. As I outline below, *mubarn* deal with powerful forces, some of which are associated with death and the perceived consequences of death. There is a belief that death may be the result of some intention on the part of another (or others), and that deliberate vengeful action may be the cause of death. Those who effect this mortal destruction are known as *jinagabi*, or 'featherfoots', since they are believed to possess magical powers that render them invisible at times, by the wearing of feather slippers that conceal their footprints. A *jinagabi* may then be said to have a 'powerful *mubarn*', while a Noongar doctor, who is a possessor of a powerful *mubarn* and thus is so named, is needed for protection against the *jinagabi* who bring death. The concepts of the *jinagabi* and the *mubarn* are best discussed together, as they constitute a body of beliefs that relate to human mediation in the spirit world when its forces are directed to human destruction.

In Noongar belief, human intervention in the spirit world as it relates to matters of mortal import is highly sensitive. Because discussion of the *jinagabi* potentially is believed to summon them, they constitute a topic that it is best not to raise in conversation. Moreover, since *jinagabi* and the corresponding power of *mubarn* are believed to be responsible for death or serious illness initiated by a person, discussion without accusation is near impossible. A ready solution is supplied in silence. It seems likely to me that beliefs about *mubarn* and *jinagabi* may be more widespread than the data would suggest.

Mubarn are believed to have special powers, including an ability to control spirits. They have the power to shape change (an ability also exercised by Alex Bibbarn, see page 130). One claimant told a story about how a man believed he had shot an emu, but he later learnt that it was in fact a *mubarn* in the form of an emu.

A *mubarn* is able to cure illness, and Harry Thorne told of two instances where he had observed these cures himself.

A number of eminent *mubarn* are remembered. There is perhaps an implication in these recollections, on the part of at least some claimants, that *mubarn* are no longer found in the Noongar population and are now sought from communities to the north and east. However, other claimants stated that some people had special powers, which could be used for good or bad, to make you sick or make you better. Another indicated that the power of a *mubarn* came from the *mumari*, who had to choose you for the role. Another considered that it was 'really old men' who were likely to have the *mubarn* power and that drinking alcohol destroyed these powers. There was also a report of a *mubarn* coming to Moora to help a family. These accounts would indicate that, for some Noongar people at least, there continue to be Noongar *mubarn*. All accounts have in common a belief in the existence of such people and their extraordinary powers.

Jinagabi are commissioned by the aggrieved relatives of a deceased person to exact revenge for a death. It may be 'payback' (revenge) for a car accident, a rape, taking a woman or doing harm to someone's family. One claimant explained the process as follows. You obtain a photograph of the person to be killed and provide it to an intermediary, who knows a *jinagabi* and instructs him accordingly, showing him the photograph. Another claimant stated that the family knew who were *jinagabi* and they could be commissioned directly if necessary. A *jinagabi* travels without leaving a trace, although it may be seen at times. A *jinagabi* has emu feathers on his feet and leaves no tracks, but a feather may remain to show where he has been. You cannot escape a *jinagabi* if they seek you. A *jinagabi* would appear to be the same as a 'splinter man'. A splinter man is able to pierce your jugular vein with a sharp splinter of bone. This does not leave a scar. Martha Borinelli told of a man whom the doctors said had died from a heart attack, but in fact he had been killed by *jinagabi* in the place of his brother, who could not be found. A man in Toodyay was reported to have simply disappeared, and it was believed he had been taken by a *jinagabi*.

According to one claimant, the belief in *jinagabi* is as strong today as it ever was and it is a part of traditional Noongar culture. They may be encountered while going about their deadly business. Several stories relating these meetings were collected. Typically, these did not result in any ill-effects for the witnesses because they were not the object of the attack. However, these encounters can cause great consternation. In these encounters, *jinagabi* exhibit spiritual characteristics, and in one case the *jinagabi* were recognised by their extremely strong smell. One claimant told how a *jinagabi* had been reported in Moora just a few days before she was interviewed.

Protection against *jinagabi* can be secured by obtaining protection from a *mubarn*, usually from areas to the north of Noongar country, like Wiluna or Jigalong. Harry Thorne told how a close family member had been cured by a *mubarn* from an illness that had been caused by those who sought to exact revenge on him for his prowess in football. Self-protection may be afforded by having a strong spirit. If *jinagabi* are known to be in your area, it is best to leave food for them.

The early accounts of Noongar culture included reference to clever men, which I have reviewed briefly above. They included the special abilities of clever men to shape change, cure illness and have power over the spiritual world in general. While the Noongar terms for clever man appear to have been replaced by a neighbouring term, *mubarn*, the belief in the existence of Noongar doctors continues to inform contemporary Noongar cultural practice.

The early accounts contained references to revenge attacks, representing action taken in response to a death or other consequence which may have been believed to have been occasioned by deliberate human action. It would appear to me that the accounts of the *jinagabi* presented here show substantial parallels with these revenge attacks. Following European settlement and the imposition of White Australian law, physical revenge attacks were discouraged and rendered illegal, so by Bates's time the practice had stopped. What had not ended, however, as she noted, was that revenge was still expected (see Bates 1985, pp. 199–200). A belief in a system of revenge exacted by beings outside and beyond the control of the European Australian criminal justice system now operates to effect the same outcomes as were wrought by physical revenge attacks. The beliefs, relating to *jinagabi* and as set out above, reflect those traditional Noongar laws and customs, but rendered into metaphysical form, so as to be beyond the reach of White Australians.

Funerals and burial practices

Funerals are important ritual events for Noongar people. There is an expectation that members of the extended family will all attend, and failure to do so is likely to attract censure. Where there have been family disputes, these should be set aside for the funeral of a family member. Male relatives are expected to act as pallbearers. Friends of the deceased are expected to attend. From the accounts provided to me, Noongar funerals are most usually conducted as Christian rituals, often utilising a Noongar pastor. However, despite the form and content of the ritual, a number of observations which were made in the course of the research reported here indicate that the substance of many aspects of the ritual of dealing with the dead remain fundamentally grounded in Noongar culture. From the evidence available to me, these would appear to extend back beyond the time of sovereignty.

While traditional funereal practices are no longer followed, their memory remains important. A number of claimants explained how funerals were conducted in the past, and two Noongar women could recall traditional funerals and had attended them. Many comments were collected about the correct way to bury the dead, in relation to the orientation of the head and feet, aspects of customary practice of which there are many examples in the early literature which I have reviewed. I will not expand on the details of these accounts, since they belong to a memory of a tradition. What has contemporary relevance is that the recollection remains an important part of the characterisation of Noongar culture.

Several practices that are observed in relation to funerals would appear to have their origin in traditional (that is, pre-sovereignty) custom. Comment was made on numerous occasions that burial in your own country was important and was preferred, as this is where a person's spirit belonged. Fred Pickett added that it was important to be buried where your family was, so that everyone was kept together. Another custom is a requirement that the body be not buried too soon after death. This is to give the spirit time to settle down before it begins its journey or new life and to allow the necessary arrangements to be made and for the many people attending the funeral to make their travel plans. Barbara Stammner-Corbett said that after death the spirit of a person journeyed to Karnet, which is 'over the ocean'; she had been told this by her grandfather and other old people. Lynette Knapp stated that her father had taught her that the spirit of the dead person went 'beyond the sun'.

There is a belief that after a death the area where the deceased was living should be vacated and later smoked. There is a belief that the name of the dead should not be used for several years after their death. It was thought unwise to go hunting too soon after a death. I was told that placing a heavy granite slab on the grave was wrong, since this prevented the free escape of the spirit from the body after death. I noted the use of grave goods, being items that were dear to the deceased. For an adult man, these included shotgun cartridges (he had been a mighty hunter) and, rather poignantly, soft toys on the grave of a child. I was told of similar practices that included placing a pannikin on a tree close to the grave and the burial of the deceased's hat and a bottle of muscat in the grave. When a family member dies, Joe Northover takes an item of clothing or other piece of personal property and places it in a special area, where he has scarred trees to mark the place and show the importance of the area to others, who should not enter without his permission. Graves are often decorated with sea shells and plastic flowers, and are quite distinctive from the other graves in a cemetery.

Bill Webb recounted how he was instructed by an older Noongar man in how to perform a reburial according to traditional practice of a Noongar skeleton, found in the Busselton region. The apparent revival of traditional Noongar burial practices indicates that the memory and knowledge of the ritual are not lost.

I have set out above material derived from the early accounts reflecting traditional Noongar burial practices. Elements of these practices remain. Grave goods are a feature of Noongar burials, as they were, in all probability, prior to sovereignty. There is one instance of the scarring of trees, which I have seen, that is a part of contemporary funereal practice, as it was in the past. Finally, and more generally, current practice reflects a consistent belief in the importance of ensuring that the passage of the departed spirit is facilitated through correct procedures, delaying burial for an adequate period and avoiding physical impediments like marble slabs on the grave top.

Conclusion

In this chapter I have set out some of the more important aspects of Noongar culture, as it has been recorded during the research reported here. In bringing these observations together, several conclusions can be drawn. First, it would appear to me that there is a singular and clearly identifiable Noongar culture, typified by customary action, belief and the adherence to a set of principles that are regarded as rules or laws. These develop from a belief in an archetypical Noongar culture, handed down from generation to generation. This is the essential quality of its considered reality as tradition. It is in its exercise, continued transmission and practice an embodiment of a fundamentally Noongar way of living, acting and believing. In Table 10.7 I have identified the various rules, or sets of rules, where I have discussed them above. This does not, of course, constitute all customary Noongar rules but only those identified in this chapter.

The characteristics of this culture have components which are evident in the accounts of the early settlers, as well as in the work of Bates at the beginning of the last century. These elements of Noongar culture are identified in Table 10.8, along with the page in this chapter where comment is made on these correspondences. In column 2 some relevant references in the early literature, along with page numbers in the book where such references may be found.

It is reasonable to conclude that many aspects of this culture are based upon or derive directly from Noongar culture as it was prior to sovereignty. In relation to

Table 10.7: Noongar rules discussed in Chapter 10

Rules relating to managing spirits of the dead	pp. 115–117; 121 and 126
Rules relating to the avoidance of spirit places	pp. 118, Table 10.3
Rules relating to the interference with dangerous places	pp. 118–119, 126–127
Rules relating to greeting country	pp. 119ff
Rules relating to the introduction of stranger to country	pp. 120ff
Rules relating to relationships	pp. 112–113ff
Rules relating to marriage	pp. 114–115ff
Rules relating to disposal of the dead	pp. 135ff
Rules relating to clever men and others	pp. 132ff
Rules relating to the domestic and social spheres	pp. 122–125
Rules relating to a totem	pp. 130–132, Table 10.6

kinship and social organisation, I have shown how elements of these systems are traceable to the accounts provided by early writers.

I have described how Noongar culture is informed by a belief in the diverse and often complex world of the spirits, and how people must work to mediate between this world and their own. Places in the countryside are regarded as spiritually dangerous, and require special treatment or qualifications on the part of those who seek to approach them. Similarly, rules and laws which relate to such things as naming and sharing also have some evidence for their practice in the early accounts I have reviewed above. Finally, I have shown that spiritual beliefs in the Dreaming, the recounting of narratives, totemic beliefs, and rituals and practices relating to death are practices which were reported by early observers.

In these accounts, it has not been my view that there have been no changes in Noongar culture. I have pointed out that some important elements would appear to have been lost, consistent with the history which is well known to have been the experience of all Noongar people. For example, the moiety system and its named totemic counterparts would appear mostly to have been lost. In writing of ritual, I have only discussed funereal rites, omitting altogether from my account any discussion of the initiation of youths, which was recorded in detail by Bates. Such rituals would now appear to be no longer practised, along with other ritual celebrations, which I identified above as 'corroborees'.

Notwithstanding these omissions, it is my view that Noongar culture remains an identifiable and discrete system of beliefs and rules, with its own integrity.

Table 10.8: Noongar customary beliefs and practices discussed in Chapter 10 and references to early literature

Custom, belief or practice	References	In Chapter 10
Kinship classification	Bates 1985, pp. 78–9, 81, 84	pp. 111ff
Social organisation	For example, Bates 1985, pp. 74–8; see also pp. 64ff	pp. 113ff
Marriage rules	Bates 1985, pp. 74–8; see also pp. 64ff	p. 114ff
Totemism	Bates 1985, pp. 191–202; Stormon 1977, p. 136; Hassell 1975, p. 32; Roth 1902, p. 53	pp. 130ff
Clever men	Bates 1985, pp. 227–33, 237; Stormon 1977, pp. 170–2; Nind 1979, pp. 42–4; Armstrong 1979, p.189; Barker 1992, p. 290; Hammond 1933, pp. 58–9; Millett 1872, p. 79	pp. 132ff
Disposal of the dead	Bates 1985, pp. 298–303; see also pp. 75ff	pp. 135ff
The spirit world and its management	Bates 1985, pp. 219–21; see also pp. 73, 125	pp. 115ff
Naming	Armitage 1836, p. 204	p. 123
Sharing	Millett 1872, p. 74	p. 122
Dreaming	Bates 1985, p. 51; Bates 1992, pp. 95–147	pp. 127ff
The telling of narratives[121]	Bates 1985, pp. 120, 133–4, 225–7; Moore 1884a, pp. 387–8; Barker 1992, pp. 289, 308, 361; Hassell 1934–35; Terry 1994	pp. 128ff

The materials provided in this discussion probably account for a small portion of the data which is potentially available, were the time and resources available to conduct a more detailed study. What is presented here provides an indication of the breadth of the culture and its complexity. The material collected demonstrates that Noongar people continue to subscribe to a distinctive culture, which is both a spiritual and a practical reference which frames action, interaction and beliefs.

121 References cited indicate that the practice of telling narratives was noted by early observers. This does not imply that the narratives themselves, as recorded by early observers, have been recorded in the research reported here. Narratives and the early literature are discussed further in Chapter 13, in the section titled 'Narrative traditions'.

Chapter 11

RIGHTS TO LAND

Introduction

Noongar people believe that individuals are the owners of areas of country. That which is owned is a right, or most usually a set of rights. Rights to country are gained by reference to a series of legitimating normative referents that are generally accepted within the Noongar community. The exercise of rights to country, or the recognition of the potential to exercise these rights, is often signalled by the use of a possessive phrase. Thus Noongar people will state 'that's his country', or make comment that an area 'belongs to' a particular family. People will commonly refer to a place as 'mine' or say 'that's my family's country'. In the use of these proprietorial terms there is a clear intention reflecting general Noongar understandings that rights to places and areas are the prerogative of individuals and groups of individuals who can therefore be said to be the owners of these places according to Noongar customary law. Later in this chapter I will examine in detail what I understand to be the corporate nature of land ownership and the social unit, whose members can together be understood to constitute the land-owning body.

In my opinion there is a normative system by which ownership of Noongar land is determined and that relies on rules which make reference to discrete principles. Given first that an individual is a Noongar person, solely by birth or adoption, rights to country may be claimed by descent or place of birth, or, in some cases, through an affinal relationship. Residency and knowledge are important attributes of realising and asserting rights to country, but in themselves do not constitute a customary ground for claiming ownership. These different pathways cannot provide for a ranking of rights to country into primary, secondary and so forth, as has been suggested for other areas of Aboriginal Australia (see Peterson, Keen and Sansom 1977; Peterson and Long

1986, p. 62).[122] This is because rights to country, while potentially realisable by reference to one or two or all of the principles noted here, are in their exercise a matter of negotiation and assertion. Thus a person who has, for example, a claim to an area of country though his father and father's father, but remains ignorant of that country (perhaps in relation to its spiritual potentialities), cannot exercise much authority in any discussion or decision that is made with respect to it. Similarly, a man or woman, however knowledgeable, who chooses to remain silent at meetings or who does not attend these meetings cannot exercise much influence in any outcome relating to their land. A second example may also be instructive. A child, no matter how strong their claim to be affiliated to an area of country, will remain only in potential exercise of their rights to country until they have reached an age of maturity that is recognised by others. However, a child will still be recognised as an owner of the country, while it is understood that they are as yet too young to either exercise their rights or discharge those duties that develop from them. While rights to country are potential, realisation is a matter of social process, reflective of time, circumstances and personalities and not of absolute ranking.

Rights to country are not exclusive. This means that a number of individuals may share rights to the same area of country. In the dealings which may eventuate over any issue which demands the exercise of rights to country, individuals may appeal to different legitimating referents in support of their claims to country. In these political exchanges (that is, exchanges which relate to an attempt to acquire power or resources), different skills, negotiations and alliances may be called into play. As in all areas of human interaction, some fare better in this process than others. Interpersonal relationships, and personal abilities and attributes, as well as personal inclination, may determine or influence the outcome. However, in matters relating to land, all claims to the exercise of a right to country are underpinned by reference to a Noongar system of laws which relate to rights to land. Claims or assertions which are not so underpinned would not be accepted by other members of the Noongar community and would be summarily dismissed.

The exercise of rights to country are consistent with the Noongar social structure, which I outlined in Chapter 10, whereby authority rests with certain

122 Peterson and Long (1986) indicate that rights may be ranked but do not imply that they form a simple dyadic of primary and secondary and that there is an interdependency between, for example, patri- and matri-filiates with respect to ritual activity as it relates to the estate of the former (p. 62).

individuals who are recognised by other Noongar people as having the right, the ability and the qualifications to exercise authority. I noted that those with these accomplishments (and they include the attaining of a certain age) are often referred to as 'elders'. In relation to land, assertions of rights to country require definitive reference to a normative system for the gaining of recognition of rights to defined areas of country. However, this process occurs within the Noongar social structure, which is also hierarchical. By reference to these rules which define rights to country, some people are able to negotiate for more, and some for less, authority in relation to the matter at hand, depending upon their authority as it is recognised by others.

The areas over which rights are asserted are of two different sorts, in principle, although these are not always distinguished. Noongar people often identify an area or a place to which they consider themselves to be particularly attached. This attachment, legitimated by reference to one or more of the rules which regulate attribution of rights to land, is often expressed in terms of a sentiment, emotion or spiritual bond to the place or area. It is special in that it affects the individual deeply in an emotional sense. The area is called by a number of terms, including 'home', 'home area', 'main area', 'main place', 'special area', 'heart country', 'heart place' and 'heart land'. Home area (as I will call it) is usually a named place, and its environs are characterised by reference to a single name and comprise what can be considered geographically as a discrete area, like a small town, suburb, mission or camp. The home area is situated within a larger area, variously called 'home country', 'run', 'family run', 'country', 'main country' or 'area'.

The use of the term 'run' was noted by Bates (Bates 1992, p. 23; White 1985, pp. 50–1), as well as by other researchers (Baines 1987, pp. 61, 194–5; Toussaint 1987, pp. 81–2; Hodson 1989, p. 99; Birdsall 1990, p. 182). It evidently became incorporated into Neo-Nyungar at some stage prior to the end of the nineteenth century. It is a term that has several meanings, according to the *Macquarie dictionary*, including a 'large area of grazing land; a rural property' and '*obsolete* the area through which an Aboriginal tribe habitually moved hunting and gathering'. The *Oxford English dictionary* gives a date of 1826 for the first meaning.[123] The use of a term that is taken from the colonial European proprietorial vocabulary is significant. A 'run' as a grazing property was (and, in some areas of northern Australia, continues to be) a significant area of land, over which an individual or family has grazing, water and access rights. Similarly, the Noongar 'run' is understood to be

123 The *Australian national dictionary* gives an example dating from 1804.

a property over which the owner exercises a range of rights, including the right of exclusion. Noongar people, so it appears to me, incorporated this term 'run' into their vocabulary to express the concept of an area over which a person (or family) could, by traditional right, exercise proprietary rights.

The run, or one of the equivalent terms noted above, may also be used to describe an area through which a person or his or her immediate forebears habitually travelled, usually in search of work. Such a use generally, though not always, indicates that the person has a special as well as a proprietorial interest in the area so defined. The meaning of the term 'run' must therefore be understood in its context, since it may be used in one of two senses. Home area and run are not always distinguished, and in cases where the run is quite small it may not be considered different from the home area. However, typically a run will comprise several named locations (towns, missions, significant natural features and so on), forming a geographic region or area, which can be delineated by reference to its peripheral named points as locations on a map or in the lived travel experiences of the listener.

A person's rights, subject to seniority and command of requisite knowledge, are exercised across the run and are not limited to the home area. However, a person's rights to his or her home area are underscored in their exercise by the sentiment which the home area evokes. This does not mean that an individual commands a superior right to a home area as opposed to the run, or that those who share rights to a run that includes another person's home area must defer to the person whose home area it is. However, where a person has a home area within a run that is subject to the exercise of rights by others, it would be a requirement that that person be included in any decisions about the run. I will consider the exercise of these rights and the body that exercises them later in this chapter.

In this chapter I examine data collected during the research reported here and the bases upon which Noongar people claim attachment to country. In doing this I build on these preliminary concepts, including the notion of the home area and the run. I examine how rights in country are held by groups of people, rather than by individuals. In the following chapter, which is an extension of this one, I examine how areas are understood to be bounded. I then look at permission and the granting and withholding of access, as well as at other rights and duties exercised by Noongar land-owners.

How rights to country are asserted and legitimated

I stated above that rights to country are claimed by one or more of three means. Table 11.1 sets out details of the home area and runs of those interviewed during the research reported here. These data are set against the individual's place of birth, the country affiliation of their matri- and patrikin, as well as their place of residence and claimed knowledge over their life, where these are known. The data represents what those interviewed explained to be their relationship to country and is not an account constructed from the archival or historical record.

There are a number of qualifications that need to be made with respect to these data and their presentation in Table 11.1. First, the details that have been summarised are often complex. In rendering them into a summary form, some of this detail inevitably has been lost. Claiming affiliation to country is a social process that occurs within a discourse. Tabulated summaries of such a discussion may provide a good overview, but will mask complexities and diversity. So, for example, the table does not show the detail of filiation at levels beyond ego's parents. Second, some interviews were conducted with more than one person. In these cases I have attempted to provide details for only one person interviewed, generally the most senior. Third, the data on the home area and run has been reduced for convenience and should not be understood to be a definitive statement as to the total geographic extent of a single individual's rights to country.

Ancestral ties to country

Noongar claimants recognise that descent is an essential requirement for the acquisition of a Noongar identity. I have set this principle out in Chapter 9. With respect to rights in country, descent is also cited as an operative principle. Many claimants referred to their ancestral ties to country. For example, Joe Walley stated that to 'come from' an area means that you have a traditional connection to that place, through descent; that is, either matri- or patrikin were affiliated to the same area. Another claimant reported that her country had been her mother's country, and saw this as providing support for her claim; another claimant made a similar point. Verna Ugle reported that her mm country was Pumphries Bridge, an area she also claimed. There are a number of other examples where mother's country is cited as being ego's country. Claimants also claimed their father's country on numerous occasions. Mal Ryder stated that his country was inherited from both his mother and father. Filiation in this system is then reckoned through either matri- or patrikin and can be called cognatic.

Table 11.1: Summary of country affiliations of some claimants

	Birth	Patrikin	Matrikin	Residence / lived at	Home / main country	Run / country	Other
1	Wagin		Narrogin, Pingelly, Beverely	Narrogin	Narrogin, Drandra, Pumphrey's Bridge	Pingelly towards Pinjarra; towards Busselton; towards Kellerberrin and Merredin	
2	Beverley	Northam	Brookton, Beverley	Shackleton, Kwolin, Wyalkatchem	Mt Stirling, Bruce Rock, Shackleton, Kwolin	Bruce Rock, Shackleton, Kwolin	Wyalkatchem; but not his country
3	Badjaling	Success Hill, Perth	Brookton	Quairading	Quairading, Badjaling	Quairading, Badjaling	
4		York, Brookton		Quairading	York		
5	Nr Narrogin	Bridgetown	Pumphries Bridge	Pinjarra, Bridgetown, Busselton, Narrogin	Pumphries Bridge, Wandering	Pinjarra, Bridgetown, Busselton, Narrogin	
6	Shackleton			Shackleton	Shackelton	Shackleton, short of Kellerberrin; Bruce Rock	
7	Badjaling	Denmark; Walpole	Katanning	Badjaling, Quairaing, Toodyay road	Badjaling	Midland, Toodyay, York, Brookton, Badjaling, Quairading (Ballardong)	
8	Pingelly	Beverely, Brookton, Quairading	Perth, Pingelly	Brookton, Wickepin, Narrogin, Harris-Smith, Kulin and Lake Grace(?)	Kulin	Brookton, Wickepin, Narrogin, Harris-Smith, Kulin and Lake Grace	
9	Pingelly	Perth, Williams		Bruce Rock, Merredin, Marvel Loch			
10	Djuring (Kellerberrin)	Beverley	Brookton, York	Kellerberrin	Badjaling; Kellerberrin	Badjaling, Kellerberrin	
11	Quairading	Mogumber, Dangin		York, Darling Ranges, Wundowie, Northam	York	York, Darling Ranges, Northam	

continued

	Birth	Patrikin	Matrikin	Residence / lived at	Home / main country	Run / country	Other
12	Gnowangerup	Ravensthorpe, Jerramungup, Bremmer Bay		Needilup, Capr Riche	Jerramungup, Bremmer Bay, Ravensthorpe	Albany, Kendenup, Gnowangerup, Rabvensthorpe	
13			Kulin, Wickepin, Dumbelyung	Kulin	Kulin		
14	Warricup station			Bremmer Bay, Cape Riche, Jerramungup, Fitzgerald	Albany, Stirling Ranges	Stirling Ranges to Israelite Bay, Gnwangerup	
15		Albany		Jerramungup	Jerramungup–Borden	Stirling Ranges, Jerramungup, Bremmer Bay	
16	Norngeri Bridge, nr Djuring	York		Djuring, Kellerberin	Kellerberrin, Djuring	Kellerberrin, Djuring	
17	Badgebup, Nyabing, Rock Well			Badgebup, Nyabing, Rock Well	Badgebup, Nyabing, Rock Well	Katanning, Badgebup, Rock Well, Nyabing	
18			Cataby, Bull Frog Well, Mingenew, Gingin	New Norcia, Moora, Cataby, Wedge Island	Wedge Island	Cataby, Wedge Island, Jurien Bay	
19	Mogumber	Bremer Bay, New Norcia		New Norcia, Moora, Mogumber area	New Norcia	New Norcia, Wyening, Mogumber, Watheroo, Toodyay to Northam	
20			New Norcia	Miling, Walebing (Moora), Mogumber, New Norcia	Walebing, New Norcia, Moora, Cataby	Walebing, New Norcia, Moora, Cataby	

	Birth	Patrikin	Matrikin	Residence / lived at	Home / main country	Run / country	Other
21	Moora		Mogumber, New Norcia		Moora	Moora, Dallwallinu, Three Springs, Carnamah	
22	Mulla Downs (Yamaji)		Dandaragan, Moora	Gnowangerup/ Borden	Dandaragan, Moora	Dandaragan, Moora	Connection through husband with Gnowangerup area
23	York	Northam, New Norcia		Northam reserve	Northam, York	Northam, York	
24		New Norcia		New Norcia	New Norcia	New Norcia area	
25		Perth, Mogumber		Mogumber, Moora	Mogumber, Moora		
26	Moora			New Norcia, Perth	New Norcia		
27	New Norcia	New Norcia		new Norcia, Three Springs, Coorow, Carnamah	New Norcia	Coolimba, Cliff Head, Eneabba, Coorow, Mingenew, New Norcia	
28	Walebing (Moora area)	Moora area		Moora	Moora area	Moora area	
29		Northam	Pinjarra	Northam	Northam	Northam area	Also Pinjarra
30			Busselton		Busselton	Busselton, Vasse	
31	Perth	Bunbury	Northam	Busselton, Bunbury, south west coastal areas	Wardandi country	Wardandi country	
32			Busselton, Margaret River		Busselton, Margaret River	Capel River, Busselton, Margaret River	
33			Mandurah, Pinjarra, Busselton,	Bullfinch			

continued

	Birth	Patrikin	Matrikin	Residence / lived at	Home / main country	Run / country	Other
34	Busselton	Manjimup		Perth, Busselton	Busselton	Busselton, Margaret River areas	
35	Manjimup		Manjimup–west coast, Ludlow, Pemberton	Pemberton, Manjimup, Perth	Pemberton	Ludlow, Pemberton, Northcliffe, Manjimup, Bridgetown, Augusta, Windy Harbour	
36		Ludlow, Bunbury		Ludlow, Bussleton, Augusta, Manjimup, Collie, Donnybrook, Bunbury	Pemberton	Pemberton, Ludlow	
37	Picton Junction		Augusta, Busselton	Busselton	Busselton, Margaret River, coastal area	Busselton–Margaret River and coastal areas, north 'toward' Bunbury, south 'toward' Augusta	
38	Pinjarra	Busselton, Walebing	Darkan	Pinjarra, Mandurah	Mandurah	Busselton, New Norcia, Mandurah, Pinjarra, Williams, Narrogin	
39	Walebing	Pert, New Norcia, Moora	Perth	Perth, Upper Swan	Perth	Perth metropolitan, Upper Swan	
40	Pinjarra	Pinjarra	Busselton	Pinjarra, Mandurah	Pinjarra, Mandurah	Pinjarra to Medina, south of Canning River, Preeton River, Boddington, Brusnwick Junction, Harvey, Waroona to Armidale	
41	Brookton	Brookton		Perth, Brookton, Beverley	Brookton, Beverley	Brookton, Beverley, and beyond?	

	Birth	Patrikin	Matrikin	Residence / lived at	Home / main country	Run / country	Other
42	Perth	Esperance, Guildford		Perth, Upper Swan, Carnarvon, Bruce Rock, eastern Wheatbelt	Hopetown, Esperance	Hopetown, Esperance	
43	More River	Wagin		Carrolup, Wagin	Wagin, Carrolup	Wagin, Beafort and Arthur rivers (upper), Norring Lake	Wife's country Busselton
44		Collie, Wagin, Cosmo Newberry	Collie, Quairading	Collie	Collie	Darkan, Bunbury, Capel River, Collie	
45	Wagin			Wagin, Harvey	Harvey	Harvey	
46	Northam	Northam	Mandurah, Rockingham Pinjarra, Capel	Northam, Perth	Mandurah, Pinjarra, Rockingham	Capel to Rockingham to Collie	
47	Josbury (Wiiliams)	Dwarda, Boddington, Narrogin, Quindanning, Williams	Wandering, Shakleton, Bruce Rock, Kellerberin	Wandering area, Williams, Bannister	Josbury, Wandering	Boddington, Wandering, Pumphries Bridge, Narrogin, Williams	Multiple connections through matri- and patrikin listed
48	Moore River	York	Gingin	Walebing, Perth			
49	Quairading	York	York	York, Quairading to Kwolyn	Yoting, Quairading	York to Kwolyn	
50	Toodyay	Yamaji	Busselton, Moore River	Perth (Bassendene)	Perth metropolitan; Busselton		Wife's country is Perth
51		Perth, Kings Park, Cannington			Perth metropolitan area		
52	Kellerberin, Bruce Rock	Perth, Pinjarra, Kings Park	Kellerberin		Perth		

Table 11.2 provides a summary of the data set out in Table 11.1, showing in each of the cases for which sufficient data are available whether home area or country as listed in Table 11.1 is derived from patri- or matri-filiation, from birth or from residence and knowledge. This is recorded by the use of a 'true' or 'false' value, or where the information is not available, by 'na' (not available). I have recorded a 'true' value where one of several places listed provides a match even though the other places named do not. Table 11.3 provides statistical data, derived from a sum of the counts of the values ('t', 'f' and 'na') recorded in Table 11.2.

The following observations regarding patri- and matri-filiation can be made in relation to these data. Nearly 65 per cent of claimants from whom relevant data were obtained cited patri-filiation as one of the means whereby they gained filiation to country. Sixty per cent made this claim in relation to matri-filiation. There were seven cases where both matri- and patri-filiation were cited. Despite the limitations of these data, they provide an indication that descent is an important means by which rights to country are established. However, it is not the sole criterion.

Birth

Birth is cited by some claimants as a determinant of gaining rights to country. However, this is balanced, at least to some extent, by an understanding that place of birth is not always a matter of choice for parents. In the past, in particular, many families were forced to live in places not of their choice, particularly as a result of government intervention or the exigencies of the labour market. This has led, in a few cases, to an ambivalent account of the status of birthplace in the Noongar system of customary laws. At least one claimant ranked it as being of less importance than descent. However, others mentioned place of birth as being important for gaining rights to country. One told how the afterbirth should be buried at the place of birth, and thereafter the place had a special significance for both the individual and their descendants. Joe Walley said that the place of birth was important because it marked the spot where you came onto the earth, and represented the spiritual relationship between a person and a particular place. Others noted the importance of the place of birth for their mother and father, while others again stressed that birthplace was important in a more general sense.

Table 11.2 shows some correspondence between place of birth and home area or run. Table 11.3 shows how these data can be translated into figures. Of the 37 cases reported, some 24 (65 per cent) show that place of birth and home area or run are the same. When families were able to follow their own inclinations, and

Table 11.2: Summary of country affiliations

Case	Birth	Patri-filiation	Matri-filiation	Knowledge/ residence	Birth or filiation count[124]	Note
1	f	na	t	t	1	
2	f	f	f	t	0	Affinal ties to run and home area
3	t	f	f	t	1	
4	na	t	na	f	1	
5	t	f	t	t	2	
6	t	na	na	t	1	
7	t	f	f	t	1	
8	f	t	f	t	1	
9	f	t	na	t	1	
10	t	f	f	t	1	
11	f	f	na	t	0	Parents buried in York, ego married in York
12	t	t	na	t	2	
13	na	na	t	t	1	
14	na	na	t	t	1	
15	f	t	na	t	1	
16	t	f	na	t	1	
17	t	na	na	t	1	
18	na	na	t	t	1	
19	t	t	na	t	2	
20	na	t	t	t	2	
21	t	na	t	t	2	
22	f	na	t	f	1	
23	t	t	na	t	2	
24	na	t	na	t	1	
25	na	t	na	t	1	
26	na	na	na	t		Insufficient data
27	f	na	t	t	1	
28	t	t	na	t	2	
29	t	t	na	t	2	
30	na	t	f	t	1	
31	na	na	t	na	1	

Case	Birth	Patri-filiation	Matri-filiation	Knowledge/residence	Birth or filiation count[124]	Note
32	f	t	t	t	2	
33	na	t	t	t	2	
34	t	f	na	t	1	
35	t	na	t	t	2	
36	na	t	na	t	1	
37	t	na	t	t	2	
38	t	t	f	t	2	
39	f	t	t	t	2	
40	t	t	f	t	2	
41	t	t	na	t	2	
42	f	t	na	f	1	
43	f	t	na	t	1	
44	na	t	t	t	2	
45	t	na	na	t	1	
46	f	f	t	f	1	
47	t	t	t	t	3	
48	t	f	f	f	1	
49	t	t	t	t	3	
50	f	f	f	t	0	Affinal link, spiritual link
51	na	t	na	na	1	
52	f	t	f	na	1	

Table 11.3: Summary data on patri-filiation, matri-filiation and place of birth

Outcome	Birth	Patrifiliation	Matrifiliation	Knowledge/residency
TRUE	24	24	18	43
FALSE	13	13	12	5
Not available	15	15	22	4
Total	52	52	52	52
Total cases available	37	37	30	48
% of cases true	64.9	64.9	60.0	89.6
% of cases false	35.1	35.1	40.0	10.4
% of total not available	28.8	28.8	42.3	7.7

124 Count of filiation through birth, father or mother (maximum is therefore three).

occupy and habitually use their runs, birth would automatically occur within the run of either the father or mother. Such an event would serve to strengthen the ties between a child and the matri- or patri-run. In the past, forced movements were quite common, while the requirement to seek medical assistance and hospital services in the larger cities, including Perth, has probably increased over time. Consequently place of birth presents some difficulties as an invariable means of establishing links to country. From the data, my conclusion is twofold. First, place of birth, particularly if it is in matri- or patri-country, is regarded as a signifier of rights to country. Second, for Noongar people, place of birth (provided it was not a consequence of the temporary hospitalisation of the mother), whether within or without an ancestral run, is of significance to the individual. It provides, in any debate, a ground for the pressing of a claim to be heard in relation to the exercise of any right in relation to that place.

Marriage

The claimants consider that marriage confers rights upon a partner in the country where they live where there is either virilocal or uxorilocal residence. For example, Dorothy Winmar told me that if you 'marry in' (that is, join another extended family) you have 'got to have a say' for your husband's country as well as your own. Another claimant stated that her mother 'come to belong' to the country of her husband because she married him and lived in his country. Lomas Roberts made the more general point that a wife becomes a part of your country and its traditions, and Joe Walley talked of two old men who taught him about Noongar traditions. Neither was Noongar, but both had married Noongar women, and consequently became a part of the Noongar community. Michael Blurton spoke of marriage as a 'ticket' to the town that was the home area of your spouse, while Katherine Penny had been told that she might have rights in her husband's country because she was 'married in' to it.

One claimant made it clear to me that he saw it as his duty to pass on the knowledge of his own wife's ancestral country to his children, although his deep attachment to it was through residence and spiritual association rather than from ancestral connection. Another claimant described the Mogumber-Moora region as her 'heart place' because she was married there and her children were born there; however, in this case her own birth at Mogumber probably underpins this view. My conclusion is that, in Noongar thinking, parents have a duty to represent and promote the interests of their children. In a cognatic system, children have rights to the country of both parents, at least potentially. A parent living in their spouse's country and raising children there is consequently eager to ensure that the children's rights in the country are promoted and realised. The rights that a spouse gains in the country of the marriage are therefore exercised vicariously and on behalf of the children. The vigour with which they are prosecuted and the degree to which they are accepted by others as legitimate would most probably depend upon the length of residence, the seniority of the spouse and their knowledge of Noongar culture, particularly as it related to land-based spirituality.

Residence and knowledge

Fred Pickett told me that he considered that he 'belonged to' the Quairading region, in part because of his long-term association with the region, but also because of his specialist knowledge of certain places there. This he could not discuss openly, as it was a matter for senior Noongar men only. He was born in Badjaling and lived in the Quairading region for a greater part of his life. His affiliation to this area was then through birth, residence and knowledge. Knowledge of country was considered to be important in asserting rights to country by other claimants. A senior Noongar claimant distinguished 'first knowledge', gained from the old Noongar people and the land, from 'second knowledge', which is gained from books — and was not deemed 'real knowledge'. Without 'first knowledge' you could not 'speak for' the country; that is, assert rights to it.

In Table 11.2 there are 48 cases where there is sufficient data to draw a relationship between run, home area and place of long-term residence. These data are analysed in Table 11.3. Of these, 43, or nearly 90 per cent, show direct correlation, indicating that residency and knowledge of country are regarded as significant requisites for claiming affiliation to country. This is borne out, very generally, by the field visits that I undertook with claimants, which were without exception to areas of country with which the individual (or individuals) were affiliated and for which they held detailed, personal and expert knowledge.

Detailed knowledge of country is not, however, of itself a determinant of ownership of country. It is rather a manifestation of such. This can be understood in relation to some additional data set out in Table 11.2. The column with the heading 'Birth or filiation count' records, for the 51 cases for which data are available, the number of affiliation references (birth, patri- or matri-filiation). There are only three cases where none of these is cited (number 2, number 11 and number 50). Attachment in these cases, as the notes in the right-hand column of the table indicate, appears to arise from either affinal ties (see above) or, in case number 11, perhaps anomalously, through burial and sentiment. The conclusion I draw from this is that in Noongar custom the assertion of rights to country are facilitated by close physical association to the areas in question. In no case, with the exceptions of those noted and explained above, did knowledge and residence of itself constitute a claim for affiliation to country. In short, residence and knowledge are the manifestation and executive practice of a land-owner's exercise of rights and duties. They do not make a person an owner, a point that was made by one senior claimant, who is knowledgeable about a particular town but does not consider it 'his country'.

Did rights change hands?

Demographic movements will affect residence patterns and long-term associations, as well as a person's ability to gain familiarity with areas. Demographic movements may also affect the birthplace of children. If rights to country are gained through marriage, in some circumstances a spouse may gain rights to country that was not their ancestral land. This results in a system where attachment to country may not always be fixed by reference to ancestral country. However, this does not mean that the system is open-ended and without referential principles.

The criteria for legitimate claim to country, apart from ancestral country, have been set out above. In all cases, claims to rights in country are legitimated by a series of requisites: residence, familiarity and knowledge, frequency of visits and spiritual associations. However, legitimation is a social process. Rights must be recognised by reference to these legitimating referents by other Noongar people.

The early literature provides references to the dynamics of shifts of rights to country over time. Bates (n.d.d, p. 54), as I noted above (p. 48), was aware that changes in land affiliation did take place, and she appears to accept this as a traditional part of Noongar culture. There are accounts of disputes over succession to country following a death, reported by Hallam and Tilbrook (1990, pp. 136–7, 211) for the Perth area. Succession to land (that is, changes of ownership over time) was noted by Moore (1978b, pp. 259–60; see Table 6.1). Barker (1992, p. 383) recounts how land could change hands, and notes that if a man had no male heir, 'his next neighbours may have his ground' (p. 383). Such accounts give support to the conclusion that traditionally the allocation of rights to country could change hands over time. Such changes were most likely subject to normative referents.

Succession and changes of allocation of rights in country are accepted by anthropologists in Australia as a feature of traditional systems, subject to rules and socially legitimating referents. Discussion of the process of succession may be found in the writings of such anthropologists as Sutton (2003, pp. 5–8, 121–2), Peterson (1983) and Peterson, Keen and Sansom (1977).

The social formation that relates to land

The Noongar family and its relationship to land

From the data considered in this book I consider that the claimants regard the extended family as the primary unit that owns country. For example, Wayne Collard said of his area that the land-holding group is collectively referred to as 'the Riley family'. This group is descended from George Riley and Elizabeth Smith, who are his MFF and mfm respectively. A number of other claimants listed ancestors and their descendants as comprising a family whose members were the owners of a specific tract of country. The country was shared between family members. These comments related to areas that included Badgebup and Nyaling, Moora, Moora and Mogumber, Narrogin, Busselton, Shackelton, Kwolyn and Bruce Rock, Jerramungup, Bremer Bay and Ravensthorpe, Albany, Jerramungup, the Stirling Ranges and the Perth area. Others stated more generally that rights to country were traced by descent, and that different families were responsible for different areas of country.

Claimants stated that a person might have rights to more than one area of country. One claimant said he had rights to the Pinjarra area because his mother was born there. Martha Borinelli claimed some rights to the Bremer Bay region because it was her fm country. Dorothy Winmar claimed both the Perth region and Ballardong country, as she could trace ancestors to both areas. One senior Noongar claimant told me that he had claims to the Perth area through affinal and spiritual connection, but he had an interest in the Busselton area through his mother's family.

Noongar people are aware of the complex and sometimes extensive network of kin that comprises the basic structure of the greater family. So, for example, Susan Pickett noted how the Fords and the Garletts were related to her through her mother and that they 'sit with' the Davis family. Harry Thorne listed seven families that were either his consanguineal or affinal kin and one other that may have been connected, but he was unsure how. Charlie Shaw recounted how he travelled to Boojin Rock (Brookton) each year to join members of his greater family for a get-together. Charlie's mz married Fred Collard. The recognition of the greater family may, then, have implications for the manner in which people define and exercise rights to country. A group of senior Noongar men told me that their families were affiliated to the Perth area and were related, so had access to each other's land.

Interests shared between families in the same area of country may not always be the result of extended family relationships. It appears that, in some circumstances, different families may share rights to the same area of country. In this regard, a number of claimants expressed the view that two or more families had a connection with the same area of land. Myrtle Yarran, for example, spoke of the Quairading–Badjaling area, and how, in addition to the families that had moved in to the mission from elsewhere, there were many families with rights to the area gained by birth or descent. Others made similar remarks about the different families associated with areas like Arthur River, Bunbury, Busselton, Pemberton, Shackleton, Williams and Narrogin, Collie, Mandurah and Pinjarra, York, Brookton and Beverley, New Norcia and Moora. While some of these families acknowledged that they shared common ancestry, not all did so. Where families share rights, these may be differentiated in their exercise by reference to knowledge and strength of attachment. However, from the data reviewed here it would appear that the principle of exercising a right to country is evidenced by the citation of the family name in connection with it, notwithstanding that the exercise of the right may be subject to qualification or negotiation, in practice.

Noongar people subscribe to the authority structure that is evident in their community in relation to the exercise of rights to country. Joe Walley said that to have authority to speak for an area and to have standing in the community, a person's knowledge should come firsthand from the elders and not be learnt from books. Much the same point was made by another senior Noongar claimant, as I noted above (p. 154). Others characterised the senior role as being taken by the eldest family member. However, Wayne Collard stated that the role of senior family member has, in the case of his family, been decided at a large family meeting. In these accounts it is evident that, while having authority in the family relies upon 'standing', achieved through age, experience and knowledge, the senior family member is accepted by (and is therefore acceptable to) the other members of the family, and does not act on his or her own account. He (or she) represents the family interests, but commands respect because of his or her standing.

The landed family: observations and conclusions

In Chapter 9, I described the family as one of the fundamental components of Noongar society. As shown above, for many Noongar families, descent supplies an important means whereby rights to country are derived, while affinal relatives are also counted into the family. Consanguineal kin of the extended family trace common ancestry by reference to named forebears. Apical ancestors, so identified, are usually associated with places which are understood to have been their own. Since descent from named ancestors who have known affiliation to country is an attribute shared by all consanguineally related members of that family, family members together share claims to ancestral country. Rights to country are therefore shared between family members, and it is the extended family, as a whole, that can be understood to be the owner of the country in question. This extended family is the country group.

In cases where an apical ancestral connection is not remembered, more recent affiliations with country are recalled. This may rely on the attachment through birth and occupation of a family member of the first or (more usually) second ascending generation. However, the principle of affiliation remains the same, and it is consanguineally related family members who together make claims to the country. In Noongar thinking, families are typically and invariably linked to country, and that is one of the ways by which they are identified. I have commented on this above, and it has been well documented for Noongar people by Birdsall (1990, pp. 151–2).

An individual exercises rights to country in the context of the family relationships that provide the reference for their existence as a Noongar person. Thus an individual may talk about an area as being their country, but will recognise that there will be other family members who have rights as owners to the same area, since family members legitimate their claims to country by reference to the same matri- and patri-filiates. Even where claims are only traced back two generations, the Noongar family of descendants is typically quite large, so it is this extended family whose members identify with the area in question.

The number of forebears increases exponentially over each ascending generation. Consequently, identification of apical ancestors in relation to claims to country must involve the exercise of discrimination and choice. The realisation of rights to country and their exercise is likely to be determined by the individual's command of the requisite knowledge and experience of the country in question, as explained above. From the data set out in the previous section, this would appear to be the operative principle that governs the exercise of this choice. However, in any cognatic system, appeal through descent may be made to more than one apical ancestor, and so to more than one area of land. Thus a person may claim rights to more than one country. In practice, then, countries of choice are determined by appeal to ancestral connection, but limited by knowledge and experience.

Over time, and as families split and divide, attachments to country will be subject to choice (matri- and patri-filiation, place of birth), determined by residence, available knowledge and opportunity. Thus a greater family, with ancestral depth, will comprise a number of different extended families whose territorial affiliations will be different and whose component parts can be differentiated by reference to these territorial references. However, members of the same greater family claim common ancestry, and sometimes other ties through marriage over the generations, so are able to assert a commonality. This extends to the way in which they can exercise rights to country. Potentially, a person can claim the right to country, subject to command of requisite knowledge, by reference to members of his or her greater family, who are regarded as having once held those rights.

Unrelated families may claim attachment to the same or overlapping areas of country. This was recognised by claimants who accompanied me on field visits, where members of different family groups, who were not, as far as I know, members of the same greater family, showed or talked to me about country that was their own.

Since extended families have an authority structure, determined for the most part by age and demonstrated knowledge of Noongar culture, a senior family member is often named as the principal person for a particular area or place. This is communicated by such a phrase as, 'he's the main one for there'. In matters relating to the country in question, such a person is understood to have the authority to speak on behalf of the rest of the family, whose members lay claim to the land. However, this does not mean that the individual has exclusive rights to the country, nor does it mean that the individual exercises these rights without due reference to other family members. It would be usual for all family members to meet and discuss any issue that affected their country and to reach a consensual agreement.

A summary of these propositions is as follows. First, rights are held by the members of the extended family, together as communal rights. Individuals comprising the extended family hold these rights not as individuals but as members of the family, and therefore do not do so exclusively. It is the sum of the members of the family that own the land, not its constituent members, singularly. Second, a family may have legitimate claim to more than one area of country, by appeal to multiple legitimating principles for claiming land. However, such choice is limited in practice by residence, familiarity and knowledge. Third, rights to country may also be asserted through claims of kinship (shared ancestry, appeal to a common lineage) to areas where members of the greater family hold land. Fourth, the right of a family to country is seldom exclusive, and may be shared legitimately by other families. Finally, Noongar authority structures and the requirement that there be a command of land-related knowledge in any dealings over country result in senior and knowledgeable members of families taking a lead role in matters relating to land. However, this role is one that represents all family members, and is often exercised in conjunction with other senior members of other families with an interest in the land in question.

The consequence of these arrangements is that, in Noongar thinking, rights to land are allocated across the members of one, two or perhaps several families. Areas of country identified as belonging to one family may overlap with those belonging to another. This complex criss-crossing of rights forms a palimpsest of territorial interests, which is marked by the non-exclusive and necessarily co-operative nature of their exercise within a population comprising the members of several extended families.

Conclusion

I have noted that there had been a consistent view, for all areas reviewed, that more or less bounded areas of land were considered to be the property of families and individuals. Bates recognised that rights extended to areas that she called 'runs', which were sometimes geographically substantial. This account would appear to accord with the contemporary Noongar view that land is divided between families which are country groups and whose members exercise rights as owners in it, and extends to include a run that can be geographically quite extensive.

The early literature makes clear that rights to country are gained through descent, and there is some evidence that descent was reckoned through either the matri- or the patri-line. This is a view supported by Bates. Rights to country could be attained through birth and marriage. This system of gaining rights to country would appear to have remained current, in its fundamentals, and is evident in the contemporary data I have reviewed above.

The early literature has many references to the family as being the basic land-owning unit. I have discussed what these early accounts may have meant by both the term 'family' and 'tribe', and noted that there may have been some confusion over what was being identified. Members of a family, according to these early accounts, evidently exercised rights to country. Individuals whose authority was recognised because of their age and their knowledge were identified as 'leaders' of these families. From the data reviewed here, it would appear to me that the social unit that relates to land, and whose members together exercise rights to an area (or areas) of land, continues to be much the same as it was formerly. An authority structure continues to be apparent, manifest by the role apportioned to senior men and women in relation to matters that relate to land. The system of land ownership and the exercise of rights would therefore appear to remain, in its fundamentals, the same as that described in the early accounts.

Finally, I set out in early parts of this book how it is I conclude that rights to country were not exclusively held, but were enjoyed together by different parts of the same family. I discussed in Part I how I considered that other alliances, and other distantly related or non-related families, might exercise rights to the same country. From the contemporary data analysed in this chapter, I have concluded that rights to country are enjoyed by a number of different groups of people (for the most part, comprising different extended families), and therefore rights to country never were and are not today the exclusive preserve of a single group. These observations would lead to the conclusion that the distribution of rights to country is today based on similar principles to those used, from the evidence available, in the past.

Noongar land ownership represents a system that relies for its legitimation and social acceptance upon a set of normative referents that remain consistently articulated and repeatedly espoused. They provide for a framework of customary values and principles whereby Noongar people today negotiate and assert their rights to their country. In short, the claim of rights to country represents a central feature of Noongar culture. By reference to the accounts provided in the early literature, we are in a reasonable position to determine whether these principles are fundamentally the same as or different from those obtaining at sovereignty. My conclusion is that they are fundamentally the same. The term 'fundamentally' is used advisedly, since there have been substantial changes in the Noongar way of life, including the Noongar people's ability to access land and exercise their rights to it. However, from these data I conclude that these changes are a matter of emphasis and accent, rather than alterations to the basic premises and values that underpin (and underpinned) Noongar customary rights to country.

Chapter 12

BOUNDARIES, PERMISSION, RIGHTS AND DUTIES

Introduction

In this chapter I first review data provided by Noongar people that assist in developing an understanding of how boundaries are conceptualised in Noongar discourse. I also examine how the concept of a boundary relates to the totality of Noongar land. I then review data illustrative of how rights to bounded areas of country are articulated by the expectation that permission must be sought by those who do not enjoy rights as owners and who wish to enter that country. Since this expectation is tempered by other rights and duties, this is no straightforward matter. I will look, in a more general sense, at the available data identifying other rights and duties which are exercised by land-owners in relation to their country.

Boundaries

In this section I seek to illustrate and support the following propositions. In Noongar geography there are two sorts of boundary. The first relates to the extent of Noongar land; that is, country that is owned by Noongar people and is a manifestation of their culture and belief, and wherein Noongar people exercise their rights as land-owners. The second relates to a subdivision of the first and provides the means by which Noongar people define their home area and their run by geographic referents. In both cases, boundaries are defined by a reference to place. This can be either a natural feature (a hill, a lake, a river) or a town or other settlement. In all cases, from my observations, boundaries are drawn conceptually and generally rather than definitively. While taking a geographic referential basis from topography, boundaries are generalised to interstices which have about them indefiniteness if probed to specific locations. Away from the boundary, the indefiniteness disappears. Noongar people talk about boundaries as a process experienced through travel, through which, in time and space, you begin to leave your own country and enter someone else's. This lack of precision should not be misunderstood as a failure to define the extent of territory or an indication that the requisite knowledge is lacking. To provide too precise an assertion of a boundary may evoke hostility among neighbours. Boundaries are as precise as they need to be, given the circumstances, a point that has been made elsewhere for other areas of Aboriginal Australia (Williams 1982, pp. 145–6).

The boundaries of Noongar land

In Table 12.1 I set out a summary of information provided by Noongar people in relation to the boundaries of Noongar land. There is a lack of consistency regarding detail in these accounts. Moreover, those providing information have tended to do so, in the majority of cases, with regard to their immediate area, rather than providing points of reference for the whole of the Noongar boundary. There are, however, some negative points of agreement. With one exception, Geraldton was considered to be outside Noongar country, as were Mt Magnet, Kalgoorlie and Norseman, while Esperance would appear to be on the margins. Generally, and in the majority of cases, the border of Noongar land would appear to be characterised as falling somewhere between Geraldton and Dongara, to pass north of Three Springs and Dalwallinu. It then passes between Merredin and Southern Cross, or to the east of the latter, includes Bruce Rock and Lake Grace to reach the coast at Hopetoun, or perhaps as far east as Esperance.

The Noongar boundary in relation to earlier accounts

I have discussed in some detail the difficulties of interpreting data presented by Tindale (1974) with respect to 'tribal boundaries' (p. 17). In part, this is because he sometimes represented dialect units (for which he was later criticised), and so created apparent territorial distinctions where fundamental social and cultural distinction were not in evidence. However, a comparison between Tindale's map ('Map Australia S.W. Sheet') and the data in Table 12.1 can be made. Tindale's circumcision line is the boundary, to the west of which resided a number of groups (which he names) whose members share a common culture, and can collectively be called Noongar, as I have argued is the case. In such a comparison it will be seen that the Noongar boundary, as the claimants have set it out, corresponds in most particulars with that set out by Tindale.

Boundaries of country and run

Boundaries of runs and home areas were typically described by reference to a notable geographic area. So, for example, Ross Story described his 'main area' as

Table 12.1: Some Noongar accounts of the borders of Noongar land

Geographic referents
West from: east of Merredin; Bencubbin; Wongan Hills
Paynes Find; a little east of Southern Cross
Kalgoorlie and Geraldton outside; Merredin inside
Yellowdine [east of Southern Cross]
West of Kalgoorlie; Paynes Find; east of Kellerberrin; Wave Rock; Southern Cross, west of Mukinbudin
Esperance and Kalgoorlie outside; Ravensthorpe, Bremer Bay, Hopetoun and Jerramungup inside
Kalgoorlie outside; Southern Cross probably outside; Merredin inside
Norseman, Kalgoorlie and Esperance outside
Dalwallinu and Paynes Find inside; Cue outside; Southern Cross 'strange feeling'; Merredin inside; Norseman outside
Dongara is the border
Paynes Find outside
Geraldton and Mt Magnet outside
Geraldton outside
Carnamah outside
Carnarvon and Kalgoorlie outside
Northampton outside
Esperance, Hyden; Bruce Rock; Dalwallinu; Three Springs, Eneabba and Dongara mark boundary
Ravensthorpe, Esperance, Southern Cross and Geraldton mark border
Salmon Gums, Wave Rock, Mullewa
Geraldton, Southern Cross, Lake Grace; Kojonup; Esperance
Meekatharra and Mullewa were different

'Dryandra country', which lies to the north-west of Narrogin and is a state forest. He stressed that country was bounded by the limits of knowledge and feelings of well-being. Once you were outside of your country, you felt strange and that you did not belong there. A similar point was made by other claimants. Kevan Davis listed a number of places as marking the extent of his country. Characteristic of each account is that the boundary is defined by reference to a series of named places (usually towns), which when linked conceptually form an area of country. There were some instances where accounts were provided of a boundary following a vegetation change. Angus Wallam considered that his country ended where the taller grass trees began to appear and some of the trees changed. Joe

Northover related the boundaries of his country, to some extent, to the occurrence of spiritual beings within the watercourses. William Reidy said boundaries were marked by rocks and trees. Where a boundary is marked by a river, as was the case with the Pallinup, the boundary is geographically fixed. There was a general view, prevalent amongst those who discussed this issue, that knowledge of these boundaries had been given to them by the old people.

Rights and duties of land-owners

Rights of access, rights to withhold access and permission

Noongar permission

My assessment of the information collected during fieldwork and set out in the data sheets is that Noongar people consider that it is a land-owner's right to have free use of and access to his or her own land. Conversely, those who do not share rights in the land should seek permission before they enter or use that land. Roy Taylor told me that when it comes to development, it is the people with a spiritual attachment to the land who must be asked. He regarded it as the right of an owner to be asked before any action took place on land to which he was spiritually connected.

Noongar permission is discussed by the claimants in several layers. First, there is a general and typically unqualified statement that a Noongar person must keep to his or her own area, and not go outside. Harry Nannup said that it was quite permissible to take resources in your own area and that of your wife, but elsewhere you should ask. Evelyn Dawson and Charmaine Walley expressed the view that you did not need permission to be in your own area, but others, including other Noongar people, should ask. Joe Northover said he was free to hunt in his own area, which he defined, but elsewhere he should ask first. William Reidy said, 'People know their country. If you went into another area you had to ask. That's the proper way.' Verna Ugle said that she did not travel to Kojonup or Albany often, as it was not her country and she would not act freely there. Another claimant said that when he visits a town outside his own area, he always asks, and when people from other areas visit his town (Northam), they come and ask him first before camping there.

These relatively straightforward views were qualified by others, who considered other aspects of the permission process. Ross Story distinguished his home area from his run, indicating that with respect to the latter, he preferred to talk to others who shared the country to let them know when he was visiting. Ken Fitzgerald said he only needed permission if he visited a site of spiritual significance, presumably because of the dangers which might eventuate from such unprotected action. He said of an old Noongar fox shooter that he had not needed to ask to shoot, 'because he was a part of the mob', implying that familial and social relations vouchsafed his entry and use of the area in question. Angus Wallam said that you were free to use country where you had family. Another senior Noongar man put his views in the context of respect. He said that 'we didn't like to step on other people's toes', and indicated that it was important to respect the rights of others to their country. He said of Kellerberrin and Quairading that these were his areas and others should keep out. If he goes somewhere else, then he must be taken by the local owners, and that this was an important aspect of showing respect.

Myrtle Yarran emphasised the importance of showing respect, which she articulated as a protocol that required calling in on the senior land-owner, to let them know you were visiting. In such a case, it was assumed that you were known to the local family, and so were free to move across the country and use the areas, subject to the observance of the protocol. She pointed out that those who were ignorant of country placed themselves in danger from it and were unlikely to have much success in hunting because they were not known to the country, which I take to mean to the spirits of the country. Myrtle Yarran indicated that it would be wrong to refuse a request from other Noongar people to share in the resources of your area, while Ken Fitzgerald stated that 'you can't say "no"'. Pat Kopusar noted the dangers of entering unknown country. She stated that while permission should be asked of owners of country, they had a duty to grant you permission, as well as to ensure your safety. So, while there was an expectation that permission be sought, there was an expectation that it would be given and that the owner would ensure your protection while on his (or her) country. Danger in country was understood to arise where a stranger was unrecognisable to the spirits of the country, in the absence of a proper ritual introduction. As a result, the stranger was placed in danger. There was a view that a person who was not a Noongar, and who wished to visit Noongar country, should always ask first. The same applied to Noongar people who visited an area of country outside of Noongar lands.

These accounts provide a range of views about the permission process. From them, four observations can be made. First, bounded country ideally is regarded as the property of the family (or families) with rights to it. Ideally, then, permission is required for members of other families to enter or use it. Second, rights to use country are extended to members of other families where there is a family connection. This would appear to relate to the use of country by members of the greater family who are also consociates. Third, the extension of rights to country requires the exercise of protocols of respect and acknowledgment of the role of the senior members of the family responsible for the country in question. Finally, while permission can ideally be withheld, there is an expectation that permission will not be withheld, and that the land and its products will be shared between Noongar people, particularly in cases where people know one another.

Understanding Noongar permission

Seeking and granting permission should be understood in the context of people's relationship to the spirituality that Noongar people believe to reside within the countryside. I have already discussed this in some detail above, particularly with respect to what I have termed 'dangerous places'. Noongar people believe that unknown country is potentially dangerous because Noongar land is possessed of spiritual potentialities which are either avoided or knowledgably managed. Ignorance of country is therefore a matter of personal jeopardy. To venture into unknown country is to imperil both yourself and those who depend upon you. This means that, for the most part, Noongar people regard country which is not their own, and therefore that is unknown to them, as country to be avoided.

In Noongar thinking (and as I have outlined above in this chapter), an owner of country has the right to exclude or grant permission to non-owners to enter and use the land. The owner has a duty to share their land with others, and a duty to ensure that no harm comes to visitors. In mutual recognition of the right of an owner (a petitioner being an owner in his or her own right), a visitor has a duty to ask permission before entering or using another person's country. The exercise of these rights and duties forms a reciprocal chain of interactions which are both complex and interdependent. This can be explained as follows.

The person who asks permission is also asking for assistance, guidance and even protection from the owner. Consequently, asking permission is as much about respecting the rights of the owners as it is about the self-interested concern for the safety of the person who makes the request. This is a matter of personal security. The granting of permission requires the exercise of both a right and a duty. While it is clear from the data that an owner has, ideally, the right to give or withhold access, this right is not unqualified. The request implies a duty on the part of the owner to share the resources of the country with others. The granting of permission implies a requirement that visitors be protected.

While the act of asking and giving permission is an important aspect of the land-owning system in Noongar dealings, it is by no means a singular or one-dimensional process. As a normative system, it operates to signal the rights of a family over an area of country. It operates to demonstrate the Noongar cultural trait of inclusiveness and sharing. Concurrently, it operates to show how a land owner has a duty with respect to their country, that relates to both caring for others and sharing their land and its resources with a community of people much wider than those members of his or her immediate family.

The right of an owner to include or exclude is hedged about with interdependent considerations which qualify that right. The act of asking is not a simple act that is akin to asking permission to camp in a farmer's paddock, or to cross private property to retrieve a ball.

Both knowledge of country and rights to country form complex webs of interests, variously distributed across the members of extended families. The rights that reside within one family are often not exclusive to a single area of country. Some areas may overlap. Given these complexities and the resonances and intricacies which underlie the giving or asking of permission, neither asking nor granting permission can be understood as an absolute indicator of the rights of an owner, as would be the case where a property is exclusively owned. So, while asking and seeking permission is a part of Noongar dealings over land, it is neither a neat nor a conclusive process that signals invariably the rights of an owner. It must be understood in the context of the asking and the giving.

Rights to the resources of the country

Consistent with the comment made in the previous section, a number of claimants related how they continued to access their country and considered that they were free to do so. This included the general right to camp, hunt and get food. More specific rights were expressed in relation to the various resources found on Noongar land. Here, claimants provided an extensive list and these data are provided in summary form in Table 12.2. Claimants also asserted their rights to medicinal plants found on their country as well as to minerals, including salt and ochre. These data represent examples of the realisation of rights to the resources of the country that the claimants consider to be theirs. For the most part, these rights were reported rather than observed in their practice. However, from my experiences during fieldwork, these rights generally were asserted in the context in which they were practised.

Rights to intellectual property

Again based on the field data and my research, I am of the opinion that the claimants are mindful of their rights to the knowledge of their culture and their land, regarding it as their property. Those claimants with whom this matter was

Table 12.2: Examples of rights to take food resources

Resources taken or activity	Area
Goannas, camping	Dryandra area
Camping, kangaroos (grey and red, *tamma*), witchetty grubs, water (drinking and washing), jilgies, lizards	Bruce Rock, Shackleton, Kwolyn
Kangaroos (grey and red), barleys,[125] bush medicine, berries, quandongs and bush carrots	Wyalkatchem
Hunting, firewood (with permission of Noongar owners)	Badjaling
Kangaroo, fish, wild honey, quandongs, *marl* (shrub berries) and *parig* (figs)	Borden, Gnowangerup, Jerramungup
Fish (groper, salmon, skippy, marron, bream)	Cape Riche and other areas
Firewood, fruits, witchetty grubs, shade, shelter, nuts, honey, bush medicine, goanna eggs, mallee hen eggs, kangaroos (meat and skins), rabbits, lizards, water, camping	Jerramungup, Gnowangerup, Bremer Bay, Ravensthorpe
Travel and camping, kangaroos, possums, wild carrots, berries and bush medicine	Kulin region, extending as far east as Wave Rock (Hyden), and as far west as Wickepin and as far south as Lake Grace
Food	Albany-Jerramungup region
Hunting	Beaufort River
Paperbark for use in paintings	Northam
Kangaroos, emu, camping	New Norcia area
Jam gum	New Norcia

discussed consistently stated that they require permission if others wish to use the land. For example, Verna Ugle considers that she has a responsibility to monitor and control the release of cultural information by other members of her family, particularly in relation to issues of land ownership, cultural activity and native title. Claimants were mindful of the fact that knowledge of a person's country is, by customary right, the property of the owner. Others should not presume to talk about narratives or other details that relate to country that is not their own. Verna Ugle made this point in relation to talking about spirit beings outside her own country. Charmaine Walley said that it was her right to talk about the spirit being

125 Nuts of trees, unidentified.

the Beemula, because her father had told her about it and it is believed to reside on country she claims as her own. Charlie Shaw considers that he has the right to deal in information about areas from Lancelin to Jurien Bay and its hinterland because he was appointed as the custodian of these areas. Lynette Knapp told me that she could not relate narratives that belonged to the north-western side of the Stirling Ranges (she identified this area as Tambellup) because this was outside her country. It was a point also made by Carol Pettersen. Perhaps the most obvious example of the exercise of this right, as well as the refusal to be seen appropriating another person's intellectual property, is to be found in the field visits I experienced. Noongar people took me to areas that they regarded as their own and in which they exercised rights as owners. Telling me about the country, the spirituality it contained and relating narratives that made intimate reference to the country, was a natural outcome of their relationship to the country and their right to command the allocation of that knowledge to others.

Rights to share in the resources obtained by others from the country

Two claimants expressed the specific view that they should receive a share of any resources taken from the land by others. Lomas Roberts said he had been active in lobbying for Noongar benefits from the abalone farm at Bremer Bay and the Ravensthorpe nickel project. Carol Pettersen and Lynette Knapp, like many other senior claimants who provided information upon which this book is based, are members of the numerous working parties convened by the South West Aboriginal Land and Sea Council to consider any proposed activity on land subject to claim. Carol and Lynette are keen to ensure that Noongar people gain benefit from developments like the Ravensthorpe nickel projects as well as from different shire or private projects. The right of owners to receive a part of the resources of their land, when it is exploited by another, is exemplified in the customary practice whereby a visitor who takes food from the land always provides the owner with a portion of his catch.

Duty to look after and visit country

I have noted above that a land-owner has a duty to care for visitors to their country. This is one of several duties about which Noongar people spoke during the research reported here. In this section, I discuss some other aspects of the exercise of duty, particularly as it relates to caring for country.

Based upon the research data, and upon my observations and discussions with Noongar people, it seems to me that land-owners have a general duty to care for their country, which is best expressed by the phrase 'to look after'. Looking after country may require quite general activity, like visits and general inspections, or more specific activity and more intense intervention by being involved in site protection and site management. There is some indication available that burning the country continues to be regarded as an owner's duty. I set out examples of the reported exercise of these duties in the following paragraphs of this section.

Looking after country typically requires a personal inspection, to check for damage, perform maintenance and ensure there is no unwelcome or unexpected development. So, for example, Ken Fitzgerald stated that he visits York at least two to three times a year, and my understanding of his statement is that he sees these visits as an opportunity to check the country, in the manner just described. Wayne Collard said that, whenever possible, he checks on the welfare of eagles in the Kulin region. He evidently sees this as a part of his duty as a land-owner, given the context in which this statement was made by him. Others reported that they regularly visit their country and check up on burial sites of family members, to check for vandalism and ensure places are undamaged, as well as cleaning out the *gnamma* holes. Harry Nannup said that he 'worried for the country', and often took drives through his area to keep an eye on it and make sure everything was in order. Harry Thorne said he 'worried for the country' because 'it's real homely to me', indicating its intrinsic value to him as his real home place. Claimants 'worry for country' in those particular circumstances where they feel they have little power or influence to ensure that the country is treated according to Noongar traditions and beliefs. Such was the case for Carol Pettersen and Lynette Knapp, who expressed concern over the clearing of firebreaks at Mt Manypeaks, east of Albany, which they considered to have damaged the important area. Bill Webb said that he likes to visit his sites at least twice a year, which he considers to be an obligation. Glen Kelly said he visits the various sites in his run during the Christmas holidays and that it is very important for him to do so. He checks to see whether things have been damaged.

Another aspect of 'looking after country' is the duty to make any representations that might be necessary to ensure its integrity. This is often called 'speaking for country' and may be necessary when development is proposed that might harm spiritually sensitive places. 'Speaking for country' is understood to be an important duty for a land-owner. Some claimants expressed the emotion of 'feeling sorry' for the country which had been badly affected by salinity or clearing. In my view, 'to feel sorry for' your country is an expression of your concern and care for it.

The claimants provided many examples of their more specific involvement in looking after their country. For convenience, these are summarised in Table 12.3. In addition, many Noongar people expressed a desire to remedy damage or prevent it, although they often have not been able to do so. Duty of care, for a Noongar land-owner, naturally occurs within the context of the possible. It is only relatively recently that Noongar people have been asked about development on their land, and have had the opportunity to reverse their relative powerlessness to discharge their duty and to look after their country. Most Noongar people would still consider that they continue to exercise very little real power and control in this regard. As a consequence, I think the examples available of the exercise of a duty to look after country are necessarily somewhat restricted. 'Looking after country', 'speaking for country' and, when the situation warrants it, 'feeling sorry for country' and 'worrying for country' are all a part of the normative system that underpins the possession of rights and the exercise of duties in relation to the land.

Colin Headland remarked about one place I visited with him that a fire needed to be put through it to clean it. Glen Kelly reported how he had been involved in burning projects with the Department of Conservation and Land Management (CALM), and that burning was a part of his custodial duties that should be exercised in relation to his land. However, in general, those with whom I worked did not have much to say about the use of fire. It was a significant part of Noongar traditional life and an important means whereby Noongar people managed their environment (e.g. see Hallam 1975). Today, many areas of the South West are privately owned, and the setting of fires is strictly controlled. This would appear to be one area of Noongar culture which it has not been practical or possible to pursue, except in a limited manner.

Duty to pass on traditional knowledge to the next generation

Based upon the research data collected, and upon my own observations and discussions with Noongar people, it is my view that the claimants consider that they have a duty to pass on their knowledge to members of the next generation, just as this knowledge was passed on to them. This ensures the continuity of Noongar tradition over the generations. It was a matter that was mentioned on a number of occasions by those with whom I worked as constituting an important part of their responsibilities as senior Noongar people. The importance of passing on knowledge to the next generation is often reported as a fact and accepted practice, rather than characterised specifically as a duty. Lynette Knapp and Carol

Table 12.3: Examples of the exercise of duty in Noongar country

Activity
Consultations with CALM about the management of Dryandra State Forest
Tourism projects; taking people to his country as a part of tourist projects
Site clearances in relation to proposed developments as proposed by bodies like the Water Corporation
Worked with the local shire to ensure environmental health of his country particularly in attempts to remedy salinity problems; also ensured that areas, such as the Wagin Reserve, were maintained and kept clear of rubbish and overgrown vegetation; worked with government agencies to promote tourist trails and information boards
Worked with CALM to protect, rehabilitate and manage significant sites within his country
Attempts to protect sites locally, particularly those threatened by motorbikes and fossickers; worked with Main Roads Department to ensure road development did not damage sites; worked with Australian Army to prevent their taking over important areas of land
Cleans up rubbish from important areas
Participates in site clearances with shire; required Main Roads Department to return sand taken from an area which they should not have disturbed; asked council to place a culvert for kangaroos to access water point
Has concern for the environment, particularly the water supply, rubbish and unregulated access; has undertaken regeneration projects with CALM and was part of the negotiations about the marine park in the area; participated in a reburial
Participated in a number of heritage and site surveys
Advised on the control and direction of tourists
Employed an archaeologist to undertake a full investigation of a site
Planning and consultation with CALM to ensure that a proposed road did not affect a burial site
Worked with CALM about the position of a proposed road; participated in a number of archaeological surveys
Participated in a number of site-monitoring and heritage surveys; at the time of the interview, was working on a site-monitoring assignment
Involvement in numerous site clearances in the Perth metropolitan area; campaigned for the protection of a number of important Wagarl sites, including the Old Brewery site and Pyrton

Pettersen told me that telling your children about the extent of their country 'almost went without saying'. This was said in the context of a discussion about duties and responsibilities for their country. Passing on knowledge of country, as well as the rights and duties of a land-owner, is understood to be in itself a duty and can be considered as such here.

Conclusion

In my review of the accounts provided in the early literature of the system of land ownership evident through areas of the South West, I draw some conclusions relating to the rights of owners. These I summarise as being, according to these accounts generally, that Noongar land-owners had 'undisputed' rights in their country (see p. 48). However, the nature of these rights, as they could be differentiated into constituent subsets of rights, was not usually set out in these early accounts. Moreover, the data derived from accounts of the Albany region indicate that not all action on another person's country required permission, indicating that some rights were shared between the members of different families (see p. 49).

I have suggested that interpersonal relationships and alliances may have played an important part here, in facilitating the sharing of rights between families and individuals. Two conclusions may be drawn from this. The first is that, at or very close to sovereignty, Noongar people exercised rights to their country and these rights were most probably comprehensive. That is to say, their exercise permitted the owner to do what he wished within his own country. Second, at or close to sovereignty there operated a system of permission whereby, ideally, a person who did not have rights to the country was required to ask permission before he or she accessed the country, took game from it or set a fire. However, it is clear that, in practice, such permission was complex in its execution and not always consistently required or sought. This reflects a situation where rights to country were variously attainable. The situation with respect to permission was one that was tied in with personal relationships, alliances, ties of kinship that rendered its practice a complex undertaking.

It would appear to me that much the same systems are in operation among Noongar people today as was the case at or close to sovereignty. People continue to regard their country as their own, as of right, and permission is an ideal requirement, hedged about with circumstantial qualifications that provide for a complex and often context specific outcome. Rights today may be articulated better than they were to the early settlers (who perhaps had little interest in such detail). I consider that while rights of access and use of resources remain important, they are probably less so today than would have been the case some 175 years ago. I conclude this to be so because of the fundamental changes to Noongar economy, where, as far as I am aware, no family now relies primarily upon the land and its resources for sustenance, as would have been the case at sovereignty. While it may be surmised that the attention paid to rights of access and use may have changed, the data indicate that the right of use and access remains fundamental to the normative system of customary land ownership amongst Noongar people. Similarly, burning, which was evidently an important part of the management of Noongar land in times past, and therefore conceivably a duty that fell on the owners, is now more or less absent. Nevertheless, to some limited extent it remains a duty of Noongar land-owners. I conclude that duties relating to the care and protection of country now probably receive greater emphasis than they did formerly, when the impact of development, clearing and urbanisation had yet to be felt across Noongar land.

From the information available to me, I conclude that the rights and duties of the Noongar people have not changed in their fundamentals and the normative system upon which an owner is understood to relate to his or her country remains founded upon the same principles that it did at sovereignty. However, the emphasis of these actions and their incidence has altered, as is to be expected, given the substantial changes that have taken place across the South West over the last 175 years.

Chapter 13

CONTINUITY OF CONNECTION: ECONOMIC AND SPIRITUAL CONNECTION WITH THE COUNTRY

Introduction

In this chapter I examine two aspects of the connection between the claimants and the application area which is evidenced in the data. The first relates to the degree to which the claimants utilise the application area for the procurement of natural resources which would appear, from the information available, also to have been exploited prior to sovereignty. In this, I distinguish between economic utilisation; that is, foraging or hunting for resources that have a substantive economic benefit, and intellectual properties that relate to the resources manifest as knowledge. In the latter case, items may not necessarily be exploited or consumed. The knowledge of the resources can be understood to be a part of Noongar traditional understanding. The use of natural resources and the demonstrated knowledge of their existence and use are operational aspects of the rights and duties of land-owners within the Noongar culture as they relate to the economic utilisation of Noongar land. The incidence of the use and knowledge of resources is therefore instructive in coming to a view about the extent of the exercise, in practice, of these rights. It may assist in understanding the degree to which customary knowledge of traditional economic practice remains a part of Noongar culture.

In this chapter I also discuss a second aspect of the connection between Noongar people and their country. This reflects the way in which spiritual connectedness with country is articulated through the belief that certain places within the countryside are of significance and embody a powerful spirituality. These places, often referred to as 'sites' or 'sacred sites', form a body of knowledge for Noongar people, and represent a significant aspect of customary belief. The manner in which the claimants consider that such places should be treated represents a notable aspect of Noongar customary behaviour. An appreciation of the extent and content of belief as it relates to places may be helpful in reaching a view as to the continuity of religious and spiritual beliefs as they are expressed through the attribution of spirituality to named locations or areas.

Economic use of the countryside

In Chapter 12, and in the context of the exercise of rights in country, I set out some details relating to the use of the application area by the claimants. Table 12.2 listed some of the resources that the claimants reported having taken from the countryside, which they regarded as their right. Here, I examine these data along with others provided during the course of the research in relation to more general discussions about the claimants' use of the resources of the country. Sometimes, those interviewed talked about past activity and did not make it clear whether such activity was still current practice. In other cases, the distinction was made clear. In the data I set out here I comment on those instances where it is evident that the practice discussed was, for the most part, an observance that was recalled rather than being a part of current practice. Where it appears clear or reasonable to assume that the practice is current, I indicate this to be the case. Where the status of the activity is unclear, I indicate that this is so. My concern here is to explore whether Noongar economic utilisation of the countryside is a continuing practice, or whether it is what might be termed a 'memory culture'.

I have divided the economic use of the countryside into five main headings. These can be summarised as follows:

- camping;
- hunting and fishing;
- food;
- medicines;
- resources (artefacts, painting, indicators), minerals and water.

These data do not represent a definitive account of the economic exploitation practised by all of those interviewed. This is because not all Noongar participants in these field studies were asked about their current hunting and gathering activities. Research that focused exclusively on the uses of the natural resources of the land would in all probability provide substantial additional data. However, as will be seen from the volume of the data analysed, the details presented are sufficiently comprehensive to provide an indication of the current status of the utilisation of the natural resources of the application area by the claimant community.

Camping

Of the 46 citations in the research data, there were 26 cases of camping activity remembered or recalled by 23 claimants interviewed. I have interpreted these data to mean that those who provided the data reported that certain places were important because it was remembered that people had camped at these specific locations. I will discuss the importance of these historical places in the second part of this chapter, along with some additional data. However, and evidently, a memory that a place had been a camping place does not constitute current use of the country.

There were some 19 cases of where claimants reported that they continued to use the application area for camping activities. These cases derived from 15 interviews. There was one additional instance where it was unclear to me whether or not the camping activity discussed was current or in the past.

These data, along with their sources, are set out in Table 13.1.

Table 13.1: Utilisation of the application area, camping

Camping	Number of citations	Number of interviewees
Camped in the past	26	23
Current camping reported	19	15
Unclear	1	1

These data are of limited assistance in providing any measure of the current use of the claim area by the claimants. As indicated above, the data are incomplete. Moreover, many parts of the claim area are alienated and not open to camping, while parks and forestry reserves have access and camping controls. Both circumstances serve to limit the availability of areas of the South West to the claimants and may also discourage access. Many of the claimants are, however, able to access their country on day visits from their own town base, or that of their extended family, making camping unnecessary. Finally, many of those interviewed were older members of the community, who might prefer not to camp out if other accommodation is available. However, on the positive side, it is clear that members of the Noongar community continue to visit and camp on their land, and this use is further demonstrated in the remaining data considered in this section.

Hunting and fishing

Table 13.2 shows, in summary form, some of the animals, fish and reptiles that the claimants have discussed as being taken from the application area. Against each species listed are the number of cases noted as current exploitation, those reported as being in the past and those where the time of the utilisation is uncertain.

Kangaroo is the most frequently hunted animal, followed by yabbies and marron, freshwater turtles, and saltwater and freshwater fish. Possum is the only

Table 13.2: Animals hunted or caught on Noongar land

Species	Now	Formerly	Uncertain
Birds (gen)			2
Birds, cockatoos			1
Birds, duck	1	2	
Black swan		1	
Crabs	1		
Emu	3	3	
Fish (freshwater)	3	1	4
Fish (saltwater)	4	3	
Goanna	1		1
Hunting (gen)	2	2	
Jilgie, yabby[130]	7	1	1
Kangaroo (Brushtail)			1
Kangaroo (gen)	13	5	2
Kangaroo (Little)	1		
Lizard (Long)	1	1	
Lizard (Blue-Tongue)	1	1	
Lizard (Bobtail)	1		
Numbat			1
Porcupine (echidna)	2		2
Possum	1	3	
Rabbits			1
Shell fish	1		
Turtle (freshwater)	5	1	
Turtle (saltwater)	1		
Witchetty grubs (*bardi*)	6		5

category spoken of as being more frequently hunted formerly than now, and Joe Walley pointed out that this animal, like many others, was now protected, and hunting them could incur heavy penalties from prosecutions mounted by CALM.[127] Overall, these data indicate that Noongar people continue to benefit

126 Genus *Cherax* but smaller than a marron.

127 CALM (Conservation and Land Management) was the department of the Western Australian government with responsibility for environmental management at the time of the research.

economically from animals, reptiles and fish taken from the application area. Of the species listed in Table 13.2, the following are documented as being recorded in the early literature on Noongar traditional practice by Meagher and Ride (1979, pp. 72–4):

- birds (gen);
- birds, cockatoos;
- birds, duck;
- black swan;
- emu;
- fish (freshwater);
- fish (saltwater);
- jilgie, yabby (Moore 1978b, p. 399);
- kangaroo (gen);
- lizard (gen) (see also Nind 1979, p. 25);
- possum;
- turtle (freshwater);
- witchetty grubs (*bardi*).

In the account provided by Meagher and Ride, lizards generally were not identified as to species, nor were kangaroo. The numbat was recorded by Grey (see Bindon and Chadwick 1992, p. 338) and the porcupine (echidna) is commonly eaten in other areas of Aboriginal Australia (Palmer 1999, p. 37); it seems reasonable to assume that both were traditionally eaten in the South West. The mallee hen is recorded as being hunted by a Noongar man by Millett (1980, pp. 223–4), although she makes no mention of their eggs. Shellfish were not eaten traditionally in the South West (Meagher and Ride 1979, p. 74) and rabbits, as is well known, were introduced by the European settlers.

Overall, the list of animals, reptiles and birds which are hunted or caught on Noongar land would appear, for the most part, to represent those species probably taken by Noongar people at the time of sovereignty.

Marine resources

Lomas Roberts identified Cape Riche and adjacent coastal areas as important fishing places for him and his family. Another claimant reported that he often took crabs from the Harvey Estuary, while Charlie Shaw stated that he fished from beaches and from the offshore island, Cillion, to which he could swim. Coastal fishing was considered by a number of other claimants to be a significant family activity.

The use of the sea was considered to have been important to Noongar people in times past. Charlie Shaw pointed to the middens round Wedge Island as evidence of the use of marine resources in the past and stated that the old people used to spear a species of small seal there, which they ate. One claimant stated that in the past Noongar people used to camp up the Yunderup River. Ellen Hill and Barbara Stammner-Corbett both talked of the importance of fishing to their family economy, particularly in the past. Attention was drawn to the springs that occurred on the beach below the high-water mark, which presumably were water sources in times past. Fish traps were also reported by Charlie Shaw, Bill Webb and Glen Kelly.

Bush foods (vegetables)

Table 13.3 summarises some of the bush foods which were identified by those Noongar men and women who provided data to the researchers. The table shows whether, from the information available, the bush resources continue to be used as a food source, or whether there remains knowledge of the use rather than actual use. Of the 33 different plants listed, 18, or 54.5 per cent, are still utilised by the claimants. An additional 10 (30.3 per cent) are of uncertain status, since the context for the collection of these data does not provide sufficient information to form a view about whether the resource is still used. Only five (15 per cent) would appear not to be used at all. However, these data were provided by a number of different Noongar men and women, and there was no consistent indication of the status of the plant in question. Many of these data were collected from the north and west of the application area, with the southern and eastern areas being under-represented. Of these plants, 48.49 per cent have a Noongar name. Additional research focusing specifically on bush foods would yield a greater variety of plants than are recorded here and, in all probability, more details as to the Noongar name, use and preparation.

My view is that the use of these plants forms a part of Noongar knowledge, and the plants which are taken are a supplement to other foods, sourced from the markets and supermarkets. While the economic value of these bush foods is therefore limited, the knowledge of the resources is exercised in its transmission to others and practised in the collection and consumption of the foods. To know about Noongar bush food and to practise its collection is, then, a signal to others of your status as a Noongar person. It remains a traditional cultural attribute.

Table 13.3: Plants utilised for food and found on Noongar land

Common name	Noongar name*	Scientific name	Status**	Use, description
Angel bread		lerp	C1, U1	Sweet edible waxy secretion, produced by young of psyllids
Banksia		*Banksia* sp.	K1	Fermented drink made from steeping flowers in water
Banksia		*Banksia* sp.	C1	Buds picked and chewed, 'like a chewing gum'
Berries	*yorna* berries		U1	Berries also eaten by Blue-Tongue Lizard
Berries (general)			C2	Berries collected and eaten
Bush potato	*carnu*		C5, U3	A small, sweet, white potato
Bush potato	*jol*		U1	Potato-like tuber
Bush potato	*joobak*		U3	Potato-like tuber
Bush potato	*kara*		U1	Potato-like tuber
Bush potato	*warrany*	*Dioscorea* sp.***	U1	Potato-like tuber
Bush potato			U1	Wild potato found around Wanaroo — probably *jol, joobak* or *kara*
Bush potato			U1	Like a *carnu*, but a different species
Chilli onion, blood roots	*born, kardang, potaij*	*Haemodorum* sp.	C4, U3	Roots, with a hot spicy taste, often compared to a chilli
Emu berry			C1	Small, green berry with a seed
Emu bush	*jeyak*		C1	Small fruit shaken from tree and eaten
Emu plum		*Podocarpus drouynianus*	K1	Small shrub with fruit like a purple grape
Fungus	*nguma*		C1	Fungus on tree bark; dark-red inside; cooked in ashes and tastes like meat
Grass tree	*balga*	*Xanthorrhoeaceae*	C2, K2, U1	Young hearts eaten, used for making fire, torch, floor covering
Jam gum	*marngart, yorgum* (name of tree)	*Acacia* sp.	C11, K1, U2	Edible gum, laxative

Common name	Noongar name*	Scientific name	Status**	Use, description
Kerbein	*norn*	*Lepidosperma gladiatum*	C2	White, fleshy part at the base of the stem is eaten, best when in seed
Kulberry	*kulberi*		C1	Low, thorny bush with yellow to white berries, with hard seeds
Little green apples			C1	Tree/bush with yellow flowers and small, apple-like fruit
Manna gum	*mana*	*Eucalyptus viminalis*	K1, C3	Gum, which is very sweet, eaten; also seeds
Mushrooms			C2	Mushrooms collected and eaten
Not named	*poojak*		U1	Flower steeped in water to make sweet drink
Onion			U1	Onion-like plant with seeds that are eaten raw
Pig face	*bane*	*Carpobrotus virescens*	C1	Sweet succulent fruits eaten
Quandong		*Santalum acuminatum*	C4	Small tree with red fruit and large stone
Stinkwood			K1	Seeds used to flavour meat
Tea-tree		*Melaleuca* sp.	K1	Leaves used as infusion to make tea
Wattle		*Acacia cyclops*	U1	Large seeds used when ground up to make a biscuit
Wild fig			C1	Fig, fruit eaten
Zamia palm		*Macrozamia riedlei*	K4	Seeds detoxified and ground to make flour

* Some assistance in identification was provided by reference to Daw, Walley and Keighery (1997).
** C = contemporary use, K = knowledge, but no evident use, U = uncertain.
*** Meagher and Ride (1979, p. 75)

The customary nature of these bush foods is borne out by reference to the early literature. Meagher and Ride (1979, pp. 74–5) record the former use of *banksia* species, the *warrany* (bush potato), *born* (chilli onion), acacia gum, wattle and zamia palm seeds. Other references to the use of the zamia palm are found in Millett (1980, p. 99) and Clark (1842, p. 3) as well as Grey (1841, vol. 2, p. 58). Salvado remarks on the consumption of yams (Stormon 1977, p. 161) and Hassell comments on the eating of manna gum (1975, p. 21). Hassell notes the use of the quandong (1975, p. 21) and the *quirting*, a hot onion (p. 22), which is recorded in Table 13.3 as *born*, *kardang* and *Potaij*. Grey (1841, vol. 2, p. 58) records *bohn*.

Moore records the use of the bush potato, *carnu*, which he calls *konono* (Moore, 1978b, 301). Roth records the fermented drink made from banksia flowers (Roth 1902, p. 49) and Crawford and Crawford (2003, p. 42) comment on its use and cite early references to its exploitation. Crawford and Crawford note, from the early literature, the eating of certain sorts of fungus (pp. 30–1).

Given the lack of detail relating to some plants listed in Table 13.3, it is not possible to either identify them all with certainty or find reference to them all in the early literature. However, given the information available to me, it is reasonable to conclude that most of the plants listed would have been used prior to the settlement of the South West by European colonists. With the exception of the mushroom, it seems most likely that all species listed are indigenous.

Medicines

Thirty-five examples of medicinal use of plants collected during the research reported here are set out in Table 13.4. Most are for common ailments, including constipation and diarrhoea, while those categorised as 'medicines' or 'tonics' appear to be more general in purpose. Of the medicines, 26 (74 per cent) would, from the context, appear to be a part of contemporary Noongar practice. In eight cases (23 per cent), it is uncertain whether the medicinal use is current or a part of memory. The snake bite cure is recalled, but the medicinal herb or plant is not remembered.

Table 13.4: Some examples of Noongar medicine

Malady or purpose	Noongar or other name	Status*	Details
Asthma	Emu plum	1C	
Bull ant and bee stings, sores and aches	Eucalyptus leaves	1C	Leaves are boiled
Chest colds	Coastal lavender	1U	
Common cold	Gum leaves	1C	
Common cold	Wattle leaves	1C	Leaves crushed
Cuts and ulcers	White gum	1U	
Diabetes	Leaves (unspecified)	1C	Boiled
Diarrhoea	Red gum	1C	
Diarrhoea	Red gum gum	1C	
Diarrhoea	Manna gum	1C	
Diarrhoea, scabies, cuts and infection	Marri gum	1C	
Insect repellent	Emu oil	1U	

Malady or purpose	Noongar or other name	Status*	Details
Laxative	Jam gum	1C	
Laxative	Rare emu	1U	
Laxative	Red gum gum	3C	
Laxative and constipation	Jam gum	1C	
Medicine	Emu fat	1C	
Medicine	Emu oil	1C	
Medicine	Liver of Bobtail Goanna	1C	
Medicine	Red gum sap	1C	
Fertility	Turtle liver	1C	
Medicine or tonic	Not named	1C	Prickly leaves; for making medicinal tea
Medicine, rubbed into skin	Emu oil	1C	
Medicines	Plants unspecified	1C	
Medicines	Tree bark	1C	
Mouth ulcers	Wild bees' wax	1U	
Rheumatism	Porcupine fat	1C	
Skin cream	Bain	1U	*Carpobrotus virescens*
Snakebite	Unnamed	1K	
Stomach ulcers	Jarrah gum	1C	
Tonic	Bush medicine (not specified)	1C	
Tonic	Reed	1C	Boiled
Tonic, aphrodisiac	*Born*	1U	
Ulcers	*Wornt*	1U	*Eucalyptus* sp. Gum used to treat ulcers
Ulcers, infections	Red gum	1C	

*C = contemporary use, K = knowledge, but no evident use, U = uncertain.

The early accounts of the South West provide little detail about medicinal use. Hassell (1975, p. 24) lists several medicinal remedies, including the use of the seeds of the red gum and more specifically the use of eucalypt gum for the treatment of diarrhoea. Hammond (1933, 59-60) lists a few general cures, but none are relevant to those set out in Table 13.4. All the medicinal plants noted in Table 13.4 are indigenous. It is reasonable to conclude that the practice of the use of these medicinal remedies constitutes a continuing part of Noongar customary practice, and represents a traditional pharmacology, the practice of which has continued from times prior to the settlement of the South West by Europeans.

The use of resources, minerals and water

Table 13.5 summarises data collected relating to the use of natural resources by the claimants. Items 1 to 6 represent what appear to be examples of current use. I have included a descriptive statement sourced from the data sheets in support of this conclusion. The status of items 7 to 13 is uncertain with respect to their current use, and again comment is provided in all but one case to contextualise the status classification. Unlike medicines, only a relatively small percentage of cases (13 per cent of the total) represent current usage. The majority of the rest relate to aspects of the material culture which are no longer practised, perhaps because they have been superseded by modern technology or materials. For example, electric torches have replaced the need for burning torches and synthetic glues have negated the need for natural ones. Nevertheless, the knowledge of these uses of natural resources remains a part of the culture of the claimants from whom these data were collected.

Meagher and Ride (1979, p. 76) list a number of the items included in Table 13.5 as being recorded in early accounts of the material culture of the South West. They make reference to a variety of spears and other artefacts, the use of bark for shelter and the manufacture of glue from grass tree resins, as well as the use of ochres (p. 77). Kangaroo skin cloaks were a notable feature of the material culture of the Noongar people, as has been well documented (p. 72; Hassell 1975, pp. 113–14). Some items included in Table 13.5 represent modern adaptations of traditionally used materials, including items 3, 4 and 43. With these exceptions, it would appear reasonable to conclude that the uses, or the knowledge of the uses, recorded in Table 13.5 represent practices which were current in the application area prior to 1829.

Economic use of the countryside: conclusion

I draw the following conclusions and make these observations relating to the data set out above. First, it is evident that Noongar people continue to visit and camp out on Noongar country. However, I consider that these data are an unreliable indicator of the degree to which Noongar land is used, since it may be accessed without a requirement to camp. Second, kangaroo, freshwater crustaceans, freshwater turtle and fish (saltwater and freshwater) appear from the data to represent sources of food for Noongar people. These would appear to have an economic value and may supplement conventional foods. These species are reported as being used by Noongar people at or about the time of sovereignty. Third, a wide variety

Table 13.5: Use of resources by claimants

No.	Resource	Use	Status*	Details
1	Animal skins	Rugs	1C	Ego commented that Noongar people make rugs from kangaroo skins.
2	Ochre	Paintings	1C	Ochre used in his paintings.
3	Paperbark	Paintings	1C	Paperbark collected off the trees and used in paintings.
4	Seeds	Revegetation of mining areas	1C	Billinue Community (Cataby Seeds) collects native seeds from the surrounding land to be used for rehabilitation of mine sites.
5	Wood	Firewood	1C	
6	Wood, wattle tree	Spears, boomerangs and clapping sticks	1C	Wood is used for spears, boomerangs, clapping sticks and fighting sticks.
7	Balga	Artefacts	1U	
8	Balga	Torch	1U	Grass tree leaves can be used for a torch.
9	Box reed	Twine	1U	Box reed is found around water. It is very strong and is used for tying things.
10	Emu bush (berries showing)	Indicates emu eggs ready to hatch	1U	The emu bush lets you know when to leave the emu eggs untouched. When the berry comes out on this little bush, that is the time when the baby emus are developing in their shell.
11	Indji plant (in flower)	Indicates skipjack season	1U	Indji plant is a type of pea with red flowers. When it flowers, it signals the season of skipjack.
12	Paperbark	Water	1U	Water is obtained from inside the bark by cutting into it.
13	Paperbark	Water	1U	Strip back the bark and there is moisture.
14	Paperbark	Fish poison	1K	
15	Balga	Floor covering of hut	1K	
16	Acacia?	Soap	1K	Possibly *Trymalium floribundum*
17	Balga	Sticks for making fire	2K	Fire drill.
18	Balga leaves	Camp shelter	1K	
19	Balga leaves	Torch	1K	

No.	Resource	Use	Status*	Details
20	Banksia	Torch	1K	
21	*Birun*, bush with spiky leaves	Fish 'net'	1K	
22	Branches	Bush mattress	1K	
23	Bulrushes	Twine	1K	The stems of bulrushes are made into rope and then bags.
24	Eucalypts	Spears	1K	
25	Kangaroo dung, ash and balga gum	Glue for artefacts	1K	
26	Kangaroo dung, charcoal and balga gum	Resin, glue	1K	
27	Kangaroo sinews	Fishing line, hook from barbed stick	1K	
28	Kangaroo skins	Process kangaroo skins	1K	
29	Kangaroo skins	Skin rugs	1K	
30	Manna gum	Glue	1K	
31	Manna gum	Glue	1K	
32	Ochre	Ritual purposes	1K	
33	Ochre	Unspecified	1K	
34	Ochre	Unspecified	1K	
35	Paperbark	Burials	1K	
36	Paperbark	Shelter	1K	
37	Paperbark	Shelters	1K	
38	Paperbark	Torch	1K	
39	Paperbark	Water	1K	
40	Peppermint tree	Spears	1K	
41	Porcupine quills	Spear heads	1K	
42	Reeds	Fishing nets	1K	
43	Salt	Unspecified	2K	Probably not traditional uses.
44	Spear wood	Spears	1K	
45	Water	Drinking	1K	

No.	Resource	Use	Status*	Details
46	Water	Drinking, washing clothes	1K	
47	Water	Unspecified	1K	

*C = contemporary use, K = knowledge, but no evident use, U = uncertain.

of plants is collected, consumed and used, while the knowledge of the use of numerous others is evident. Fourth, medicinal plants comprise a substantial body of pharmaceutical knowledge, there being 35 different species recorded, of which 74 per cent would appear, from the data, to be in current use. These plants and their uses, which would appear to represent a part of traditional Noongar knowledge, represent an important part of contemporary knowledge and use of the natural world. Fifth, the use of natural resources for other purposes (artefacts, shelter, art and ritual) would appear to be limited, reflecting the substantial changes which have occurred in the material culture of the Noongar people. However, continuing knowledge of the use of natural resources is evidenced in the data.

In these accounts I have distinguished between three varieties of data: incidence of contemporary use; incidence of past use; and cases where incidence of use is uncertain. These assessments cannot be regarded as conclusive, since they require an interpretation of the data based on the context of its collection and reportage. However, it is evident that the contribution of natural resources to the Noongar domestic economy is likely to be quite limited, with the possible exception of some meat and fish. The economic benefit of the use of medicinal resources is likely to have some direct economic benefit, although this would be hard to quantify. However, occasional and opportunistic utilisation of natural resources, with limited economic benefit, would appear to be a continuing part of Noongar culture and to have some importance as an activity that typifies the following of a Noongar lifestyle. Knowledge of the use of resources, where evidently dissociated from practice, would appear to have cultural value and represents a continuing and non-diminishing intellectual property. This is concluded as follows. The economic use of many of the natural resources employed in traditional Noongar material culture would have ceased as soon as alternative (and more convenient) materials came to hand. While this would have varied with the resource, it seems likely that this would have occurred, for the most part, several if not many generations ago. This means that the knowledge of the use of items of material culture has survived well beyond the generation whose members utilised and employed the resources. The knowledge (but not the use) would then appear to represent a continuing aspect of Noongar traditional knowledge. In short, the knowledge has been passed on from generation to generation and has become a commodity quite separate for the practice of which it was formerly a part. In reaching this conclusion, then I would reject a view that the knowledge of the use of material culture without concomitant practice represents merely a remnant of decaying cultural practices.

Sites in Noongar country

Introduction

During the course of the research reported here, claimants showed the researchers numerous sites or places which were of particular spiritual importance. Knowledge of sites, the duty to care for and protect them and the authority to talk about them are features of Noongar cultural observance and practice which I explore in the following paragraphs.

Not all sites are the same. Some sites are more specifically associated with spirituality than others. Thus spirituality is differentiated by the claimants. For example, some sites are believed to be the spiritual home of particular named spirit beings. Others are associated more generally with unnamed spirit beings. Some sites are considered to be significant because of their historical or emotional importance, but are regarded as having a spiritual component. Sites can be understood to be important because of other attributes, including their potential as places where natural resources can be found, or because they have a historical importance but are not considered to be intrinsically spiritual. Heuristically, then, sites can be divided up categorically for convenience. However, many claimants consider the metaphysical aspects of their world to comprise parts of a whole, and differentiations for the purpose of classification do not always sit comfortably with this understanding.

The term 'site', in common English usage, can imply a more or less specifically bounded area, as in 'building site' or 'campsite'. The use of the term 'site' for places and areas which are spiritually significant to Aboriginal people is, again, a convenience. However, this use can be misleading. This is because spirituality, as the phenomenon is commonly understood, is not considered to be restricted or bounded. While a single physical feature (like a pool or rock) may be the marker of a site (and so is clearly bounded), spirituality is not so confined.

In this section I briefly review some of the data which have been collected in relation to sites on Noongar country and provide an overview of each type of site and its incidence. Some spiritually significant areas are associated with the travels or other activities of spirit beings, which are believed to have journeyed in the long distant past during the Dreaming. Their activities and the consequential modifications to the countryside are recounted as narratives. In the second part of this section I examine some of these narratives and their sequelae as they are believed to have affected the physical and social Noongar world.

The sites data

The sites or areas of cultural significance in Noongar country which were recorded during the research reported here may be classified as follows for the purposes of this analysis:

- spiritual;
- habitation;
- burial;
- historical;
- resources.

Spiritual sites include those associated with named spirit beings, other spirits, sites associated with healing and birthing, as well as places where rituals were formerly conducted. Habitation sites are those which show signs of archaeological deposits, and these may not strictly be limited to places where there was habitation. Burial sites are graves. Historical sites are those places remembered for past associations, like old camping places or missions. Resources are divided into meat (1), vegetable (2), water (3), fish and reptiles (4), minerals (5), medicines (6) and other raw materials (7). In cases where the resource was not specified, the site is coded 'R'.

Many sites had multiple uses and were significant for several reasons. For example, a site might be of spiritual importance as well as being a burial site and a resource area. The categorisation of sites by only one of the classifications listed above does not reflect the complexity, diversity and richness of the cultural significance of place to Noongar people.

Table 13.6 sets out a summary developed from the data collected of the incidence of site types classified according to the five categories noted above. The second column in Table 13.6 shows how a site or area was first recorded in terms of the classifications listed above. The figure at the foot of this column sums to the total number of sites recorded (290) during the research reported here. Column 3 records the incidence of the identification of the same site type recorded as supplementary or additional classifications for a site recorded during the research. Thus

Table 13.6: Types of sites recorded

Type	No of sites	Additional classification	Total	% of all sites
Spiritual	116	25	141	49
Habitation	21	14	35	12
Burial	15	6	21	7
Historical	97	36	133	46
All resources	41	57	98	34
Totals	290			

of the 116 sites recorded as being of spiritual importance there were an additional 25 sites that were also classified as important because of their spiritual associations. Consequently 141 sites were classified as being of spiritual importance to the claimants. Similarly, there was a total of 35 sites identified as significant on account of their association with habitation, 21 burial sites, 133 sites that had historical significance and 98 that included recognition of the importance of resource exploitation and use.

The attribution of site categories is not exhaustive, so some sites may have attributes of more than three categories. It is evident to me that many areas associated with the collection or hunting of natural resources were not recorded as sites, so are not counted in the table. It is important to remember that the list of sites represents only a sample of the areas and places of significance to Noongar people and, while representative, is in no way an exhaustive account of all the many thousands of sites and areas of significance to Noongar people in Noongar land.

Resource sites have been pooled in Table 13.6 but a detailed break-down of resource site types is presented in Table 13.7. Field data indicate that 98 of the 290 sites recorded included reference to their resource use or potential. Generally, however, the data in Table 13.7 are of limited assistance in determining the break-down of the figures to specific resource use, since nearly 33% of the total cases (32) were not broken down by resource type.

From these data I conclude that spiritual attachment to places and country is an important aspect of Noongar relationships to country. Based on these multiple classifications overall nearly half the 290 sites recorded included reference to the spiritual significance of the place. A little under half were considered to have historical significance while just over a third of sites recorded were considered associated with the procurement of natural resources.

Table 13.7: Sites relating to acquisition of resources

Type	Total of all listings
Resource gen	32
Meat (1)	8
Vegetables (2)	9
Water (3)	17
Fish (4)	20
Minerals (5)	5
Medicines (6)	3
Raw materials (7)	4
Total	98

Site categories: discussion

Spiritual

The spirituality of a site is explained by reference to one or more spirit beings, which are believed to reside at or inform the site and its environs. These may be named. The most ubiquitous spirit being is the Wagarl, a huge serpentine being with creative powers associated with springs, creeks, pools, rivers and estuaries. I will discuss the numerous narratives in Noongar tradition relating to the Wagarl later in this chapter. Other spirit beings include the Emu, Kangaroo, Moon, Dog, Parrot and Mallee Hen, as well as those that appear to have originally had a human form, but are now metamorphosed into the countryside as mountains or other natural features. Sites are also variously associated with other named spirit beings, including *mumari* and *wutarji*, and other supernatural creatures, like the *jimba* and *jarnak*. Unnamed spirits of deceased and unknown forebears of the claimants are believed to reside at many former camping places. I have discussed this aspect of Noongar belief above. There are spiritual associations recorded relating to natural species, including the bullfrog, currawong, kangaroo and eagle.

Former ritual grounds (including those often referred to as 'corroboree' grounds) may be regarded as having a spiritual importance, providing for a significance that extends beyond a historical value. This is particularly so for places that are considered to have been associated with the rituals of initiation. Public rituals, often performed, so it would appear, close to reserves or other living areas, are common in the site inventory. While ritual sites are no longer used, they continue to have a spiritual significance for the claimants, and knowledge of them remains a part of Noongar culture.

Finally, some sites are spiritually important because they are considered to be 'healing places'. These sites are regarded as places to which people go when they need emotional as well as spiritual healing. Carol Peterson and Lynette Knapp told of how a young woman with a serious drug problem had spent time at such a site and been cured of her addiction.

Habitation

Habitation sites are archaeological sites, including stone arrangements and places where artefact scatters have been reported. The research reported here was anthropological rather than archaeological; hence few sites of this category were recorded.

Burial

Many Noongar people have been buried within town cemeteries. Generally, these places have not been recorded in the site inventory, unless they were places where specific data were recorded. Some cemetery sites were established close to former missions or settlements, while a number of other graves are known to exist either in the bush or on what is now agricultural or even suburban land.

Historical

Historical sites are numerous, and comprise places which have a particular place in the claimants' history and personal life experiences. Many of these are former camping areas, reflecting the numerous places of residence that older claimants occupied while pursuing agricultural work across their runs. More permanent places of residence are also represented. These include a number of the old reserves, which were a common feature of most towns throughout the South West until the 1970s. The site list contains some of the major missions and settlements, including those at Carrolup, Badjaling and Djuring. The list of official settlements represents only those that came to the attention of the researchers, and is far from complete. Other camping places represent places where Noongar people have lived, often by arrangement with the local farmer for whom they worked. These often lacked basic facilities. Camping areas are often associated with the collection of natural resources.

All resources

I have discussed above the acquisition of resources from the land and made comment on the degree to which this can be understood to represent contemporary practice as distinct from remembered practice. Not all places from which resources are taken today were recorded as sites. My evaluation of the data collected in relation to sites and the acquisition of natural resources is that, for the most part, they represent places that are remembered as being rich in resources that were exploited during periods when Noongar people camped or lived close to them. These data are not of much assistance in determining whether these sites are so utilised today, although, as I have already concluded, the claimants do continue to exploit their country for its natural resources.

Narrative traditions

Narratives relating to specific places, or a series of places, form a part of the oral tradition of the claimants. These serve to explain how the creative forces evident in the Dreaming, when the activities reported in the narratives are considered to have taken place, resulted in modifications to the landscape. The narrative event is explicatory text. The knowledge of the narrative is an indication to others of the possession of an understanding of Noongar cosmological processes. Generally, its enunciation is reserved to older members of the community, who are regarded as having the authority to speak of such things. Some claimants told me that narratives, since they relate to a family's country, should ideally only be told by members of that family. Consequently, narratives represent more than an oral tradition, as their social reproduction signals both authority within the community and a relationship to ancestral country.

It is not my intention to reproduce, verbatim, the narratives collected during the fieldwork. I will summarise aspects of some of the principal accounts in order to provide an overview of the relationship of the narratives to place, as well as to furnish material upon which to base my opinion as to the prevalence of the narrative traditions in Noongar culture today.

Wagarl

The Wagarl represents the best-known Noongar spirit being. The Wagarl is a huge serpentine being, sometimes characterised as having a hairy face or mane of hair. There are many Wagarl traditions through the South West. The extensive travels of the Wagarl are believed to have occurred during the creative period, in time long past that is sometimes referred to as the Dreaming. In some cases, the Wagarl is believed to have travelled down a river system and eventually to have breached the coast to form an estuary or inlet where the river now enters the sea. In other cases, and perhaps where the narrative tradition is developed by those whose geographic association is aligned to the coast, the Wagarl is believed to have moved from the sea and then created estuaries, coastal lagoons and rivers by moving upstream. It is believed that the Wagarl created the rivers and pools during its travels, being responsible for the purity of the water, its constancy of supply and the safety of those it protects. However, it is an ambiguous figure, and must be treated with great respect. These aspects of the Wagarl (and other supernatural beings) have been discussed in detail in Chapter 10 and elsewhere in this book.

Today, the Wagarl is usually considered to be confined to a pool or reach of a river where it may be encountered by the unwary. The Wagarl is a multiple being, with many manifestations. In one account, it had children (baby Wagarl), while in another it appeared as two different beings that were in conflict. The Wagarl is also recorded as the Beemula in some accounts collected from the north of the claim area. The narrative traditions are rich and diverse, with a commonality of spiritual characteristics that can be understood to typify Noongar beliefs.

I recorded data relating to seven principal Wagarl traditions. The first is a Wagarl that appears to have moved from the inland areas round Miling and Moora, following what is now the Moore River, passing Mogumber and reaching the sea at the Moore River mouth. The narrative details of this track are poorly developed in the data. Another Wagarl is reported to have followed a more northerly route, to reach the sea between Lancelin and Cervantes, a track that is marked by the extensive sand plain lagoons and limestone caves that are believed to have been created by the Wagarl in its journey to the coast. There, freshwater springs, which flow from the beach below the high-water mark, are the present-day manifestation of the Wagarl and its track.

A third Wagarl track follows the Avon River from some point south-east of York, passing Northam and Toodyay. The Wagarl broke through the Darling Ranges at Walyunga and formed the extensive coastal lagoons, river reaches and lakes that are now the site of modern Perth.[128] A fourth Wagarl track is believed to have entered the sea at the site of what is now the Peel inlet, where the Wagarl gave birth to progeny. These offspring made the Serpentine, Murray and Harvey rivers, while the mother made Lakes Clifton and Preston and the estuary at Australind when she travelled south. A fifth Wagarl commenced travel in the vicinity of Wave Rock and followed the drainage system south-west towards Wagin, incorporating

128 R. Bropho made some comment on this Wagarl when giving evidence in the Metro native title claim. See WAG142/98. Richard Wilkes Albert Corunna and others (Applicants) and the State of Western Australia and others (Respondents), 7.3.03, p. 851ff.

the Hotham River to join with the Arthur River and the Blackwood and so to the sea. A sixth Wagarl is associated with the Collie River. A seventh Wagarl narrative, featuring a pair of the mythic beings that travelled from the sea at the present site of Albany, making in their conflicts the coastal features round Albany, and the King and Kalgan rivers. A variety of individual Wagarl, not recorded as being a part of a longer narrative sequence, were recorded at such places as Margaret River, Canal Rocks, Hotham River and Bremer Bay.

The Wagarl was recorded by early settlers, and it seems reasonable to conclude that it was a significant part of the religious belief of the people of the South West at this time.[129] It would appear reasonable to conclude that the narratives of the Wagarl represent an oral tradition and concomitant beliefs that date back to a period before sovereignty.

Emu

In the area round Wagin, the Emu spirit being is associated with the Wagarl, but is also associated in its own right with a number of sites in the vicinity. The town of Wagin is probably derived from the Noongar word for emu, *watj*.

Dog

The Dog man (Twert) travelled from Jerramungup with many dogs and two women as his wives who were not of the correct moiety. He went to a place in the Fitzgerald National Park that is now called Twertup, where he was turned into a dog, either as a result of his wrong marriages or because he mistreated his dogs, or both. The place now has many dogs, and is dangerous, especially at night. The narrative is recorded by Hassell (1975, pp. 31–5). The track followed by Twert is recorded as a site. Another story collected from the Jerramungup area, and relating to a particular site, tells of an interchange between the Kangaroo and Moon, both now being represented in the features of a large granite dome. The narrative is included in a more extensive account provided by Hassell (p. 221).

Stirling Ranges, Barren Ranges and Fitzgerald Ranges

There is a suite of narratives relating to these locations, which account for the tracks or route of spiritual beings. The first relates to the Kangaroo people and the Emu people, who originally lived together in the Stirling Ranges. They had a fight and the Emu people were badly injured. They escaped to the Fitzgerald Ranges,

129 A brief summary of some of the relevant early references is provided by Vinnicombe (1989, pp. 8–13). See also Stormon (1977, p. 128); Armstrong (1979, p. 189); Clark (1842, p. 4).

spilling their blood on the ground as they went. This blood is now manifest as a red rock outcropping across the area between the Stirling Ranges and the Fitzgerald Ranges.

A second narrative relates to the Kangaroo people of the Stirling Ranges and the Emu people of the Barren Ranges. The former had promised a girl as a husband to an Emu man. When the time came for her to leave, a party of Emu people assembled to accompany her. She was saddened by the thought of leaving her pet dog, which was in turn upset at her departure. As they left, in the middle of the day, the dog howled. The party turned around to see why the dog had howled and were all turned to rocks. The girl became the Stirling Ranges, now seen as the 'Sleeping Lady', the profile of the ranges viewed from the Chester Pass to Albany road, which resembles a supine woman.

A third narrative relates to two brothers who lived near Ongerup. They were Parrot Men. They had a competition to see who could fly the fastest. They ran so fast that they collided with Mt Trio in the Stirling Ranges, making a cave in the mountain, through which they passed to emerge on the other side. This caused many of their feathers to fly about, which formed the many wildflowers across the countryside.

Finally, there is a narrative of a narcissistic Kangaroo Man who spent his time preening himself in his reflection in a pool. His wife, tired of his vanity and consequential failure to supply her needs, cooked herself and her baby some meat. He returned to the camp to discover this and beat her as a punishment. She crawled away, mortally injured, forming the Kalgan River. She died and her pet dog buried her. Her grave is now Green Island, while she is also the Sleeping Lady of the Stirling Ranges. Her family, much aggrieved at her treatment, killed the Kangaroo Man, who became Bluff Knoll. The Noongar name for the mountain is Meilya, which means 'many eyes' and is a reference to the fact that the face of the Bluff alters as the mist blows across it, but can be seen to represent the face of the warrior. Seen from afar, the mist covering the mountain is understood to be his hair blowing in the wind, showing that he is still alive.

Hassell (1975, pp. 171–3) records a story with a similar motif to that contained in the story of the Two Parrot Men (loss of feathers); however, to the best of my knowledge, these narratives are not recorded by Hassell as presented here. Hassell did record that Bluff Knoll was inhabited by a malevolent spirit being called Noatch, whose shape-changing attributes were reflected in the many faces that can be seen in the Bluff. Hassell gives the name for Bluff Knoll as *Bullah Meual*, which she interprets as 'Great Many Face Hill' (Hassell 1936, p. 702). Hassell's account has some similarities to the last one provided above. Hassell tells a story of Balyet, who died in and now haunts the mountains (Hassell 1975, pp. 128–9; 1934–35, pp. 272–3), although she does not make it clear to which mountains she is referring. The author recorded some narratives relating to the Stirling Ranges in 1973 (Palmer 1976). Some aspects of the narratives collected have similarities with those reported here, including the motif of the ranges appearing to take a human form and a battle between two groups. However, the traditions collected in 1973 from Gnowangerup would appear to be substantially different from those collected from helpers with affiliations to areas to the south and east of the ranges. Narrative complexity, variety and the occurrence of different versions of narratives are common features of oral tradition and cannot be interpreted correctly as showing decay or breakdown. By their very nature, oral accounts are inconsistent, and the process of oral tradition spawns variety. There is therefore no such thing as an original or 'correct' version of a narrative.[130] My conclusion is that the narratives I have reported here represent a continuing cultural tradition, based on materials, concept and beliefs that are a part of customary practice and that represent a cultural continuity with the past.[131]

Sites in Noongar Country: conclusion

Sites in Noongar country are often the focus of comment, attention and debate in the media. It is my experience that they evoke strong emotions in Noongar people. This is a consequence of the fact that they are believed to represent a focus for spirituality, and because any undue interference with them is believed to be damaging to the world order as it is conceived. It is therefore not surprising that many of the sites discussed here are associated with a spiritual presence. Given the nature of this spirituality, which I have discussed in other sections

130 In relation to oral traditions, an accepted anthropological view, see, for example, Vansina (1973, p. 27).

131 Brunton (2003, pp. 87–8) cites my 1976 article in support of a view that literary sources may have modified traditional narratives (and perhaps other beliefs too) and that consequential transmutations may render them substantially different to those that would have been in evidence prior to European sovereignty (p. 89). The quotation to which Brunton refers in my 1976 article is footnoted as sourced from 'Father Dwyer, Gnowangerup, 1973'. To the best of my knowledge, Father Dwyer was not a Noongar man. My interest was in exploring how oral traditions may change in all cultures. I suspect, on rereading Dwyer's quotation, that he had sourced his information from Hammond, a conclusion that Brunton also supplies. However, Brunton's point is somewhat blunted in the absence of a Noongar recital supporting his conclusion.

of this book (its potency, its danger, its life-giving attributes), sites represent a part of Noongar culture that cannot be taken lightly. I have commented on the extent to which I consider the nature of sites to be traditionally based and have concluded that from the information available to me, they would appear to be based upon beliefs, traditions and cultural ideals that extend back to a period prior to sovereignty.

I have shown that many sites have a strong historical and emotional importance to Noongar people. This means that these places figure in Noongar accounts of how they and their immediate forebears have lived their lives in close proximity to the land. I have no reason to suppose that such sentiments did not inform Noongar views traditionally as well. However, there is no way that this can be demonstrated.

In my opinion, the narratives and traditions I have set out as examples of the genre relate to whole areas of country, rather than to specific places within it. However, places may be identified within a narrative complex as the location of a specific event. The narratives serve to explain the form of the physical world, as well as its concomitant spiritual presences. The narratives and their constituent spirit beings form an ontological system that explains the natural and supernatural worlds, as well as the Noongar people's relationship to it and their place within it.

While I have emphasised that the data I have considered here are likely to be only a portion of those available, I conclude that it is likely that knowledge of sites, narratives and spirit beings has been lost within the claimant community. Any comparison with the narratives collected by Hassell, for example, shows that she was able to draw on a rich diversity of material, which was readily to hand. However, and to balance this conclusion, I point out that Hassell lived at Jerramungup for eight years, with one group of people whom she came to know well. A similarly extended period of fieldwork might provide copious additional material. Moreover, Hassell (and most other early observers) were silent on the spiritual and metaphysical aspects of Noongar culture. These remain central to the culture while the means of manifestation may have changed.

Chapter 14

RELATIONSHIP TO THE SEA

Data collected

Several claimants spoke of their association with the coastal areas which comprised their country. For example, Lomas Roberts identified Cape Riche as being particularly important to him, as was the entire coast east from Albany. He and his family fish along this coast. Lomas Roberts also reported that he conducts a ritual of introduction in relation to the ocean. Another claimant reported that he often took crabs from the Harvey Estuary, while Charlie Shaw stated that he fished from beaches and from Wedge Island, which is part of his country, to which he could swim. Coastal fishing was also considered by a number of other claimants to bc a significant family activity.

The use of the sea was also considered to have been important to Noongar people in times past. Charlie Shaw pointed to the middens round the settlement of Wedge Island as evidence of the use of marine resources in the past and stated that the old people used to spear and eat a species of small seal there. One claimant stated that, in the past, Noongar people used to camp along the Yunderup River to fish. Ellen Hill and Barbara Stammner-Corbett both talked of the importance of fishing to their family economy, particularly in the past. Attention was also drawn to the springs which occurred on the beach below the high-water mark, which presumably were water sources in times past. There were also fish traps reported by Charlie Shaw, Bill Webb and Glen Kelly.

The use of offshore islands is restricted to the comments (noted above) made by Charlie Shaw about Wedge Island. The island is close to the shore and it might be possible to wade to it at the lowest tide. Lomas Roberts described Doubtful Island (east of Bremer Bay) as a *markabal* place (meaning dangerous) because many Noongar people had died there.

Charlie Shaw said that his mother had taught him that dolphins were the family totem. Lomas Roberts reported that gropers and dolphins were 'brothers' to his family, which in my view is likely also to be a totemic reference. Bill Webb reported that dolphins meet up to have corroborees, 'like Noongars'. He also told a story about the origins of the whale.

In the narratives relating to the Wagarl, discussed in previous chapters, the spirit being emanates in some cases from the sea, making coastal features and forging its way into the estuaries or creeks, which it made.

Observations on the data collected

From the accounts reviewed here, fishing and the procurement of other marine species appear to be effected from coastal rocks or from the banks of rivers and tidal estuaries, or in shallows where wading is practical and safe. Accounts of the exploitation of areas of the sea beyond the beach, littoral zone and areas generally accessible without the requirement for the use of a boat or other watercraft are absent. It is possible that fishing has been (and is) conducted by means of a boat, since these became available, but this is nowhere stated. Accounts of past practice would appear to be consistent with this current use. Consequently, it is my opinion that the area beyond what I will call the low-water mark does not appear to be used by any of the people whose information has contributed to the production of this book. It is possible that additional research might challenge this view, but from the available data, this would appear to be a reasonable conclusion.

On the other hand, it is evident that Noongar people believe that there is a spiritual presence within the sea, reefs and offshore islands, as is evidenced by the existence of some coastal sites that are within the sea, such as reefs, areas of ocean or islands. The spirituality that is so central to the Noongar belief system is thought to sanctify these areas of the sea or islands, and will therefore be of significance to Noongar people — who would, it could be assumed, exercise their duties to ensure the well-being of these places. In the accounts I have provided of Noongar country areas (runs) there is little reference to or inclusion of offshore islands or reefs an exception being Wedge Island. Otherwise islands do not appear to form a component of any person's account of their country. In the absence of an ability to exercise rights in relation to these places, it may be that the rights, if claimed, are potential or inchoate. However, insufficient data exist upon which to draw a conclusion in this regard.

The accounts provided by early settlers and observers generally point to the fact that, traditionally, Noongar people did not access areas below the low-water mark. Fishing from the shallows, from lagoons, creek and tidal estuaries, on the other hand, undoubtedly represented an important component of the traditional economy. These activities would appear to relate to areas above the low-water mark. Lyon, for example, reports that the people with whom he was acquainted in the Perth region had no boats and were unable to swim (Lyon 1979, p. 150). Barker comments on the Albany groups' aversion to swimming and their antipathy to water (Barker 1992, p. 248). Fishing does, however, appear to have been an important economic activity, and Salvado reports the use of nets, particularly close to the sea (Stormon 1977, p. 159). For the Perth region, Moore states that spears were used to take fish (Moore in Green 1979, p. 122) and Nind reports on coastal fishing from the Albany region (Nind 1979, p. 25), as does Barker (1992, pp. 270, 294). Collie reports on Aboriginal people fishing in the shallows (1834, p. 83), while Hassell records that water spouts were believed to be spirits of *janak* (Hassell 1975, p. 66).

Meagher and Ride conclude that the Noongar traditional economy was not a maritime one, since the Noongar people were not seafaring and had no water transport (Meagher and Ride 1979, p. 73). However, they indicate that fishing was an important economic activity (pp. 73–4). Keen draws the same conclusion (Keen 2004, pp. 50–1), reporting that Noongar people did not access offshore islands (p. 98). Crawford and Crawford, basing their views on the early literature like the previous two sources, conclude that fishing in estuaries, river mouths and from weirs was an important part of the local economy, especially in the summer months in the far South West (Crawford and Crawford 2003, p. 37).

A lack of access to water transport and a disinclination to swim seems to have meant that offshore islands were not a part of traditional country. However, offshore sites continue to be spiritually important to Noongar people, an issue that was not addressed in the early accounts. In relation to the taking of marine resources, the incidence of exploitation is probably less now than it was formerly. Modern methods (hook and line) have replaced spears and fish traps, and weirs are no longer employed. However, the situation that the current research reflects is broadly consistent with the practices that characterised the exploitation of marine resources, as evidenced in the early literature. Noongar people continue to take marine resources from the coast, from estuaries and from inlets.

Chapter 15

CONCLUSION: CONTINUITY, NOONGAR LAWS, CUSTOMS AND RIGHTS TO COUNTRY

The copious early ethnographic accounts considered in this book provide an opportunity in relation to the South West of Western Australia which is not afforded in many other areas of the continent. It is possible to recreate a view of the society that existed not long after the acquisition of sovereignty by the British Crown. Such a reconstruction is an enterprise to be embarked upon with caution. The early accounts were limited in scope, narrow in their view and sometimes blinkered by prejudices and preoccupations of the time and are incomplete as ethnographies. Consequently, an absence of a current belief in the early literature is no proof of innovation. Nevertheless, and despite these limitations, together they furnish a starting point for any analysis that seeks to provide a view as to whether contemporary practice, belief and custom are consistent with that which can be supposed to be extant in about 1829. While this early literature has formed an important part of my analysis and conclusions, it is not the only measure of traditionality.

I have placed reliance on Noongar people's own views as to what constitutes tradition, that is, a system of customary rules, beliefs and concepts which claimants have been taught and that they consider they have always known to be a part of the thinking and knowledge passed down from their forebears. Practices and beliefs which are culturally ascribed by those who practised them to a time before imagining are not of the recent past. This conclusion is bolstered in this book by evidence drawn from the more general anthropological literature that a traditional practice or belief resonates with those found elsewhere in Aboriginal Australia.

Both from the early literature and from our general knowledge of the culture of Aboriginal Australia as it is likely to have been prior to European settlement, it is evident that there are some notable omissions in the contemporary Noongar account. Gone, it would seem, is any reference to the moiety or semi-moiety system. Modified kinship reckoning and ideal marriage rules remain, but these are no longer reliant on social categorisation. Religious observances, exemplified in the major rituals of male initiation and subsequent neophytic submissions, ceased — or so it would appear— long before living memory. Public ritual performances, often called corroborees in the Noongar account, are recalled by older claimants but appear to have ceased about 40 or 50 years ago. With the cessation of these rituals, much oral literature (songs, poetry), as well as dance and decorations, has also vanished from the lived culture. Funereal rites, as described in detail by a number of early observers, are no longer current, although beliefs associated with death and the spirit world, along with accompanying practices, remain. The ritual of the funeral remains of considerable importance in Noongar society. I have concluded that parts of the oral literature that relate to narratives of place, as well as (perhaps) more generalised narratives, are less numerous today than they once were. It is likely that the corpus of materials dealing with the aetiology of the landscape is diminished. Finally, the economic revolution that accompanied the introduction of European food, particularly flour and manufactured goods, spelt the end, at a fairly early date following European settlement, of the traditional subsistence hunting and gathering life style. This has implications for material culture and the exploitation of resources. However, as I have shown above, use of the countryside and knowledge of its resources remains, even though exploitation does not yield (in most cases) a significant economic benefit.

In the compilation of a list of losses there is a danger that the culture in question will be seen by some as incomplete: a fractured vessel that no longer contains all that is required to sustain its own integrity. The evidence, as I have presented it in this book, does not support such a conclusion. Cultures are the product of those who create and perpetuate them. A concomitant attribute of a viable community is a culture. I find no evidence for the demise of the Noongar community. On the contrary, the data I have considered in the preceding accounts support the view that Noongar culture remains vibrant, although not unaltered. The degree of change and the nature of that change is one of the questions I have sought to address in this book.

The Noongar community is a social aggregation of many groups of people who live (and whose forebears traditionally lived) across the South West of Western Australia. I have set out above how the community can be characterised and how it is structured. In an elementary sense, members recognise a commonality founded upon common belief and practice and a shared recognition of cultural unity. Members understand that they share a language style that contains elements of the Noongar language and its constituent dialects. They recognise that they share cultural similarities in relation to beliefs, practices and observances. Nothing exemplifies this better than the belief in the Wagarl, the major spirit being that is believed to be the source of waters, river and pools and the great creator of inlets, bays, creeks and springs. Spiritual correspondences extend far into Noongar belief and culture. Religious belief is founded on a land-derived spirituality, exemplified in many forms as malevolent, benevolent or a dangerous mixture of the two. Spirituality is manifest at certain places within the countryside where an embedded spirituality provides focused exemplars of a pervasive spirituality.

Members of the Noongar community recognise common ancestral ties, developed through affinal links, sometimes traced back many generations. While not all Noongar greater families are known to be related, common ancestry and affinal links over time are important parts of the cement that binds the community together. Together, the shared cultural practices and the holding of beliefs, values and mores provide legitimation for the claim that Noongar people together constitute a body whose members recognise more in common with one another than they do with others. This is a fundamental process in the claiming and perpetuating of an identity. It enables a public discourse where Noongar is distinguished from non-Noongar for the inclusion and promotion of the former, and the exclusion and potential detriment of the latter. It may be that the geographical extent of known consociates within the community is today greater than it was traditionally, when travel was limited to foot walking, although, as I have pointed out, there is evidence that people traditionally moved over wide areas. However, the boundaries of the Noongar community, based on cultural similarities and common practices, would appear to be much as it was first recorded by White Australian researchers.

Within the Noongar community, I have identified land-owning groups, which can be called country groups, and in Noongar exchanges are called families. The family (or extended family) comprises a cognatically recruited descent group, with affines who appear to become incorporated into the country group over time. The country group has a structure, a system of authority and perdures over time. It is therefore able to hold title to land and to ensure, through the principle of descent, that rights to that land are passed on to succeeding generations. I have noted how several early writers provided instances were land changed hands and that such a change of rights was not inconsistent with a traditional system of succession.

I have expressed the view that rights to country are exercised by country groups, but these rights are not exclusive since two or more country groups may share rights within the same area. The often complex interrelationship between families underscores and validates the operation of the exercise of these shared rights. Rights relate to the use, management and control of access of others to the country, as well as a right to share any benefit derived from the country by others. Rights imply duties, which I have set out in detail. While I have observed that the opportunity for the exercise of rights has been severely restrained in the past, I conclude that for Noongar people, the exercise of their rights in relation to their land remains at the heart of their understandings about their relationship to their country. The recognition of country, its ownership by a country group and the exercise of rights of access, and rights of use and benefit constitute a rule-based system, intrinsic to Noongar culture, which would appear, from all the information available to me, to be fundamentally consistent with that described in the early accounts for the South West.

In total, this constitutes a system of laws and normative rules which govern action. These rules extend to all aspects of Noongar practice and tradition. They certainly include how rights to land are ascribed, apportioned and executed. They are systemic in that they reside within the social structure of the community and are intrinsic to it. They are rules believed to have been given at some time in the far distant past by metaphysical agency, and are immutable and inviolable. Change notwithstanding, these elements of Noongar beliefs and practice would appear, from the data available to me, to be an important part of contemporary practice and observance.

Birdsall (1988, 1990) notes that many anthropologists had written off Noongar culture as one that was a victim of assimilationist policies and bureaucratic inhumanity.[132] In my opinion, this prejudiced academic view identified by Birdsall merely mirrored the equally biased populist view. There is no doubt that Noongar people and their culture have been hard hit in the South West of Western Australia. The now empty and echoing halls of Carrolup and Mogumber settlements stand in mute testimony to the forces that impacted upon Indigenous culture. However, the conclusion that Noongar culture was decimated as a consequence, or that it became fragmented and is consequently now without integrity, does not necessarily follow. The drawing of a conclusion developed from a view that a particular culture was hard hit by European settlement is understandable. However, deriving conclusions without reference to data, or without seeking it out, is an error. I consider that in the case of Noongar culture, the matter has sometimes been determined more by reference to assumption than by reference to facts.

It was not until comparatively recently that in-depth studies were undertaken into Noongar culture, based on extended field research. These recent researchers (notably Birdsall and Baines) have concluded from their data that Noongar culture is complex, diverse and has structural integrity. This work reversed the

132 I discuss relevant anthropological writings in this context in Chapter 8, where citations are also to be found.

former academic view that Noongar culture was remnant, perhaps in the process of innovative reconstruction. I too have based this book and my opinions on a comprehensive data set representing a substantial body of materials relating to Noongar culture. I conclude that Noongar culture constitutes a cultural system, in its own right, with its own tenets, laws and beliefs, and its own community of practitioners and believers. There is a normative system of land ownership, regulated by reference to a set of rules that determine the constitution of the land-owning body and the rights and duties of its members. I reach this conclusion not based on the assumptions developed where there is an absence of data, but rather after due consideration of the extensive and detailed materials that resulted from field research in the South West of Western Australia.

Appendix A

ACKNOWLEDGMENT TO CLAIMANTS

The following Noongar claimants gave their permission to SWALSC for their material to be included in this book.

Ross Story, Kevan Davis, Myrtle Yarran, William Reidy, Verna Ugle,* Roy Collard,* Susan Pickett, Yurleen Dorothy June Winmar, Lomas Roberts,* Wayne Collard, Ken Fitzgerald,* Carol Pettersen, Lynette Knapp, Fred Pickett, Janet Beattie, Harry Nannup, Joe Walley, Richard Walley, Angus Wallam, Joe Northover, Ruth Hayden, Charlie Shaw, Martha Borinelli,* Harry Thorne,* Mal Ryder, Charmaine Walley, Evelyn Dawson, Katherine Penny, Ron Gydjup, Faye Gydjup, Sheila Humphries, William Worrell,* May Taylor, Michael Blurton, Ellen Hill, Sue Kelly, Glen Kelly, Pat Kopusar, Barbara Stammner-Corbett, Bill Webb, Colin Headland, June Headland, Diane Yappo, Beverley Port-Louis, Roy Taylor,* Tom Taylor, Margaret Drayton.

*These people are among the many Noongar people who have passed away since participating in the research for this book in 2004. In these cases, SWALSC contacted relatives of the deceased in relation to permission for material to be included.

Appendix B

RESEARCH DESIGN

The following data sheets were used in the collection of materials that later were used in the production of the expert's report.

SINGLE NOONGAR CLAIM (SNC) RESEARCH PRO FORMA

(Complete in electronic form)

This pro forma sets out the sort of data that may be helpful to the anthropologist when he writes his expert report. The suggestions that follow are not meant to be the actual questions you might ask, but are provided as guidance for the areas that you might wish to cover. Each area is introduced by a 'Key Concept' which suggests the overall area for inquiry. Within this are supplementary areas to pursue. Follow alternative leads if this appears fruitful. Note examples of reported and, where possible, observed practice in support of statements. Probe the hows and the whys whenever possible.

Do not ask leading questions; use prompts only when necessary.

Field note ref:

Person interviewed (ego)
Noongar Name
Address
Phone Number

Date

Place

Note on circumstances

PART 1: LAND OWNERSHIP

1. Key concept: Association with claim area

(Use witness profiles, other previously collected data; pay attention to the basis for links)

Prompts

1.1. What is ego's relationship to the claim area?
1.2. Has ego lived on the claim country all his/her life?
1.3. How do you define a 'home'[133] area?
1.4. How do you define 'run'?[134]
1.5. What are ego's 'home' areas? Where is ego's run?
1.6. What are the 'home' areas of ego's M, F, MM, MF, FM, FF? Where were their runs?
1.7. What is meant by phrases like, 'come from' or, 'belong there' 'speak for' etc.?
1.8. What is the basis of this association (descent, birth, residence, parent's/grandparents life history, burial of ancestors)
1.9. What of ego's spouse; children?
1.10. Where do these rules/principles governing association come from? How were they learnt? Are they a part of Noongar traditional knowledge?

Comment

Keywords: [descent, home area, run, birth place, burial or death place, residence, marriage, connection] Others:

133 Centre of affiliation. Use local term if appropriate and note what it is.

134 Range or region over which person travels and feels comfortable. Use local term if appropriate and note what it is.

2. Key concept: Boundaries

2.1 How are the boundaries of ego's area defined? (see 1.3 above)
2.2 How are the boundaries of Noongar country defined?
2.3 Where do these boundaries come from? Where did ego learn about them?
2.4 Are they a part of traditional Noongar knowledge?
2.5 Do these boundaries go beyond the claim area?
2.6 Do others (non-Noongar) agree and recognise these boundaries?

Comment

Keywords: [boundaries] Others:

3. Key concept: Family connection to apical ancestors

(Use genealogies, witness profiles, other collected data)

3.1 What is the exact nature of the connection?
3.2 Is the genealogical data clear and correct?
3.3 Does ego know anything of the apical ancestor? (where born, lived, died) How did ego get this knowledge, from family members or books/research?
3.4 If not, how far back is remembered?
3.5 Is there a view about the ethnicity of oldest remembered forebear?

Comment

Keywords: [apical ancestors] Others:

4. Key concept: Social formations that relate to land

4.1 Is ego's right to his/her home area shared with others?
4.2 Who are these others? (Other consanguineal kin? Others not consanguineally related?)
4.3 How is the group(s) that relates to an area identified? (Family name, group name?)

4.4 Do some people have a stronger say than others? Why (principle)? How is this agreed?
4.5 What is the relationship of the group to other Noongar groups?
4.6 What is the relationship of the group to the Noongar community?
4.7 How do you get to be a member of the group that's linked to an area? What are the principles for recruitment? How does the group get a connection to the area?
4.8 Is this way of being linked to country a part of Noongar traditional knowledge and thinking?

Comment

Keywords: [continuity, recruitment to group, recruitment to community, local group, family/families,] Others:

5. Key concept: Permission and access protocols

You may need to differentiate traditional ideas from what now occurs in towns and public areas.

5.1 Is there a concept of asking permission in relation to land and activity on it?
5.2 Is 'run' and 'home area' different in this regard? Does ego have more say over one rather than the other? How does this work?
5.3 How does asking permission work in practice?
5.4 Where can ego go without asking permission?
5.5 Is there a difference between asking and 'letting people know'?
5.6 If so, what does 'letting people know' mean and involve?
5.7 How do people ask permission? Are there ways of doing this without actually asking in person?
5.8 Is there such a thing as 'standing permission'?
5.9 Does ego have to ask if he/she goes into a Noongar area with which he/she is not associated?
5.10 Does ego have to ask if he/she goes into an area which is not Noongar?
5.11 Do non Noongar people need to ask when visiting Noongar country?
5.12 Where do these ideas about permission and letting people know come from? Where did ego learn about them? Are they a part of Noongar traditional teaching and rules?

5.13 Ask for practical examples of who needs permission and when — e.g. someone wants to build a house/run a tourist venture on ego's home area; will it make a difference if that person is part of ego's family, a Noongar person, a non-Noongar (e.g. desert person)? What about on ego's run? Is it the same?

Comment

Keywords: [permission, protocols, access, rights to exclude] Others:

6. Key concept: Rights and Duties

(Collect examples of when right last exercised, how often do people do these things, did they do them as a child, who taught them, did their M, F, MM, MF, FM, FF do these things, does ego teach their children, grandchildren, others. But see also 14.)

6.1 What can ego do in those areas where he/she does not need to ask permission?

6.2 What examples of rights to access area? Collect examples of when right last activated.

6.3 What examples of rights to hunt, forage etc.* in area? Collect examples of when right last activated.

6.4 What examples of rights to camp and use area? Collect examples of when right last activated.

6.5 What examples of rights to exclude others from area? Collect examples of when right last activated.

6.6 What examples of rights to take minerals or other resources from area? Collect examples of when right last activated.

6.7 What examples of rights to control activities of others in area and their use of the area? Collect examples of when right last activated.

6.8 What examples of rights to share in any benefits derived from area? Collect examples of when right last activated.

6.9 What examples of rights to protect places in area? Collect examples of when right last activated.

---

* fish, bush medicine, bush tucker, gathering, use of resources, (artefacts/implements, build and use shelters, ochre and minerals, camping, burn/light fires, use and protect water.

6.10 What examples of rights to trade in the resources of the area. Collect examples of when right last activated.
6.11 What examples of the right to maintain, protect and prevent misuse of the cultural knowledge of the land of the claim area. Collect examples of when right last activated.
6.12 Are these rights limited to some areas or do they extend to the whole of the claim area?
6.13 Are there duties that ego has in relation to his/her area or the whole claim area?
6.14 Are there duties to protect places? Visit country and inter-act with it in some way? Look after visitors to your country? Do other things?
6.15 Are rights and duties a part of Noongar tradition? Where do they come from?

Comment

Keywords: [permission, protocols, access, rights to resources, rights to camp and use, rights to exclude, rights to benefit, duty to protect, duty to care] Others:

PART 2 NOONGAR CULTURE

7. Key concept: Kinship and social organisation

7.1 What words are used for immediate family members? (incl. mz, mb, FB, FZ and their children)
7.2 Are families important? Why? How?
7.3 Are Noongar families related? How? (Specific families; all families?)
7.4 Are there relationships between Noongars that go beyond the consanguineal?
7.5 Where do these ways of classifying kin come from? Are they a part of Noongar culture?
7.6 Are there other groupings within Noongar society (moieties, totemic groups etc.)?
7.7 If so, are these a part of traditional Noongar ways of understanding the composition of groups?

7.8 Are families connected/associated with different areas? How? What does this mean?
7.9 Does this connection yield the right to exclude others? Noongars? Non-Noongars?

Comment

Keywords: [moieties, social structure, relationships (non-consanguineal), kinship]
Others:

8. Key concept: Noongar laws and customs

(How is the community defined and united through its observation/acknowledgment/practice of laws and customs.)

8.1 Evidence that the laws and customs govern people's behaviour. Evidence of continued observation each generation since 1829.
8.2 Laws and customs that determine people's actions as members of the Noongar community
8.2.1 Rituals associated with birth
8.2.2 Naming rules or customs
8.2.3 Initiation
8.2.4 Marriage rules
8.2.5 Distribution and sharing of resources
8.2.6 Regulate and resolve disputes
8.2.7 Attendance at funerals
8.2.8 Rituals associated with death
8.2.9 Ceremonies/meetings on country
8.2.10 Calling out to country
8.2.11 Any other laws and customs.

Comment

Keywords: [birth place, birth ritual, customs, dispute management, death rituals, death beliefs, funerals, meetings, names, marriage, rituals, sharing]

9. Key Concept: Spiritual basis for applicant's traditional beliefs

(You could follow with section 15)

9.1 What is the fundamental belief system? Explore Dreaming, spirits, spiritual beings, *maban*, narratives, birth songs/corroborees/stories, etc.
9.2 Is there a name for this fundamental belief?
9.3 How does this belief system relate to the land? Is this Noongar land?
9.4 Is the spiritual belief important? Does it affect all aspects of life or just a few?
9.5 Totemism? Is there a relationship with natural species? Examples?
9.6 How do you get these relationships with natural species?
9.7 What does this relationship mean in practice (food taboos, special care, feeling for)?
9.8 Where do all these beliefs come from? Are they a part of Noongar traditional knowledge and belief?

Comment

Keywords: [totemism, ritual, sites, spiritual] Others:

PART 3 NOONGAR IDENTITY

10. Key concept: Identity

10.1 How does ego normally identify? (Noongar, other named group; other?)
10.2 How did ego obtain this identity? (from parents? Grandparents? Other?)
10.3 What does this identity mean to ego? Does it relate to an area of country? Does it relate to the past? How?
10.4 How did ego's M, F, MM, MF, FM, FF identify?

Comment

Keywords: [identity] Others:

11. Key concept: Membership of claimant community

11.1 Who are the Noongar?
11.2 Are there rules (principles) that govern recruitment?
11.3 What is importance of descent? From mother or father or both?
11.4 Can people be adopted into the Noongar community? (As children, as adults, how?)
11.5 Does place of birth make you a member?
11.6 Does a non-Noongar become a Noongar by marrying in?
11.7 Are the Noongar people one community? If so, explain how this is so.
11.8 Do Noongar people come together? Do they share things? Do they have a common culture? Does this make them distinct from non-Noongar people?
11.9 Where did these rules about being a Noongar come from?

Comment

Keywords: [outsider recognition, insider recognition, descent, adoption, marriage, birth place, residence] Others:

12. Key concept: Community structure

12.1 Who has authority in the community? Why?
12.2 How are those with authority expected to behave and what are their duties?
12.3 How should others treat those with authority?
12.4 Was this authority structure always so, as far as ego knows or has been taught?

Comment

Keywords: [authority, elders] Others:

13. Key concept: The language (or use of language words)

13.1 Is the Noongar language different to other languages spoken by people outside the claim area?

13.2 Are there different dialects of Noongar (different language styles)?
13.3 Are different styles of Noongar associated with different areas?
13.4 Does language or the words used from it identify ego as a Noongar? To other Noongars? To non-Noongars?
13.5 Where did ego gain his/her understandings of Noongar language?
13.6 Examples of how the language is used today, including language teaching programs.
13.7 Where does the language come from? (a part of traditional Noongar learning?)

Comment

Keywords: [language styles, language names, language groups, language] Others:

PART 4 ATTACHMENT TO COUNTRY

14. Key concept: Connection to country — economic

(May have been covered, in part, in 6 above.)

14.1 Does ego visit country? When, where, how often?
14.2 What does ego take from the country (e.g. of hunting, gathering, fishing, use of resources, minerals, fibres)?
14.3 Are there medicines in the country? What are these, when taken and used last?
14.4 Is the use of the country important? Why?
14.5 Did Noongar people always use the country in this way or are there now differences? Explain.

Comment

Keywords: [connection to country economic] Others:

15. Key concept: Connection to country — spiritual

Collect details of location of sites and areas of spiritual importance. Document ethnography as fully as possible. Avoid sensitive or gender restricted material.

15.1 Are there spiritual places in the country?
15.2 What are they and where are they?
15.3 Why are they important?
15.4 Are there stories for these places? What are the stories?
15.5 Do the stories link one place to another? Document this within claim area.
15.6 Who taught ego about these places? Does ego teach others?
15.7 Where does this knowledge come from? Is it a part of Noongar tradition?
15.8 Protection of sites.

Comment

Keywords: [connection to country spiritual] Others:

PART 5 SEA COUNTRY

16. Key Concept: the sea environment ('Sea country')

Complete only if ego has an association with an area of coast and adjacent sea.

16.1 Is there 'sea country' over which ego has rights and duties ['sea country' includes islands]?
16.2 Is this the same as or different from the rights and duties exercised in relation to land country?
16.3 What is the extent of sea country?
16.4 How are rights acquired in sea country?
16.5 Check questions in sections 2, 3, 4, 5, 13 and 14 above.

Comment

Keywords: [sea country, food-marine, littoral zone] Others:

Appendix C

SINGLE NOONGAR CLAIM (SNC) OBSERVATION PRO FORMA

(Complete in electronic form)

Complete as many of these as you can. Firsthand observation usually makes for good ethnography. Complete a new pro forma for different sorts of activity. However, if a series of activities are closely related, use one form.

Field note ref:

Person observed (ego)

Date

Place

Note on circumstances

1. Observation

REFERENCES

Armstrong, F 1979 [1836], 'Manners and habits of the Aborigines of Western Australia, from information collected by Mr F Armstrong, interpreter, 1836', in N Green (ed.), *Nyungar, the people: Aboriginal customs in the South West of Australia*, Creative Research and Mt Lawley College, Perth, pp. 186–206.

Bagshaw, G 2003, *The Karajarri claim: A case-study in native title anthropology*, Oceania Monograph 53, University of Sydney, Sydney.

Baines, P 1987, 'The heart of home: The intergenerational transmission of a Nyungar identity', PhD thesis, University of Western Australia.

Barker, C 1992, 'Journals', in J Mulvaney and N Green (eds), *Commandant of solitude: The journals of Captain Collet Barker 1828–1831*, Melbourne University Press, Melbourne.

Bates, D 1907–09a, unpublished manuscript, 'Social organisation of tribes', DB4a.

——1907–09b (approx.), unpublished manuscript, 'List of names of dialect map'.

——1909, unpublished manuscript, 'Totemic map of Western Australia', DB3a with notes to totemic names.

——1966 [1938], *The passing of the Aborigines*, Heinemann, Melbourne.

——1985, 'The native tribes of Western Australia', in I White (ed.), *The native tribes of Western Australia*, National Library of Australia, Canberra.

——1992, *Aboriginal Perth and Bibbulmun biographies and legends*, PJ Bridge (ed.), Hesperian Press, Carlisle, WA.

——n.d.a, unpublished manuscript, 'III 2e Genealogies. From Geraldton to Northampton Southward to Gingin Eastward to Peak Hill', H350.

——n.d.b, unpublished manuscript, 'Native vocabulary compiled by Baaburgurt alias Bulyen alias George Eliot of Wonnerup (Vasse) and Capel Districts', MS 12/2 B, 13.

——n.d.c, unpublished manuscript, 'Native vocabulary compiled by James Whitworth Busselton Incorrect', MS 12/2 B, 48.

——n.d.d, unpublished manuscript, Notebook 15, MS 73.

—— n.d.e, unpublished manuscript, 'Class divisions, etc southwestern WA', III 4c iii, H347.

——n.d.f, unpublished manuscript, 'Social organisation S.W. of W.A. Yaburgurt's information', III 4a, ii, H352.

——n.d.g, unpublished manuscript, 'Kinship terms, Southern W.A.', III 5d, H348.

——n.d.h, unpublished manuscript, 'Information re marriage laws', Notebook 21, III 4a iii, H349 (Questions to Jubych and his answers: early MSS) S.W. Area.

——n.d.i, unpublished manuscript, 'JL Wall vocabularies, Hassell's station'.

——n.d.j, unpublished manuscript, 'Vocabularies, Ngalbaitch Jerramungup'.

——n.d.k, unpublished manuscript, III 2c, 'Genealogies, Western Australia South West Division'.

Berndt, RM 1959, 'The concept of the "tribe" in the Western Desert of Australia', *Oceania*, no. 30, pp. 81–107.

——1965, 'Law and order in Aboriginal Australia', in RM Berndt and CH Berndt (eds), *Aboriginal man in Australia*, Angus & Robertson, Sydney, pp. 167–206.

——1969, *The sacred site: The West Arnhem Land example*, AIAS, Canberra.

——1972, 'The Walmadjeri and Gugadja', in MG Bicchieri (ed.), *Hunters and gatherers today*, Holt, Rinehart and Winston, New York, pp. 177–216.

——1979, 'Aborigines of the south-west', in RM Berndt and CH Berndt (eds), *Aborigines of the west: Their past and their present*, UWA Press, Nedlands, WA, pp. 81–9.

Berndt, RM and Berndt, CH 1977, *The world of the first Australians*, Ure Smith, Sydney.

Biernoff, D 1978, 'Safe and dangerous places', in LR Hiatt (ed.), *Australian Aboriginal concepts*, AIAS, Canberra, pp. 93–105.

Bindon, P and Chadwick, R 1992, *A Nyoongar wordlist: From the South-West of Western Australia*, Western Australian Museum, Perth.

Birdsall, CL 1987, 'Family history and social network among Nyungar people', *Aboriginal History*, vol. 11, pp. 129–42.

——1988, 'All one family', in I Keen (ed.), *Being Black*, Aboriginal Studies Press, Canberra, pp. 137–58.

——1990, 'All one family: Family and social identity among urban Aborigines in Western Australia', PhD thesis, University of Western Australia.

Brandenstein, CG von 1977, 'Aboriginal ecological order in the south-west of Australia: meaning and examples', *Oceania*, vol. 47, no. 3, pp. 169–86.

——1986, 'Address of Nyungar people, Albany 21st July 1986, "Noongar as it was"', unpublished typescript, AIATSIS, Canberra.

——1988, *Nyungar anew*, Pacific Linguistics, series C, no. 99, RSPacS, Australian National University, Canberra.

Browne, J 1856, 'The Aborigines of Australia', paper read before the Canadian Institute, 16 February 1856, *The Nautical Magazine and Naval Chronicle*, London.

Brunton, R 2003, *Preliminary anthropological report*, Crown Solicitor, Western Australia.

Bunbury, HW 1930, *Early days in Western Australia*, Oxford University Press, London.

Cane, S 2002, *Pila Nguru*, Fremantle Arts Centre Press, Fremantle.

Charlesworth, M 1984, 'Introduction', in M Charlesworth, H Morphy, D Bell and K Maddock (eds), *Religion in Aboriginal Australia: An anthology*, University of Queensland Press, St Lucia, Queensland, pp. 1–20.

Clark, WN 1842, 'An inquiry respecting the Aborigines of South-Western Australia', *The Inquirer*, 16 February.

Colbung, K 1979, 'On being an Aboriginal: A personal statement', in RM Berndt and CH Berndt (eds), *Aborigines of the west: Their past and their present*, UWA Press, Nedlands, WA, pp. 100–7.

Collie, A 1834, 'Anecdotes and remarks relative to the Aborigines at King George's Sound — from an original manuscript by a resident at King George's Sound', in N Green (ed.), 1979, *Nyungar, the people: Aboriginal customs in the south-west of Australia*, Creative Research and Mount Lawley College, Perth, pp. 59–96.

Crawford, P and Crawford, I 2003, *Contested country: A history of the Northcliffe area, Western Australia*, UWA Press, Nedlands, WA.

Curr, EM 1886–87, *The Australian race: Its origin, languages, customs, places of landing in Australia, and the routes by which it spread itself over that continent*, vols 1–4, Victorian Government Printer, Melbourne.

Daw, B, Walley, T and Keighery, G 1997, *Bush tucker plants in the south-west*, Department of Conservation and Land Management, Perth.

Dench, A 1994, 'Nyungar', in N Thieberger and W McGregor (eds), *Macquarie Aboriginal words*, Macquarie Library, Sydney, pp. 173–92.

Douglas, W 1976, *The Aboriginal languages of the south-west of Australia*, AIAS, Canberra.

Elkin, AP 1933, *Studies in Australian totemism*, Oceania Monograph 2, University of Sydney, Sydney.

——1945, *The Australian Aborigines: How to understand them*, Angus & Robertson, Sydney.

——1977, *Aboriginal men of high degree*, Queensland University Press, St Lucia, Queensland.

——1979, 'Aboriginal–European relations in Western Australia: An historical and personal record', in RM Berndt and CH Berndt (eds), *Aborigines of the west: Their past and their present*, UWA Press, Nedlands, WA, pp. 285–323.

Ferguson, WC 1987, 'Mokare's domain', in DJ Mulvaney and JP White (eds), *Australians to 1788*, Fairfax, Syme and Weldon, Sydney, pp. 120–45.

Fox, R 1967, *Kinship and marriage*, Penguin, Harmondsworth.

Gould, RA 1967, 'Notes on hunting, butchering, and sharing of game among the Ngatatjara and their neighbours in the Western Australian Desert', *Kroeber Anthropological Society Papers*, no. 36. pp. 41–66.

Green, N (ed.) 1979, *Nyungar, the people: Aboriginal customs in the South West of Australia*, Creative Research and Mt Lawley College, Perth, WA.

——1984, *Broken spears: Aborigines and Europeans in the southwest of Australia*, Focus Education Services, Cottesloe, WA.

——1989, *Aborigines of the Albany region, 1829–1898*, UWA Press, Nedlands, WA.

——2003, 'Aboriginal presence in metropolitan Perth since 1829', preliminary history report filed on behalf of First Respondents, Crown Solicitor, Perth.

Green, N and Tilbrook, L 1990, *Aborigines of New Norcia 1845–1914*, UWA Press, Nedlands, WA.

Grey, G 1840, *A vocabulary of the dialects of south western Australia*, T&W Boone, London.

——1841, *Journals of two expeditions of discovery in north-west and western Australia during the years 1837, 38 and 39*, T&W Boone, London.

Haebich, A 1988, *For their own good: Aborigines and government in the south-west of Western Australia, 1900–1940*, UWA Press, Nedlands, WA.

Hallam, S 1975, *Fire and hearth*, AIAS, Canberra.

Hallam, SJ and Tilbrook, L 1990, *Aborigines of the southwest region 1929–1840*, Bicentennial Dictionary of Western Australia, vol. VIII, UWA Press, Nedlands, WA.

Hamilton, A 1982, 'Descended from father, belonging to country: Rights to land in the Australian Western Desert', in E Leacock and R Lee (eds), *Politics and history in band societies*, Cambridge University Press, Cambridge, pp. 85–108.

Hammond, JE 1933, *Winjan's people*, P Hasluck (ed.), Hesperian Press, Victoria Park, WA; facsimile edition (1980), Imperial Printing Co., Perth.

——1938, 'Native laws, rites, customs, ceremonies and religious belief when in their primitive state', ms typescript.

Hassell, E 1934–35, 'Myths and folktales of the Wheelman tribe of south-western Australia', *Folklore*, vol. 45, nos. 3 and 4, pp. 232–48 and 317–41 (1934), and vol. 46, nos. 2, 3, pp. 122–47 and 268–81 (1935), selected and revised by DS Davidson.

——1936, 'Notes on the ethnology of the Wheelman tribe of south-western Australia', *Anthropos*, vol. 31, pp. 679–711.

——1975, *My dusky friends*, CW Hassell, Fremantle, WA.

Helms, R 1896, 'Anthropology of the Elder Scientific Exploration, 1891-2', *Transactions of the Royal Society of South Australia*, no. 16, pp. 237–332.

Hiatt LR 1962, 'Local organisation among the Australian Aborigines', *Oceania*, vol. 32, pp. 267–86.

——1966, 'The lost horde', *Oceania*, vol. 37, no. 2, pp. 81–92.

——1968, 'Ownership and use of land among the Australian Aborigines', in RB Lee and I DeVore (eds), *Man the hunter*, Aldine, Chicago, pp. 99–102.

Hodson, S 1989, 'Nyungars and work: Aboriginal labour in the Great Southern Region, Western Australia 1936–1972', MA thesis, University of Western Australia.

Horton, D 1994 (general ed.), *The encyclopaedia of Aboriginal Australia*, AIATSIS, Canberra.

Howard, MC 1976, 'Nyoongah politics: Aboriginal politics in the south-west of Western Australia', PhD thesis, University of Western Australia.

——1978, 'Aboriginal leadership in the southwest of Western Australia', in MC Howard (ed.), *Whitefella business*, Institute for the Study of Human Issues, Philadelphia, pp. 11–34.

——1979, 'Aboriginal Society in south-western Australia', in RM and CH Berndt (eds), *Aborigines of the west: Their past and their present*, UWA Press, Nedlands, WA, pp. 90–9.

——1981, *Aboriginal politics in southwestern Australia*, UWA Press, Nedlands, WA.

Keen, I 1997, 'The Western Desert vs the rest: Rethinking the contrast', in F Merlan, J Morton and A Rumsey (eds), *Scholar and sceptic: Australian Aboriginal studies in honour of LR Hiatt*, Aboriginal Studies Press, Canberra, pp. 65–94.

——2004, *Aboriginal economy and society*, Oxford University Press, Oxford.

Laves, G n.d., unpublished field notebooks for the Albany region, c. 1929–30, photocopies, SWALSC Library, Perth.

Layton, R 1983, 'Ambilineal and traditional Pitjantjatjara rights to land', in N Peterson and M. Langton (eds), *Aborigines, land and land rights*, AIAS, Canberra, pp. 15–32.

Le Souef, S 1993, 'The Aborigines of King George Sound at the time of early European contact: an ethnohistorical study of social organisation and territoriality', in BK de Garis (ed.), *Portraits of the south west: Aborigines, women and the environment*, UWA Press, Nedlands, WA, pp. 1–56.

Lefroy, CEC 1934, *Memoir of Henry Maxwell Lefroy (1818–1879)*, Billing and Sons Ltd, Guildford, Surrey.

Lyon, RM 1979 [1833], 'A glance at the manners, and language of the Aboriginal inhabitants of Western Australia; with a short vocabulary', in N Green (ed.), *Nyungar, the people: Aboriginal customs in the South West of Australia*, Creative Research and Mt Lawley College, Perth, pp. 148–80.

Maddock, K 1974, *The Australian Aborigines: A portrait of their society*, Penguin, Harmondsworth, UK.

——1981, 'Warlpiri land tenure: A test case in legal anthropology', *Oceania*, vol. 52, no. 2, pp. 85–102.

Malinowski, B 1922, *Argonauts of the Western Pacific*, Routledge and Kegan Paul, London.

Marcus, J 2001, *The indomitable Miss Pink*, UNSW Press, Sydney.

McGregor, W 1994, 'Introduction', in N Thieberger and W McGregor (eds), *Macquarie Aboriginal words*, Macquarie Library, Sydney, pp. xi–xxxv.

Meagher, SJ 1973, 'A reconstruction of the traditional life of the Aborigines of the south-west of Western Australia', unpublished MA thesis, University of Western Australia.

——1974, 'The food resources of the Aborigines of the south-west of Western Australia', *Records of the Western Australian Museum*, vol. 3, pp. 14–65.

Meagher, SJ and Ride, WDL 1979, 'Use of natural resources by the Aborigines of South-Western Australia', in RM and CH Berndt (eds), *Aborigines of the west: Their past and their present*, UWA Press, Nedlands, WA, pp. 66–80.

Millett, E 1872, *An Australian parsonage*, Edward Stanford, London; facsimile edition (1980), UWA Press, Nedlands, WA.

Moore, GF 1978a [1884], *Diary of ten years eventful life of an early settler in Western Australia*, facsimile edition, UWA Press, Nedlands, WA. 1978b [1884], *A descriptive vocabulary of the language of the Aborigines*, facsimile edition, UWA Press, Nedlands, WA.

Mulvaney, J and Green, N 1992, *Commandant of solitude: The journals of Captain Collet Barker 1828–1831*, Melbourne University Press, Melbourne.

Myers, FR 1986, *Pintupi country, Pintupi self: Sentiment, place, and politics among Western Desert Aborigines*, Smithsonian Institute Press, Washington and AIAS, Canberra.

National Native Title Tribunal 2001, *South West Trial Area 2, Western Australia*, MA Jebb (ed.), National Native Title Tribunal, Perth.

——2003, 'Native Title Determination Application: WC03/6 — W6006/03 (Combined Single Noongar Claim), map showing claim boundary and boundary data from Tindale (1974).

Nind, S 1979 [1831], 'Description of the natives of King George's Sound (Swan River Colony) and adjoining country', in N Green (ed.), *Nyungar, the people: Aboriginal customs in the South West of Australia*, Creative Research and Mt Lawley College, Perth, pp. 15–55.

Palmer, K 1976, 'Aboriginal oral tradition from the south-west of Western Australia', *Folklore*, vol. 87, pp. 76–80.

——1999, *Swinging the billy: Indigenous and other styles of Australian bush cooking*, Aboriginal Studies Press, Canberra.

——2007, 'Anthropology and applications for the recognition of native title', *Land, rights, laws: issues of native title*, vol. 3, no. 7, viewed 30 January 2013, <http://www.aiatsis.gov.au/ntru/docs/publications/issues/ip09v4n1.pdf>.

——2010a, 'Societies, communities and native title', in L Strelein (ed.), *Dialogue about land justice*, Aboriginal Studies Press, Canberra, pp. 139–58.

——2010b, 'Understanding another ethnography', in T Bauman (ed.), *Dilemmas in applied native title anthropology in Australia*, AIATSIS, Canberra, pp. 72–96.

——2011, *Anthropologist as expert in native title cases in Australia*, AIATSIS Native Title Research Unit resource, viewed 26 September 2015, <http://www.aiatsis.gov.au/publications/products/anthropologist.html>.

Palmer, K and Brady, M 1991, *Diet and dust in the desert*, AIATSIS, Canberra.

Peterson, N 1976, 'Introduction', in *Tribes and boundaries in Australia*, N Peterson (ed.), AIAS, Canberra, pp. 1–11.

——1983, 'Rights, residence and process in Australian territorial organisation', in N Peterson and M Langton (eds), *Aborigines, land and land rights*, AIAS, Canberra, pp. 134–45.

Peterson, N, Keen, I and Sansom, B 1977, 'Succession to land: Primary and secondary rights to Aboriginal estates', submission to the Ranger Uranium Environmental Inquiry, in Joint Select Committee on Aboriginal Land Rights in the Northern Territory, official *Hansard* report, pp. 1002–14.

Peterson, N and Long, J 1986, *Australian territorial organisation: A band perspective*, Oceania Monograph 30, University of Sydney, Sydney.

Piddington, R 1969, 'Wrong marriages in Australia', *Oceania*, vol. 40, no. 4, pp. 331–42.

Pope, A 1956, *Alexander Pope's collected poems*, B Bobrée (ed.), Dent and Sons, London.

Radcliffe-Brown, AR 1930, 'Former number and distribution of the Australian Aborigines', in *Official year book of the Commonwealth of Australia*, Government Printer, Sydney, pp. 687–96.

——1930–31, 'The social organisation of Australian tribes', *Oceania*, vol. 1, no. 4, Oceania Monograph 1, University of Sydney, Sydney.

Richards, S 1994, *The Bibbulmun: Land of many breasts*, Access Press, Perth.

Rose, DB 1992, *Dingo makes us human: Life and land in an Australian Aboriginal culture*, Cambridge University Press, Cambridge.

Roth, WE 1902, 'Notes of savage life in the early days of West Australian settlement', *Proceedings of the Royal Society of Queensland*, no. XVII, pp. 45–69.

Rowley, CD 1972, *Outcasts in White Australia*, Penguin, Harmondsworth.

Shapiro, W 1981, *Miwuyt marriage*, Institute for the Study of Human Issues, Philadelphia.

Smith, M 1982, 'Late Pleistocene Zamia exploitation in southern western Australia', *Archaeology in Oceania*, no. 17, pp. 117–21.

South West Aboriginal Land and Sea Council, J Host with C Owen 2009, *'It's still in my heart, this is my country': The Single Noongar Claim history*, UWA Press, Nedlands, WA.

Stanner, WEH 1965a, 'Aboriginal territorial organisation: Estate, range, domain and regime', *Oceania*, vol. 36, no. 1, pp. 1–26.

——1965b, 'Religion, totemism, and symbolism', in RM Berndt and CH Berndt (eds), *Aboriginal man in Australia: Essays in honour of Emeritus Professor AP Elkin*, Angus & Robertson, Sydney, pp. 207–37.

——1979, *White man got no dreaming*, ANU Press, Canberra.

Stormon, EJ 1977, *The Salvado memoirs*, UWA Press, Nedlands, WA.

Sutton, P 2003, *Native title in Australia: An ethnographic perspective*, Cambridge University Press, Melbourne.

Symmons, C 1841, 'Grammatical introduction to the study of the Aboriginal languages of Western Australia', in *The Western Australia almanack*, C Macfaull (ed.), UWA Press, Perth.

Terry, FM 1994, 'Woodyche tales', comp. JM Seabrook, unpublished typescript, Western Australian Museum, Perth.

——n.d., *They came to the Margaret*, Margaret River Print, Margaret River, WA.

Tilbrook, L 1983, *Nyungar tradition: Glimpses of Aborigines of south-western Australia 1829–1914*, UWA Press, Nedlands, WA.

Tindale, NB 1940, 'Distribution of Australian aboriginal tribes: A field survey', *Transactions of the Royal Society of South Australia*, vol. 64, no. 1, Adelaide, pp. 140–231.

——1974, *Aboriginal tribes of Australia*, ANU Press, Canberra.

Tonkinson, R 1978, *The Mardudjara Aborigines*, Holt, Rinehart and Winston, New York.

Toussaint, S 1987, 'Nyungars in the city: A study of policy, power and identity', MA thesis, University of Western Australia.

Vansina, J 1973, *Oral tradition*, Penguin, Harmondsworth.

Vinnicombe, P 1989, *Goonininup: A site complex on the southern side of Mount Eliza: An historical perspective of land use and associations in the Old Swan Brewery area*, WA Museum, Perth.

White, I (ed.) 1985, *The native tribes of Western Australia*, National Library of Australia, Canberra.

Williams, D 1998, 'Foreword', *Native title: Legislation with commentary*, 2nd edn, Government Printer, Canberra, pp. iii–v.

Williams, N 1982, 'A boundary is to cross: Observations on Yolngu boundaries and permission', in *Resource managers: North American and Australian hunter-gatherers*, N Williams and E Hunn (eds), American Association for the Advancement of Science, Boulder, Colorado, pp. 131–54.

Wilson, J 1958, 'Cooraradale', thesis as part-requirement for BA (Hons), University of Western Australia.

Wilson, K 1958, 'Kinship at Coorara-dale — a part-Aboriginal housing settlement', thesis as part-requirement for BA (Hons), University of Western Australia.

—— 1964, 'Co-operatives, leadership, and assimilation', in M Reay (ed.), *Aborigines now*, Angus & Robertson, Sydney, pp. 133–32.

Wilson, TB 1968 [1835], *Narrative of a voyage around the world*, Dawsons, London.

Wollaston, JR 1975 [1848], *Wollaston's Albany journals*, ed. PU Henn, UWA Press, Nedlands, WA.

Worsley, P 1967, 'Groote Eylandt totemism and totemism aujourd'hui', in E Leach (ed.), *The structural study of myth and totemism*, Tavistock, London.

Cases

Bennell v State of Western Australia [2006] 153 FCR 120

Bodney v Bennell [2008] 167 FCR 84

Jango v Northern Territory (No. 2) [2004] FCA 1004

Mabo v Queensland (No. 2) (1992) 175 CLR 1

Members of the Yorta Yorta Aboriginal Community v Victoria [2002] 214 CLR 422

Legislation

Evidence Act 1995 (Cth)

Native Title Act 1993 (Cth)

INDEX

www.ingramcontent.com/pod-product-compliance
Lightning Source LLC
LaVergne TN
LVHW010054110826
845155LV00028B/336

* 9 7 8 1 9 2 2 1 0 2 2 9 4 *